Digital Online Culture, Identity, and Schooling
in the Twenty-First Century

New Frontiers in Education, Culture, and Politics

Edited by Kenneth J. Saltman

New Frontiers focuses on both topical educational issues and highly original works of educational policy and theory that are critical, publicly engaged, and interdisciplinary, drawing on contemporary philosophy and social theory. The books in the series aim to push the bounds of academic and public educational discourse while remaining largely accessible to an educated reading public. *New Frontiers* aims to contribute to thinking beyond the increasingly unified view of public education for narrow economic ends (economic mobility for the individual and global economic competition for the society) and in terms of efficacious delivery of education as akin to a consumable commodity. Books in the series provide both innovative and original criticism and offer visions for imagining educational theory, policy, and practice for radically different, egalitarian, and just social transformation.

Published by Palgrave Macmillan:

Education in the Age of Biocapitalism: Optimizing Educational Life for a Flat World
By Clayton Pierce

Schooling in the Age of Austerity: Urban Education and the Struggle for Democratic Life
By Alexander J. Means

Critical Pedagogy and Global Literature: Worldly Teaching
Edited by Masood Raja, Hillary Stringer, and Zach VandeZande

Culture and Structure at a Military Charter School: From School Ground to Battle Ground
By Brooke Johnson

Digital Online Culture, Identity, and Schooling in the Twenty-First Century
By Kimberly N. Rosenfeld

Digital Online Culture, Identity, and Schooling in the Twenty-First Century

Kimberly N. Rosenfeld

palgrave
macmillan

First published in 2015 by
PALGRAVE MACMILLAN®
in the United States—a division of St. Martin's Press LLC,
175 Fifth Avenue, New York, NY 10010.

Where this book is distributed in the UK, Europe and the rest of the world,
this is by Palgrave Macmillan, a division of Macmillan Publishers Limited,
registered in England, company number 785998, of Houndmills,
Basingstoke, Hampshire RG21 6XS.

Palgrave Macmillan is the global academic imprint of the above companies
and has companies and representatives throughout the world.

Palgrave® and Macmillan® are registered trademarks in the United States,
the United Kingdom, Europe and other countries.

ISBN: 978–1–137–44259–8

Library of Congress Cataloging-in-Publication Data

Rosenfeld, Kimberly N.
    Digital online culture, identity, and schooling in the twenty-first
century / Kimberly N. Rosenfeld.
        pages cm
    Includes bibliographical references and index.
    ISBN 978–1–137–44259–8 (hardback)
        1. Virtual reality in education. 2. Shared virtual environments—Social
aspects. 3. Education—Effect of technological innovations on. I. Title.

LB1044.87.R682 2015
371.33′44678—dc23   2014029745

A catalogue record of the book is available from the British Library.

Design by Newgen Knowledge Works (P) Ltd., Chennai, India.

First edition: January 2015

10 9 8 7 6 5 4 3 2 1

To Alexander, my son, and his future

Contents

List of Figures		ix
Acknowledgments		xi
1	Virtualization and Digital Online Culture	1
2	A Case Study: Sherry Turkle and the Psychological Role of Computers	31
3	Down the Rabbit Hole: Identity and Societal Mutation	63
4	Manufactured Consciousness and Social Domination	91
5	Virtualization and Neoliberal Restructuring of Education	121
6	Toward a Critical Theory of Technology for Schooling	151
Notes		169
References		171
Index		195

Figures

1.1 Early twenty-first-century realities   6
1.2 Cultural intersections   13
4.1 Friction model   94
6.1 Schooling-technology-identity model   155

Acknowledgments

A number of generous individuals were instrumental in the shaping of this book. I would like to thank Douglas Kellner for his true mentorship and confidence in this project. He brought sharp insights and inspiring thoughts to our discussions, never held me back, and encouraged me to be bold with my ideas. I also thank him for introducing me to Ken Saltman, the editor of this series. I thank Ken Saltman for welcoming this book to his New Frontiers on Education, Culture, and Politics series. His expertise in neoliberalism helped refine my thoughts on the subject.

A very special note of appreciation to my husband, Eric Rosenfeld, who in many ways, influenced the ideas presented here. His out of the box perspective, thorough critiques, and keen insights challenged my conceptualization and analyses for the betterment of the end product. This book is stronger because of his contributions and I owe him a debt of gratitude.

I would also like to recognize Jeff Share whose review of this book introduced me to the writings of some excellent contemporary thinkers. Finally, I would like to acknowledge Leah Lievrouw, Carlos Alberto Torres, Rhonda Hammer, Jaana Flávia Fernandes Nogueira, and Dora Chen, all of whom are encouraging people I crossed paths with. They are my sources of inspiration, and ultimately helped shape my thinking.

I

Virtualization and Digital Online Culture

Contemporary citizens live in complicated times where fundamental understandings of reality are being expanded and challenged. A growing number of people no longer reside in just one physical reality but live, play, and work in multiple realities: real life reality, simulated reality, augmented reality, virtual reality, and hyperreality. As each crosses over from specialized functions (i.e., military training and scientific research) into everyday use, it impacts modern ontological states. Multiple realities are so pervasive that we see them across different contexts, such as at our local mall in the form of advertisements, on our smartphones in the form of applications, and at home in our appliances.

This book maps some of the sociological and psychological changes to our lives as a result of computer technology. This work's aim is to initiate a conversation about how schooling should understand, respond to, and help individuals live out the information revolution. To achieve these goals, I will deconstruct two distinctions fundamental to my writing during a time when each reality's delineation is dwindling. The first distinction is between real life (RL) and virtual life (VL) and the second is between humans and machines.

Within the context of this book, computer technology includes artificial intelligence, human–machine hybrids, computer devices, and various stages of simulation. When I reference technology, I also mean the material and immaterial aspects of both virtualization and digital online culture that play an active role in constructing users' identities. This includes the physical objects that serve as portals to virtualization such as smartphones, the software that runs them, and the software that runs on them in the form of applications and games. The immaterial refers to the social and culture practices around the use of these objects, including but not limited to changes to our social norms around language, disclosure, privacy, access to and use of information, social networking, and activism.

It is also important to keep in mind that technology is not all good or all bad, so as this topic is explored, I make an effort to consider the positive as well as the negative. Thus, along with the magical utopia of freedom, democracy, and unfettered learning the virtual represents, there is ideology and materiality to it that is not always so idealistic. There is physicality to the virtual that relies on the actual bandwidth, pipelines, wires, towers, servers, and the myriad sophisticated objects with their unique affordances. A human factor accompanies the physicality in the form of social class, race, gender, and hegemony that accompany the armada of service providers, designers, creators, and marketers who are tangible parts of this fantastic world and are often implicit actors in our virtual experiences. Both sides to this materiality are fueled by a neoliberal undercurrent that is implicated in many of the ideological battles playing out in both RL and VL.

I use neoliberalism here in reference to political and economic practices that uphold the doctrine that the best way to advance human well-being is to allow unfettered individual entrepreneurial freedom through competition in a self-regulated market (Harvey, 2007). As Ken Saltman notes, "In the view of neoliberalism, public control over public resources should be shifted out of the hands of the necessarily bureaucratic state and into the hands of the necessarily efficient private sector" (2010, p. 23). This is achieved largely through open markets, free trade, privatization, deregulation, and a state at the service of the private sector (Harvey, 2007; Lee & McBride, 2007; Torres, 2009). As Saltman continues to argue, "By reducing the politics of education to its economic roles, neoliberal educational reform has deeply authoritarian tendencies that are incompatible with democracy" (2010, p. 25). As I outline neoliberalism's influences on education, I will demonstrate its destructive effects on the schooling process by critiquing the ethics of such practices as they pertain to upholding the ideals of social justice and the democratic state.

In order to be clear about the terminology used to describe these multiple realities and to outline my own conceptualizations, I begin this chapter by defining the terms I will use to broaden the discussion on the virtual, identity formation, identity change, and culture. This will be done through first historicizing the concept of the virtual then moving on to clarify virtual reality, augmented reality, simulation, virtual culture, and digital online culture. This is followed by a brief summary of some important voices on identity, virtualization, and culture. The chapter closes with my own perspective on virtualization and digital online culture as well as previews of subsequent chapters.

As I proceed, I would like to situate the historical, technological, and political perspectives from which I write. As a US educator who completed my graduate studies in Los Angeles, California, writing this in the second decade of the twenty-first century, I am critically aware that my experiences are grounded in the overdeveloped, high-tech Western world. I am also aware that I am from a generation at the cusp of the digital revolution. Although I did not grow up digital, I was introduced to cyberspace as a young adult through largely neoliberal education programs designed to position the United States as a global leader in the information age. I recognize this is not the same for everyone, yet whether readers are living in virtualized environments or not, all will be touched in some way by the realities I outline here.

I would also like to recognize that unlike many past inventions such as the automobile, computer technology is still changing shape. Although the automobile had different iterations, it settled into a rather predictable product early on whereas computer technology of the digital age is in constant flux. We have moved from personal computing to cloud based computing, employing tools that are also dramatically redefining the way we use the medium ranging from the mouse (i.e., drag, point, and click mechanisms) to complete gesture control. In light of this reality, I capture the essence of this phenomenon at a given moment in time. This is not to suggest that scholars should refrain from writing or theorizing about the subject but rather readers should understand that this book is a snapshot in time designed to aid in understanding the impact of this revolution. Therefore, the issues discussed in this document may be similar or very different in the near future.

Gibson's Cyberspace

The first signs of a developing vocabulary to describe the "virtual" was born out of a term coined in science fiction and credited to William Gibson's 1984 novel *Neuromancer* (Jones, 1997; Turkle, 1997) in which he defines cyberspace to be:

> Cyberspace. A consensual hallucination experienced daily by billions of legitimate operators, in every nation, by children being taught mathematical concepts...A graphic representation of data abstracted from the banks of every computer in the human system. Unthinkable complexity...Cyberspace is infinite but starts with each person who chooses to step into it; and I speak now of he who in the first place dreamed it into life.
>
> *(Gibson, [1984]2004, p. 271)*

Neuromancer was published at the start of the "information revolution"—a time when the computer was being ushered into the general public's consciousness. During the same time, the Macintosh computer, dubbed the "people's computer," was introduced, just one year after the release of Microsoft's Windows software. We also saw continuous improvement to the ARPANET (the precursor to the Internet), which was still limited to specialized communities within the United States, such as scientists, selected departments within universities, and the military. These technological gains were beginning to seep into the larger cultural landscape and Gibson was one of the first to articulate the next step.

Thirty years later, the concept of cyberspace no longer lives within the imagination of science fiction writers and readers nor is it limited to specialized communities, rather it is a fundamental part of our everyday lives. Every time users log on, open, or plug into Internet enabled devices they are entering cyberspace. Gibson's most salient points are cyberspace's "unthinkable complexity" and "infinite" dimension. Before exploring these terms, I want to mention an important element missing from Gibson's definition.

There is a side to cyberspace that goes hand in hand with stepping into the "consensual hallucination." This includes the equipment we use to login and navigate, the infrastructure that enables us to join, and the software, including the graphic user interface, that so often mediates the entire process. These tools are intentionally designed to be in sync with how we think, how we train our bodies to navigate them (e.g., the mouse, drop down menus), and how they ultimately influence our experiences (J.J. Gibson [1979] 1986; Norman, 1988). Working in conjunction with our visual and psychological cyberspace environments, they too impact who we are becoming. This is especially true of the next hardware iterations intended to help users function simultaneously and seamlessly in both the virtual and the real such as Google Glass and Oculus Rift, a virtual reality headset.

Gibson's notion of complexity is evident in cyberspace's exponential expansion. Take a moment to consider multiuser domains. In the 1980s, these were text based cyber environments (e.g., MOOS and MUDS, both refer to a form of multiuser domains) where participants interacted using avatars constructed via text. Now envision today's multiuser domains such as *Second Life* and *World of Warcraft*, where interactions are visually complex, real time mash ups. This point is particularly interesting because today's users are able to absorb these sophisticated systems without a steep learning curve. The expanding area of design tailored to user intuition discussed in chapter 3 provides further insight on this subject.

For Gibson, cyberspace is infinite in that its nature is analogous to space exploration where the canvas appears to be never ending. Users quickly learn that it is almost impossible to fully explore the depth and breadth of information and communities available. Especially noteworthy is that in a world defined and made predictable by boundaries, users seem to accept cyberspace as a new frontier: a modern day open prairie of the Wild West. In fact, some pour their hopes into this new environment the same way the pioneers were looking to the prairies as a representation of their hopes for a better life. Thus, cyberspace, also known as the Internet and the World Wide Web, is an environment defined by the nature of its essence, a pure communication world devoid of clear boundaries. It is also the vehicle by which we enter a state of psychological immersion. Psychological immersion happens when we are intellectually and emotionally transported to another environment that often exists in cyberspace but is not limited to it. A video game player can be fully immersed into an online multiplayer game or can be immersed in an offline game played against the computer. In both cases, the gamer is psychologically immersed while still being present in an RL environment. This reality of today is rapidly morphing into a different state of being where the two worlds cohabitate, a new high-tech existence where the early twenty-first-century concept of RL is disrupted.

The Abstraction of Realities

The notion of abstraction is at the heart of the distinction among terms. Gibson argues that cyberspace encompasses "a graphic representation of data abstracted." Today, the differences among RL reality, simulation, augmented reality, virtual reality, virtualization, and hyperreality lies in levels of abstraction beginning with the real and extending to the hyperreal. The further we are detached from references to RL, the more undefined things become and the more we function in the psychological state of the virtual. This idea is illustrated in figure 1.1. The continuum represents a graduated state moving from least abstract (RL reality) to most abstract (hyperreality). Abstraction is used here to describe the non-physical qualities of technological immersion. Real life space refers to the physical world including the physicality of the Internet mentioned earlier, whereas virtual space refers to technology enabled psychological

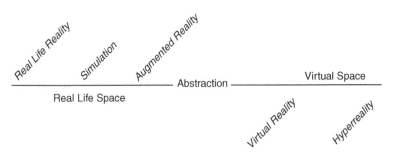

Figure 1.1   Early twenty-first-century realities.

immersion such as cyberspace and offline gaming. To better illustrate the nuances, I will briefly explain each term.

Real Life Reality

Real life reality is life experienced without computer representation, when users are not plugged into, logged on, or directly interfacing with technology. It may be influenced by technological immersion as in the case of changed perspectives or newly built relationships, but it refers to what is happening in the tangible world. It also refers to the powered off physical devices, hardware, and infrastructure that enable cyberspace entry and level of participation.

Simulation

Simulation is computer imagery that mirrors the real world, striving to directly copy the real. It often presents an idealized representation of the real or a simulacrum of it. This is seen in flight simulators, virtual tours, and computer games. Simulation can also be a combination of the real and its simulation such as in the case of many smartphone applications. The popular application called Waze, for instance, provides a simulated view of traffic patterns, while simultaneously incorporating real time data feeds from actual drivers, which appear as simulated vehicles. Users can then navigate their real world using a social, real time, virtual, simulated helper.

Augmented Reality

Augmented reality is a blending of physical reality with virtual reality: A presentation of RL augmented by virtual elements such as graphics, objects, or text. It includes aspects of simulation in that augmented things mimic the real. Although simulation and augmented reality utilize computer imagery, they still reside in RL space because they directly reference and rely upon the real.

Augmented reality is cyberspace enabled and can be controlled by gestures; "it sometimes uses facial recognition; and is often in three dimensions" (Britten, 2011). Retailers are now using augmented reality to allow customers to virtually try on clothes, and fashion shows are being augmented with a mix of RL models and augmented reality models who share the catwalk (Britten, 2011). Additionally, smartphone and tablet computer applications allow users to overlay what they see in real time with digital photos, video or text. Augmented reality is also revolutionizing tourism in the form of hardware and smartphone applications that allow museum visitors to make otherwise static content come to life leading to an interactive, dynamic and interesting adventure. Augmented reality browsers allow travelers to identify a city's most important and interesting points of interest and learn more about their general surroundings. Furthermore, they can reconstruct historical sites by pointing their smartphone toward the original location. This is currently the case with the former Berlin Wall where augmented reality users are able to see its virtual representation as a realistic 3D model by simply pointing their smartphone at its former location (Augmented Reality in Tourism, 2014).

Virtual Reality

Virtual reality represents a shift away from referencing RL. It is a state that begins to function independent from the real, where abstraction is the norm. This is a space where users enter and build, or join, new environments, often from scratch with their own rules. Although there continues to be allusions to RL, these can be more implicit such as the way we communicate and interact within this created world. It occurs within cyberspace resulting in an environment defined by the user so that the physical rules of the "real" do not apply. For example, a player of the video game series *Elder Scrolls* can create a nonhuman avatar and accrue special powers not possible in the real world. Thus, virtual reality more easily crosses over into what postmodern theorists like Baudrillard have dubbed hyperreality (1994).

As Howard Rheingold describes, "Virtual Reality (VR) is also a simulator, but instead of looking at a flat, two-dimensional screen and operating a joystick, the person who experiences VR is surrounded by a three dimensional computer-generated representation, and is able to move around in the virtual world and see it from different angles, to reach into it, grab it, and reshape it"

(*Virtual reality*, 1991, p. 17). For Rob Shields, "The virtual tricks the mind and body into feeling transported elsewhere…virtual worlds make present what is both absent and imaginary" (*The virtual*, 2003, p. 11). The film *Disclosure* (Crichton & Levinson, 1994) provides a window into how, at the time, technologists were projecting the evolution of cyberspace to include virtual reality through physical body attachments that enable one to project the self into a cyberworld. Today, such attachments still exist and are used in career-technical education, the military, and video gaming (VanHampton, 2012; Wingfield, 2013). Oculus Rift provides a glimpse into the next generation of virtual reality technology, a world where users are seamlessly and effortlessly immersed into virtual reality through what will soon become inconspicuous and wearable or even embedded electronics. As described by Wired Magazine, "by combining stereoscopic 3-D, 360-degree visuals, and a wide field of view…it [Oculus] hacks your visual cortex. As far as your brain is concerned, there's no difference between experiencing something on the Rift and experiencing it in the real world" (Rubin, 2014). However, the term "virtual" is more commonly used to describe half-immersive experiences where there is an amount of interactivity such as with a mouse or game controller combined with a visual experience that includes user navigated three-dimensional spaces such as in video games and Google earth.

The term "virtual" has also been used in computer jargon to refer to situations that were substitutes for something else. Mark Poster, the University of California Irvine professor of Media Studies and History used the following example to illustrate this point, "virtual memory means the use of a section of a hard disk to act as something else, in this case, random access memory" (2006, p. 538). For Poster, virtual reality "is a more dangerous concept because it suggests that reality may be multiple or take many forms" (p. 538). In other words Poster notes, "modifying the word 'reality' to introduce another type of reality, puts into question the general assumption that there is only one reality" (M. Poster, personal communication, January 30, 2011). The idea that we live within multiple realities is something postmodern theorists have acknowledged for years (see works by Derrida; Foucault; Lyotard, Baudrillard, Jameson, and Best & Kellner), a point I discuss in chapter 3.

It should be noted that the term "virtual" has been appropriated and repurposed according to new media contexts, and therefore a singular meaning cannot be assumed. Subsequently, virtual reality falls into four categories: professional, consumer, psychological, and technological. *Professional virtual reality* implies sensatory experiences with the use of dedicated hardware enabling users to feel and manipulate a virtual environment such as in the original professional military flight simulators. *Consumer virtual reality* is a partial sensatory experience (i.e., just audio, visual, or tactile in the form of a headset and vibrating controller) as experienced through virtual tours, ride simulators, and video games. *Psychological virtual reality* is a cyber experience devoid of sensatory components such as MOOS and MUDS, virtual banking, and online shopping. *Technological virtual reality* refers to the mechanics of a computer such as random access memory or cloud computing that uses an application to provide access to data stored on a distant server. I use a definition of the virtual in line with both consumer and psychological virtual reality. Virtual reality is virtual and/or cyber experience that often, but not always, includes partial sensatory level immersion. Unless specified, it is no longer limited to an immersive experience achieved by requiring hardware to be attached to the body. As a whole, virtual reality represents a step away from RL. Within this environment, we have become accustomed to fully functioning either by ourselves or within a community. This act of being in the virtual is virtualization.

Virtualization is a term used to describe being fully immersed in a virtual society. It occurs when we find relationships and communities in cyberspace that stand on their own without reference to the real. Participants do not need validation through a face-to-face meeting or a visit to a physical location, yet this is not to suggest these experiences are mutually exclusive from RL. Our perspectives, experiences, and interactions in the virtual impact our RL identities, a point explored further in chapter 3.

The idea that virtualization is so engrossing that it has the power to influence our views of the real is best explained perhaps through Sherry Turkle's 1997 book *Life on the screen: Identity in the age of the Internet,* where she outlines three signs that virtual reality is beginning to skew our experiences of the real. First, denatured and artificial experiences seem real. Second, the virtual can seem more compelling than the real. Finally, virtual experiences become so captivating that we believe that within them we have achieved more than we actually have.

Although virtualization is not completely devoid of connection to RL, it often starts from a strong allusion to the real that rapidly evolves into a completely new society. For Rob Shields, virtual worlds are simulation in that they "usually start out as reproducing actual worlds, real bodies and situations, but, like simulations, they end up taking on a life of their own. Somewhere along the way they begin to diverge, either when it is realized that no map can be so complete that it represents an actual landscape fully, or when they become prized as more perfect than messy materiality" (2003, p. 4). The idea of leaving "messy materiality" behind is illustrated through the concept of hyperreality.

Hyperreality

Hyperreality is a condition that no longer needs to reference the real. It can also be understood as a psychological state, where the virtual and the real blend in unpredictable and rapidly evolving ways. Hyperreality positively connotes a new reality that is better than the real. More things are possible, limitations are overcome, and life is more evolved. An example of a hyperreal environment can be found in the film *Avatar* (Landau et al., 2009), in which paralyzed veterans can walk again and the environment is an indescribable blend of ocean life and rain forest with extraordinary hues. Furthermore, the characters are very liberated, and superhuman in their capabilities. It is a world where viewers feel empowered and even euphoric at the idea of actually living a life that transcends the discomforts and challenges of RL, a state that people are beginning to experience in virtual environments (Rosenfeld, 2010). The concept of hyperreality is elaborated further in chapter 3.

Virtual Culture and Digital Online Culture

As virtual experiences become shared, they begin to create a new culture. In the early 1990s when the World Wide Web's accessibility was expanding to laypeople, users found themselves alone in most of these virtual environments. As we clicked and searched through rather static pages of text and occasionally images, we had our own private time in that virtual space, unless we had a friend or family member sitting next to us watching the screen as we "surfed" the Web together. Today, this is no longer the case. Once we use virtual tools, we join others as we enter into a parallel culture with its own population, rules, and relationships. Virtual culture can be viewed as a public sphere where social, political, economic, and cultural interactions take place (Jones, 1997), only these actions are mediated through an electronic medium. Virtual culture, as I see it, is a paradigm that ranges from simulation to hyperreality, whether we are on our own (i.e., in a simulator) or with others in cyberspace, we are in a virtual space with its own culture.

Within virtual culture, digital online culture represents the current form of acting and communicating through a fully high broadband network. Users by default become part of a cybersociety. Analogous to a tribe, this population adopts new societal norms in relation to both RL and VL behaviors. The terms themselves, "digital online culture," represent a snapshot of what the information revolution is today. However, in the near future, tools and mediums by which virtualization is achieved may be replaced by more sophisticated technologies and these terms may become obsolete; yet the notion of culture will remain.

Interreality culture resides at the nexus of RL and VL. It refers to a broader culture in which digital online culture operates. Whereas digital online culture is specific to the medium it operates under, interreality culture exists whenever there is an intersection of RL and VL, whatever the medium. As long as we function as humans in the technological context, we will have moments when both cultures are mixed. Although interreality culture is a more enduring concept, I will use the specific yet temporal digital online culture to refer to experiences that reside in cyberspace and often propagate into RL culture (see figure 1.2).

Digital online cultural practices can be likened to an RSS (Rich Site Summary) feed mechanic where two-way updates are provided and consumed while functioning in RL: a population of people who regularly broadcast information about their personal life, interests, or projected identities in real time. Since there is no dedicated time

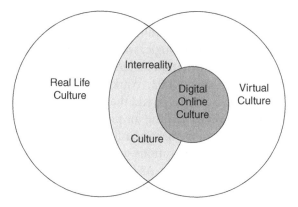

Figure 1.2   Cultural intersections.

or place for the broadcasting, RL norms naturally develop such as glancing down at a smartphone and actually typing in mid-conversation or micro-blogging, uploading, commenting during major events (i.e., graduations, births, operas, recitals). Although this behavior is considered rude in RL culture, it is an accepted norm in digital online culture.

Those who participate in this culture, also exhibit a change in language use and semantic understandings in the form of basic computer culture terminology (i.e., upload, download, compress, shoot an email, text). It encompasses the idea of mixed interactions between humans and machines. Such interactions already occur in forums where human and artificial intelligence (AI) users chat together and in multiplayer games that contain both human players and AI players. This extends to more complex understanding as seen with the concept of metadata tags such as hashtags, a symbol used on a particular Web platform to classify or categorize text where "key words" are used to identify an online event, document, image, audio, or video. The concept of "search terms" that enables one to access information and make it accessible to others is also part of this mixed interaction. Another example can be found in the attitudes toward privacy within this context, as I discuss in chapter 2; Sherry Turkle reveals some fairly radical attitude and behavioral shifts around the notion of privacy, where those operating in digital online culture see privacy violation as a natural part of digital life.

Virtual culture and digital online culture, however, are not benign. Outside of the hacker culture and creative commons (i.e., the open source movement) logic, which espouses free, collaborative, open access to information including the Web as well as software programs (Stallman, 2002; Wark, 2004), virtual spaces are mirroring RL's intricacies. As in RL, there are both hegemonic and counterhegemonic forces battling for power over user identity and more importantly the movement of information. This is illustrated through the fact that corporations and politicians are using virtual spaces to fight their battles. As NYU marketing professor Scott Galloway observed in a recent NPR interview with Steve Henn, "If someone chooses to follow you [on Twitter] you own them—and that is you own the relationship and have license to communicate with them" (Henn, 2010). Since the rules of RL do not apply in the virtual, we now have to renegotiate issues of privacy, censorship, social justice, freedom, and boundaries.

At the same time Gibson published Neuromancer ([1984]2004), an intellectual conversation about ideology and cyberspace began emerging. Philosopher Jennifer Slack (1984) points out the tendency for scholars to direct attention toward the examination of political, economic, and technological determinants of the information revolution while directing very little attention toward the examination of the information revolution at the ideological level (p. 247). Additionally, she notes that society engages in an ongoing ideological struggle over how the information revolution is to be articulated: How should we understand it? How should we live it? And how should it live within us? Over 25 years later, few education scholars, although this number is increasing, have critically engaged and theorized how society (e.g., schooling) should understand, respond to, and live this information revolution. One of my goals in writing this book is to begin addressing this shortfall.

On the other hand, many people look to virtual spaces to help them fight social injustice, extend democracy, and remedy social ills. The reality is the seductive nature of the virtual can be both a tool of manipulation and control and at the same time a tool of liberation, empowerment, and rebellion. This dialectic results in struggles being fought on a daily basis over control. This contested terrain is evidenced by the open source versus proprietary software movement, the battle over privacy, and the controversy over data mining by government agencies to name just a few. Facebook, for example, is on one hand an online tool that helps express individualism yet is also a tool highly prescriptive and open to corporate data mining (Helft, 2010). The Brazilian education philosopher Paulo Freire's ideas can be applied here in that Facebook and other social networking sites are virtual programs used en masse where people are seduced into a collective exercise for personal satisfaction and improvement via the appeal to individualism (Freire, [1968]2000). However, their participation helps to feed capitalist agendas in the form of advertising and the process of Knowledge Discovery in Databases also known as KDD, a point I interrogate further in chapter 4.

Another, more optimistic, reality is the role today's technology plays in facilitating global collaboration. In the 1960s media scholar Marshall McLuhan argued that automation (i.e., computers, the Internet) "ends the dichotomies between culture and technology, between art and commerce and between work and leisure" ([1964]1994, p. 346). One example of the way technology is resolving such divisions can be found in Rice University professor Richard Baraniuk's *Ted Talk* presentation, "Open Source Learning" (2006), in which he uses the music industry's rip, burn, mix, and create culture to describe one of the next evolutions in information dissemination. For Baraniuk, the concept of the textbook is becoming passé in light of cyberspace tools such as Web 2.0. Subsequently, he calls for a reinvention in the way we think about writing and editing textbooks, using them and teaching from them. From kindergarten to universities, a vision is shared for a knowledge ecosystem in which teachers, instructors, and professors can become writers as well as editors of their own textbooks, openly sharing them and constantly innovating on them. This collaborative relationship resonates with the Freirean concept of the teacher–student relationship in which each learns from the other in a reciprocal cycle. Baraniuk's vision would be accomplished within the creative commons framework in which quality control is monitored via peer review, illustrating another of McLuhan's points that automation is "a way of thinking as much as it is a way of doing" ([1964]1994, p. 349); just one example of the multiple facets of society that are collaborating, thinking, and doing business differently as a result of McLuhan's notion of automation as it applies to the twenty-first century.

Richard Baraniuk's (2006) knowledge ecosystem also represents the deterritorialized world of Arjun Appadurai's -scapes (1996), an online community of practice where authors from around the globe can contribute to the creation of textbooks. Appadurai explains that the new global cultural economy cannot be taken in the traditional sense of nation-state boundaries with static populations, isolated technologies, mutually exclusive financial systems, insular information sources, and territory specific worldviews. This cultural flow is "a complex, overlapping disjunctive order, which cannot any longer be understood in terms of existing center-periphery models" (p. 6). Instead, these mechanisms of encounters are landscapes extending beyond local boundaries, and when applied to Baranuik's idea of knowledge construction and dissemination reveal a method by which individual agency and global collaboration can more easily play a role in one's identity formation.

Appadurai's theory corroborates McLuhan's central nervous system analogy in which he argues that one of the principle aspects of the "electric age" is that it establishes a global network that is much like our central nervous system. For "our central nervous system constitutes a single unified field of experience," and as biologists so aptly point out, "the brain is the interacting place where all kinds of impressions and experiences can be exchanged and translated, enabling us to react to the world as a whole" ([1964]1994, p. 348). Today, cyberspace is the interaction place where experiences are being globally exchanged. Identity transformations are bound to occur as individuals use technological artifacts to function in their real and cyber lives. Elements of these changes are mediated through the use of new media tools with which individuals intuitively develop skills in identity management and exploration. Lives are being virtualized on a scale that is restructuring everyday reality as we know it, and where the global virtual self and the actual self cohabitat. This constant flow of deterritorialized information and perceptions has an impact on all of us, particularly on RL identities.

Identity Flow

As Charles Taylor notes, "In order to have a sense of who we are, we have to have a notion of how we have become, and of where we are going" (1989, p. 47). Since the time of the world's most notable ancient Greek philosophers, researchers have theorized about identity. In the nineteenth century, such theorizing inspired the work of memorable researchers (see Erikson, 1980; Freud, [1989]1923; Piaget, 1986; Tajfel, 1974; Vygotskiĭ, 1978) who espoused a variety of these theories crossing multiple disciplines: psychology, child development, sociology, education, and communications. Identity in a broad sense comprises characteristics that constitute who we are. They are largely constructed through our lived experiences including the family and societal role modeling, expectations for gender, age, class, race, ethnicity, and so on. Portions of our identity are also shared with members of groups to which we belong such as our culture, sex, ethnicity, and race. As we live out our lives, identity evolves with us, so naturally our interactions within virtual contexts and tools also influence who we are (Leary & Tangney, 2003).

Psychology based identity research is the most widely cited and well known. It falls into one of two frameworks: Freudian theory, which emphasizes the impact of the unconscious and early experiences on identity; behavior theory, which emphasizes that all behavior is determined by the environment either through association or reinforcement (Culatta, 2011). Learning theories emanating from these traditions are constructivism and constructionism. Constructivist psychologies present a more recent approach arguing that humans actively interpret the world around them and construct meaning rather than see it. For constructivists, identity is constructed, fluid, and multiple. Constructivists believe that we are active creators in our own reality and often create self-fulfilling prophecies based on the choices we make when responding to a situation (Katz, 1981, p. xiv). Identity frameworks have also extended to the realm of technology and human interaction. MIT computer scientist and education scholar Seymour Papert, a student of the famous developmental psychologist Jean Piaget (1986) who among other accomplishments fathered the idea of constructivist learning theory, expanded the notion of constructivism into a learning theory called constructionism wherein he argues the best way to learn is to construct something tangible in the real world (Harel & Papert, 1991).

In my view, the act of becoming virtualized plays a role in how we construct our identities. Through our creation of digital selves within our unique digital spaces we compose something tangible yet still virtual, and through this construction we build who we are and create who we would like to be. Although society has changed as a result of the information revolution, these theories of identity construction are still valid within this new paradigm. Nevertheless, virtual environments today are altered from the real in the sense that they provide partial sensory experiences whether it is sight (nonverbal), touch, sound, smell, or taste due to the limitations of the hardware and software used, which invariably affects the identity construction process. Thus, the way virtual environments and experiences influence our identities are not as holistic as the way RL environments and experiences influence them. I assert that technology is working to overcome these limitations by directly accessing the mind through brain sensing wearable devices (Bilton, 2013). Once this is resolved, we will witness another level of variables affecting identities.

Over 40 years ago, theorists began to recognize the identity shift occurring as a result of computers. Marshall McLuhan and Quentin Fiore ([1967]2005) articulated the fact that new technologies shape our identities by providing us with a different perception of the world. Likewise, affordance theory highlights that objects project how they allow themselves to be used in a given context and therefore influence users' behaviors with the object (J. J. Gibson, 1977). In the context of digital online culture, design theorists have applied this theory to understand the influence of design and environment on an artifact's (material or virtual) properties. In essence, such artifacts are active agents in presenting themselves to users and thereby instructing how to use them. Thus, there is a psychological dimension to identity construction that is influenced by the tools we use, the practices those tools afford, and the contexts we create using them. The concept of figured worlds, first introduced by Holland, Lachicotte, Skinner, and Cain ([1998]2001) in their book *Identity and agency in cultural worlds*, suggests that the environments, real or imagined, we create for ourselves and our interactions within them impacts our identities. Given that each of these aforementioned identity perspectives sheds insight on the numerous facets of identity construction, they will be employed as I unpack modern day identity formation.

Today, perceptions are often manufactured through virtualizing utopian experiences, relationships, and self-presentations. In McLuhan fashion, it is not humans who are driving this identity change. Rather, as Sherry Turkle predicted, the control is being transfered to the technological invention (2009; 2012a). Juxtaposed with cyberspace's portal to utopia is the material reality that experiences are manufactured. The manufacturing is orchestrated through the unseen and often taken for granted aspect of the affordances of the very technological tools we use to enter cyberspace, the interface design that both enables and inhibits individual agency as well as the new media inventions that intentionally push or pull us into uncharted ways of behaving.

Ted Nelson (1987) talked about computers being personal in the sense that "if you get involved, it involves all of you; your heart and mind and way of doing things and your image of yourself: A whole way of life" (p. 3). In the 1980s Byron Reeves and Cliff Nass, lead researchers on a Stanford University researcher project entitled *Social responses to communication technology*, noted computers are social actors and that "old brains, however, have not yet caught up with new media" (1996, p. 26) in the sense that although we know computers are not social or human, we nevertheless interact with them as social actors. As Zimmerman (2006) argues, the interface of a product is the mediator where one can find social, cultural, and economic forces at play. Thus, computers contain identity embedded within their database design, their user interface design, and their functionality. This is also echoed throughout Turkle's work as well as Howard Rheingold who writes, "Virtual reality demonstrates that our social contract with our own tools has brought us to the point where we have to decide fairly soon what it is we as humans ought to become, because we are on the brink of having the power of creating any experience we desire" (1991, p. 386). The process of virtualization results in identities that are constructed for us and also by us.

Whether we are involved in the act of creating new media tools or others create them for us, the artifacts we use turn into a piece of our identity. To a large extent, they are emotional (Coutu, 2003; J.J. Gibson [1979] 1986; Norman, 1988; Reeves & Nass, 1996) because they are imprinted on us and are loaded with cultural and historical associations that hold a powerful appeal to our psyche. This point is further corroborated within the constructivist psychology framework, which also argues that our perceptions are affected by the tools we use. These devices are an extension of who we are: members of a global community who reside in the technoscape of information and identity flow where we slide in and out of realities at will. To ignore this new reality is to deny who people are today.

Identities are produced both through the practices we engage in and through practices we do not engage in. Relationships with technology fall on a continuum mediated to a large extent by age, class, gender, and other experience that work to shape how we perceive, interact with, and process this technology. Our identities are further shaped by both active and passive participation in communities of practice (Wenger, 1999). The Web enables both types of participation, thus, as long as we are in cyberspace we are changed by the experience whether we are active participants or passive voyeurs. According to Katz (1981), "what people see and do will always be affected by choices they make, by their early interpretations, and their readiness to see—via the tools they bring to the situation" (p. xxi). The extent to which identity is impacted by virtual culture is linked to our own level of engagement with the information revolution. Those who enter cyberspace are required to construct and present a sense of self. Some do this tangentially while others do so pervasively and finally some not at all.

As noted in Erving Goffman's influential book *The presentation of self in everyday life* (1959), when we are in the face to face presence of others, we give expressions such as verbal symbols or their substitutes to convey information and we also give off a wide range of cues that tell others about who we are. For Goffman, many of the crucial facts about a person lie beyond the time and place of interaction but are still concealed within it. Although not all digital interactions are visual, many of Goffman's points about the presentation of self can be extended to our digital online performances. We present an image of who we are, or want to be, to an online community that in turn either confirms or denies that identity. As McLuhan notes, we do not necessarily store and move corporeal substance in the electronic age, rather we store and move perception ([1964]1994).

The impact virtualization has on identity formation is supported by Anthony Giddens' observation that identity establishment is influenced more by different beliefs and practices than in traditional societies. Those who are proponents of the digital generation's "explosion" (Prensky, 2006; Tapscott, 1999) argue that technology provides new ways of forming identity and hence new forms of personhood; and by offering communication with different aspects of the self, it enables young people to relate to the world and to others in more powerful ways (Buckingham, 2008). For instance, through online game playing people engage in social actions and create online identities that may result in sharpened decision making abilities, learning by doing and creating, and developing an understanding of physics by learning the laws of a specific computer generated world, such as whether you can jump over a canyon wearing armor (Johnson, 2006). Other studies have found those who engage with digital online culture vis-à-vis the Internet tended to also be more tolerant and openminded. Where an individual falls on the technology continuum shades who he/she is in relation to the information revolution including the values, practices, and habits of mind it imparts.

The correlation between new media, identity, and behavior warrant a brief discussion on the debated area of media effects. Scholars argue that mass media consumption in the form of TV programs or video games, for example, influences how recipients think and act in the real world. New media researchers such as Turkle argue that the difference between contemporary media's (i.e., video games) impact on identity and old media's (i.e., TV) impact is that contemporary media is active and old media is passive. Turkle observes, "Television is something you watch. Video games are something you do, something you do to your head, a world that you enter, and, to a certain extent, they are something you become... Some of them [games] begin to constitute a socialization into the computer culture" (2005, p. 67). Other researchers such as Kellner (2008) and Newman et al. (2005) argue that real world violence such as school shootings are a result of multiple societal factors including the construction of "violent masculinity as a cultural norm" (Kellner, 2008, p. 24). They do not exonerate media culture from this equation but mention it is only one of several potential factors influencing real world behavior. The issue of media effects is an unsettled one with many perspectives as to the link between old or new media and real world violence and other psychosocial behaviors that are beyond the purview of this book. However, I will briefly share my stance on this issue as it relates to identity formation.

In line with Kellner and Newman et al., I believe new media plays an important role in the numerous factors influencing behavior. Let us move beyond the violence in the media example to look at new media's impact on identity. Interactive media such as Web 2.0 are moving users beyond the active–passive dichotomy to voyeur–actor simultaneously placing users in subject–object positions. As users of social networking, people become voyeurs of other people's lives, and in doing so, they become the fans of their "celebrity." Likewise, as actors in social networking sites, people become the spectacle: The "object" on display for others (Kellner, 2003a). They become their own paparazzi posting the minutia of their lives for all to scrutinize. These actions shape perceptions, values, and behaviors ultimately demonstrating our changing culture and identities.

Varying perspectives on technology exist: some embrace the current value and future potential of technology to liberate and evolve identities, some reject technology as begetting more problems than it solves, still others fall in between these two poles. Thus an exploration of several contemporary technology theorists most of whom have written specifically about these challenges and their impact on identity is in order.

Contemporary Technology Perspectives

Although MIT professor Sherry Turkle's work will be analyzed in the next chapter, I would like to juxtapose one of her most enduring books, *Life on the screen: Identity in the age of the Internet* (1997), with the works of other technology scholars to provide an overview of varying scholarly perspectives on the topic. Turkle argues that Frederic Jameson's vision of postmodernism has arrived: it is a clear discontinuous break from the past. For Turkle, this is happening through technology that is increasingly more easily navigated on the surface level. The shift from understanding a computer at the programming level to one's ability to point and click popularized the use of the computer. It is of little surprise that the Macintosh computer paved the way for a new population of people learning through tinkering, fragmented exploration, and direct action. For Turkle, it was the shift from seeing what is under the hood characterized as the depth of understanding associated with modernity to just driving the car or surface level usage associated with postmodernity.

In Turkle's view, the computer "offers us new opportunities as a medium that embodies our ideas and expresses our diversity" (1997, p. 31). Some of the benefits to the change she articulates include an easier and happier interaction with computers, a new way of learning that functions in nonlinear fashion via exploration, and a postmodern way of being where we are consistently navigating multiple realities at the expense of depth but at the benefit of breadth. Additionally, she posits that computers are now being programmed to evolve beyond human control via emergent artificial intelligence that will result in a new relationship between humans and technology. Conventional knowledge about notions of spirituality and God are called into question with Turkle's discussion of the extent to which artificial intelligence and artificial life researchers have borrowed from medicine, biology, and psychology's behaviorism. She identifies the race among the biological, medical, and computer programmer communities for pushing innovation to the point of questioning what it means to be human. Subsequently, Turkle leads readers to reconsider the central components of identity, faith, and what it means to be alive.

Although Turkle raises awareness and increases understanding through her historicized accounts, her observations at times fail to balance the technological benefits with their counterpoints. This leaves plenty of room for British researchers Robins and Webster to add their strongly oppositional perspective.

Kevin Robins and Frank Webster's *Times of the technoculture: From the information society to the virtual life* (1999), written just four years after Turkle's *Life on the screen*, presents a technophobic view immediately discerned through the book's opening and lengthy discussion of Luddites and their assertion that Luddites are still needed to question the possibilities that technological change offers. They uplift Luddism as a "necessary force in the new global society" (p. 45). For Robins and Webster, efficiency based on technology is just another capitalist mechanism of control and domination. They warn readers to proceed with caution and to draw on our history with inventions to understand the potential implications of today's technological pervasiveness. Unlike Turkle, Robins and Webster argue for users to beware of modern technology's potential use as yet another tool for control and manipulation.

For all their pessimism, Robins and Webster make some valid points about technology's potential dangers. They raise questions about the relationship between technology, information, and power by arguing that "the mode of information enormously extends the reach of normalizing surveillance, constituting new modes of domination that have yet to be studied" (p. 94). They see society moving toward becoming anesthetized objects of technocrats. In contrast to Turkle, who sees identities as actively evolving through virtual interactions, Robins and Webster see identities as being passively "programmed."

Robins and Webster do not believe society is in the midst of a discontinuous break from the past. Rather innovation is a continuation of processes begun at the dawn of the industrial revolution. In essence, the information age is about a reassertion and streamlining of control strategies from capitalist economic drives, and high-tech capitalists are still driven by neoliberal agendas. In their discussion of the information revolution's long history, they demonstrate the reality that technology is an extension of Marxist's critiques of power, exploitation, and domination.

They also interrogate arguments made by researchers like Turkle, and others, as to the types of new identities that are being created in the midst of this technological rise. They especially chastise the artificial intelligence and cybernetics researchers who value instilling in people logic, rationalism, and quantification. For them, the indoctrination of these values comes at the expense of the intuitive, emotional aesthetic side of human experience privileging analytical thinking over holistic forms of understanding.

Although Robins and Webster present valid concerns about the potential downfalls and abuses associated with the technological age, they stop short of recommending or theorizing what could be done to counter the negative effect they so fervently warn against. This is accentuated even more by their view that the identities forged in this new era lack intuition, emotion, and comprehensive thinking. Interestingly, these points are refuted by Turkle's observation that although the technological community began with a more logical approach, it has now shifted to a more intuitive one. Furthermore, Robins and Webster's pessimistic portrayal is imbalanced. They fail to acknowledge the power of human agency and the relative autonomy of technology. A huge oversight is the fact that increasingly more people are using technology to resist the weaknesses Robins and Webster outline. Perhaps this is also because cyberspace represents a utopia of freedom and democracy in the population's psyche despite the fact that there is no longer a clear delineation between the real and the virtual.

Nevertheless, Robin and Webster's critique is needed at a time when a majority of Western societies are on a "technology high." The tendency is to valorize technology's impact, which points to a need for critics who are willing to go against the grain and present a skeptical voice. However, their critique would have more credibility if it were to take a more balanced approach. Steven Best and Douglas Kellner's work provides this balance.

Best and Kellner's book *The Postmodern Adventure: Science, technology, and cultural studies at the third millennium* (2001) employs a multiperspectival approach to bridge the dichotomy between technophiles' and technophobes' perspectives. They agree with the belief that technology represents a shift in identity; however, they extend the realm of this change beyond technophilia to include areas of warfare, ethics, globalization, transhumanism, and posthumanism. Likewise, they agree with Robins and Webster that there is a strong capitalist agenda behind technological innovations serving the interest of corporations and the military over humanity. For Best and Kellner, the two major forces of destabilization and novelty in the contemporary era are the Internet and globalization, which for them are interconnected.

Best and Kellner's multiple modes of mapping allow them to explain the cultural and capitalistic forces behind the many changes society is undergoing, highlighting the ways humans are coevolving with technology to create novel configurations of society. They portend a fundamental alteration of the human being into transhumanism (i.e., improved humans via melding body with electric "parts" and nanoparticles) and posthumanism (i.e., becoming a new species). They warn of the Frankenstein Syndrome, the pursuit of knowledge at the cost of examining potential consequences. This is poignantly illustrated with detailed discussions of xenotransplants, cloning, and cyborgs. They, however, overlook the fact that we cannot explore the ethics of posthumanism without examining the destabilizing consequences on human equilibrium. The notion of destabilization can be explained as the potential for new categories of humanity based on varying states of one's human–machine merger, such as the natural hierarchies that will be created when the population is subdivided based on where they fall on the fully human–fully machine continuum.

Best and Kellner theorize our future to include human fusion with technology through what they have termed the fifth discontinuity. With the fifth discontinuity, humans no longer maintain a superior position in the world. As we move to an era of posthumanism, technology is becoming more human and the human species is becoming more technological. Best and Kellner extend Turkle's recognition that technology is causing us to reexamine what it means to be human. Whereas Turkle explores this in light of emerging artificial intelligence systems, Best and Kellner examine the implosion of biology and technology including cloning and enhanced human abilities made possible by nanotechnology. Like Turkle, and diverging from Robins and Webster, they recognize the process of identity transformation will continue to evolve along with technology.

The perspective I use for analyzing digital online culture draws on each of these theorists as well as my own background in communication studies, cultural studies, and education. I build upon a cultural studies methodological approach involving the analysis of how artifacts of media culture affect people. Multicultural and multiperspectival lenses are used to interrogate the categories of hegemonic and counter-hegemonic forces. These influences are found through examining the production of media culture's artifacts within their political and historical contexts (Kellner, 2003b). Diagnostic critique is used to decode and interpret the meanings embedded in artifacts. This also includes analyzing how "culture deploys power and is shaped and organized within diverse systems of representation, production, consumption and distribution" (Giroux, 2004, p. 59). Practitioners also reveal how hegemonic and counterhegemonic ideologies are transposed to audiences via the politics of representation including race, class, gender, sexuality, and religion revealing emergent and sustaining dominant beliefs and behaviors. Furthermore, I employ George Lakoff's work on framing (Lakoff & Wehling, 2012) to illustrate that the language we use and artifacts we are exposed to are made up of ideas, viewpoints, and agendas. I also rely on Henry Jenkins's work on convergence culture, which describes the collision between old and new media, grassroots and corporate media, and power of the media producer and media consumer interacting in unpredictable ways. Convergence also describes a shift in culture where spectators (i.e., consumers) seek out new information and make connections among dispersed media content (Jenkins, 2009). These perspectives serve as important forms of analysis helping to ultimately cultivate media literacy and develop critical thinking perspectives on media culture.

The ubiquitous nature of technology is contributing to the blurring of lines between what started as two distinct realities: real and virtual. Although it is still possible to enter cyberspace through a desktop computer, there are a multitude of fragmented ways to jump in and out of it throughout a given day. This is evidenced by our abilities to tweet, take a quick snapshot and in an instant send it to a family member, navigate through a new neighborhood by checking a virtual map while walking down the street, and so on. The state I am describing is not entirely one or the other. It is dual and despite the fact that people in high-tech cultures still primarily exist and operate in the real, the real is becoming peppered with the virtual. This peppering is going to become more important as the tools become more wearable, prevalent, and integrated into our day-to-day operations, such as with Google Glass.

Subsequent chapters explore identity formation as it relates to ideology presented in cyberspace opening up new ways of thinking about society's responsibility in this evolution. Scholars have spent time mapping the political, economic, and technological determinants of the information revolution, in which virtualization is now a part, providing a solid starting point for examining digital online culture at the ideological level in terms of what this means for the citizenry and how society should respond. One of the most prominent ways society can respond is through schooling. Since few education scholars have critically engaged and theorized how we should understand, respond to, and live this information revolution, a critical studies approach is needed to provide a cultural, ideological analysis of identity construction in the context of virtualization and to draw some conclusions for schooling in light of the analysis. The purpose of the subsequent chapters is to do just that. Each chapter represents a different facet of the real–virtual and human–machine lines to help deconstruct the ontological distinction between the two realms of being.

This Book

In this book, I begin by analyzing the work of new media scholar Sherry Turkle. She is an apt starting point due to her contemporary, original, and prolific writings on the subject of technology and personal identity. As an MIT professor and director of MIT's Initiative on Technology Studies, Turkle authored four books on the subject. Her unique access to cyberspace participants in the burgeoning stages provided her with the opportunity to intimately study and think about a world that was unknown to most of the population. Her approach is also unique for the psychological perspective and ethnographic tools she brings to the analysis. Furthermore, it is interesting for the fact that she was writing within a neoliberal time that continues to work toward capturing the information revolution for hegemonic gains as opposed to personal liberation. Chapter 2 begins with a historical and political contextualization followed by a brief summary of each book to provide insight into some of the hegemonic and counterhegemonic forces at play at the time of their publication. Turkle's books are then analyzed for their contributions and omissions across themes of identity, authenticity, digital conformity, surveillance, self-censorship, race, class, gender, and schooling.

The third chapter begins with a brief discussion of symbolic interactionism and its use for analyzing digital online culture. Using numerous cultural artifacts, I take a closer look at technology as a vehicle of celebrity culture in order to articulate the prevailing thinking and practices behind the virtualization of identity. This begins the mapping of numerous cultural changes that sheds insight into ideas about identity evolution from modern identity to postmodern identity, and currently to identity grounded in digital online culture.

The fourth chapter unravels a form of manufactured consciousness most of the population engages in when interacting in online environments. This includes analyzing issues of domination and control of user data: manipulation of identity where loss of privacy is trivialized and surveillance is the new norm. It closes by outlining several fringe yet emancipatory movements against these neoliberal acts.

The fifth chapter begins by summarizing observations about the relationship among users' digital objects, identities, and knowledge acquisition. I then map schooling's past and current responses to virtualization. From there, I interrogate the use of virtual schooling as part of a larger neoliberal agenda toward privatization at the expense of human development.

The sixth chapter concludes with the role schooling should play to guide the citizenry through this area of profound and complicated changes. The chapter begins with an explanation of the intersection among schooling, technology, and identity. This is followed by a sketch of an initial critical theory of technology for schooling that includes its constitutive elements and closes with some thoughts about the future as it relates to today's morphed population and their philosophical and practical needs.

2

A Case Study: Sherry Turkle and the Psychological Role of Computers

Part of deconstructing the real–virtual and human–machine distinctions begins with a look at their impact on identity. Despite the pervasive use of computers and the World Wide Web, there is surprisingly very little sustained analysis and theorizing on the interrelationship among identity, culture, and the virtual. Although some scholars have looked at the social and personal implications of human interaction with new media (Buckingham, 2008; Johnson, 2006; Nelson, 1987; Norman, 1988; Reeves & Nass, 1996), few are examining the impact digital online culture is having on our identity in general, and specifically on how we see ourselves and live out our lives. One of the few but most prolific and long-standing researchers in this area is Sherry Turkle, a leading scholar of human–computer relations at the Massachusetts Institute of Technology (MIT). She is also the director of MIT's Initiative on Technology and Self (ITS), which investigates the social and psychological dimensions of technological change (Turkle, 2003). Her work is unique and recognized across myriad disciplines for both its subject matter and the psychoanalytical, sociological, and ethnographic perspectives it employs, making it a logical choice as a case study for this chapter. Given the ITS mission to be "a center for research and reflection on the subjective side of technology and to raise public discourse on the social and psychological dimensions of technological change" (Turkle, 2003), it is no surprise that Turkle's work engages the cultural implications of the computer, early virtual environments, and the cultural practices they provoke. *Harvard Review* referred to Sherry Turkle as "one of the most distinguished scholars in the area of how technology influences human identity" (Coutu, 2003, p. 1), and *Newsweek* identified her as one of the most important people to watch in cyberspace ("50 for the Future," 1995).

Turkle's writings are also interesting for the perspective she brings to the real–virtual and human–machine divides. Her earlier writings represent an idealized virtual world full of possibilities for releasing human potential that is described to be separate from the real world. Her later writings demonstrate another kind of separation, where in light of her interpretation of technology's encroachment on the real, she advocates users actively retreat from the virtual back to the real. In both cases, Turkle's conclusions exemplify her belief in demarcations between the real and the virtual and humans and their machines. Another point to consider as I discuss her writings is the level to which the prevailing neoliberal political agenda is evident in her observations, which is revealed as I historically and politically situate her writings.

A point made clear across Turkle's books is that like it or not technology and the virtual are not only here to stay but are also fundamentally changing human identity, culture, and society. Of particular interest are the four books she authored over a span of 30 years, as they analyze personal and cultural changes as they relate to early computing and then to virtualization. Beginning in 1984, she published *The second self: Computers and the human spirit*, one of the first analyses of computers as tools to think about the self. A decade later, one of her most well-known books *Life on the screen: Identity in the age of the Internet* hit the bookstores (1995). This book uses the then-novel world of multiuser domains (MUDs) to document both user behaviors and the role virtual participation plays on their sense of self. In 2009, *Simulation and its discontents* was published with a lengthy introduction by Turkle; she includes four in-depth essays written by other authors on simulation culture across a variety of scientific disciplines. Her most recent book, *Alone together*, was published in 2011. The strong stance that it takes on technology's negative impact on identity is surprising.

This case study will first summarize and contextualize each book then present and analyze key themes relevant to identity, ideology, manufactured consciousness, and education juxtaposed with Turkle's position on them. Contextualization is used to examine Turkle's books within their political, economic, and sociological context; other cultural artifacts of the time such as films and books are also used. Additionally, in the case of Sherry Turkle, I include the noteworthy direction of several MIT research initiatives because MIT's culture invariably impacts her thinking.

The Second Self: A Burgeoning Human–Machine Relationship

Turkle's first book *The second self* is an examination of how people are changing as a result of their involvement with technology. Using a theoretical framework drawing on developmental psychology, she looks at several groups of computer users: children, adolescents, video gamers, programmers, and hackers to document how the computer is used as an evocative object to reflect on themselves, society, humanity, and spirituality. She notes that computers affect how users think about concepts such as animate and inanimate; conscious and not conscious; life and death. Specifically, she finds the acts of computer programming, game playing, and even hacking as gateways to entering into a relationship with the computer. Her central argument is that it is through these relationships that users begin to experience the computer as a second self: a mirror of identity.

This book was one of the first of its time to uncover the computer's impact on users' psychological and emotional development. As Turkle asserts, it provokes the reader to move beyond viewing the computer as a tool that does something for us to looking at the computer as a companion that does something to us. Although I appreciate her focus on its impact on personal identity and metaphysical questions, it would be helpful to see her situate this point within the larger sociopolitical context. Considering the collective identity and ideology of 1980s US society would help the reader to comprehend and evaluate better some of her conclusions. Furthermore, Turkle does not explore the 1980s neoliberal corporate interests in getting individuals to join computer culture via mass consumerism. She mentions that purchasing a computer means entering a "new world of information to be gathered, assimilated and discussed" and "participation in this world is part of what people are buying" (p. 173), yet stops short of analyzing the dark side to the relationship between corporations and computer culture despite the fact that the cyberpunk genre of the time was critiquing it at length.

Thus, a huge oversight is her failure to discuss the ethical dilemmas and tensions around this hegemony.

At the time *The second self* was written in 1984, computer technology was still at its beginning stage with the Internet limited to scientific, military, and commercial research institutions. Although the Internet was still seven years away from its official debut to the masses, the emerging technology explosion was manifested in several advancements. The 1980s are the years of supercomputer machines such as Cray XMP, The Connection Machine, and the initial introduction of the PC, such as IBM's Commodore 64. The same period also sees the start of the open source movement with the creation of MIT graduate student Richard Stallman's Free Software Foundation (FSF). Consistent with this part of MIT culture at the time, technology presents, for Turkle, all the hopes for a better tomorrow evident in her focus on computer programming as a means of empowerment and control. Another point to consider is that although she had her finger on the pulse of technological gains, she does not engage the fact that there were two opposite perspectives at the time both linked to MIT. The first was a hegemonic position, supportive of the closed US economic culture of the 1980s, and the second was a counterhegemonic perspective pushing for an open cybersociety.

In the political sphere, society was consumed with the Reagan administration's Star Wars defensive initiative justified in Reagan's 1983 speech, "It took one kind of military force to deter an attack when we had far more nuclear weapons than any other power; it takes another kind now that the Soviets, for example, have enough accurate and powerful nuclear weapons to destroy virtually all of our missiles on the ground" (1983). The arms race against the Soviet Union compelled the US government to spend extraordinary amounts of money developing the most sophisticated technology possible in the form of a Strategic Defense Initiative (SDI) adding computer technology as a new kind of military force. The purpose was to position the United States as the most militarily sophisticated in the world, resulting in collective awareness on the need for technological advancement. In doing so, Reagan was able to continue the Cold War of the 1950s and its culture of fear was absorbed into the population's consciousness.

The 1980s was also a time of economic ups and downs. Trickledown economics promised higher income for the population by cutting taxes (Cannon, 2000). The outcome generated a high national deficit and opened the door to imported goods in the form of electronics and foreign cars, starting a swing in consumer spending from US-made products toward cheaper yet well-made Asian ones (Cannon, 2000). Although Reaganomics benefitted the service sector, specifically businesses related to defense programs such as in California, it hurt states with high manufacturing jobs, dramatically increasing unemployment. Ultimately, this decade moved the United States from a production to a service economy. The technology sector was not yet a critical player in the US economy; however, opening the import door enabled the PC clones of the 1990s to offer much more affordable prices creating a market for middle class families to afford these machines. People suffered under Reagan's $30 billion cuts to several social programs such as housing, job training, and school lunches resulting in a rise in the number of Americans living in poverty and homelessness (Cannon, 2000). Additionally, there was a conservative atmosphere supportive of Reagan evidenced by the strength and power of Jerry Falwell's Moral Majority organization. This is also made clear in Reagan's frequent references to the early American Puritan John Winthrop (Yager, 2006). While Reagan seemed to be trying to reestablish the conservative values of the 1950s, the cyberpunk genre of the same period projected an ultrafuturistic society devoid of values.

Defense spending inevitably spilled into our colleges with MIT's research historically being "heavily dependent on defense department funding" (Glenn, 1989). At the time, MIT was the top nonprofit Department of Defense contractor in the nation. Additionally, the Draper Institute, working on classified applied weapons research, collaborated with MIT graduate students in joint research activities. This is further corroborated by the fact that many of MIT's key administrators were "closely linked to the Pentagon" (Glenn, 1989). Thus, on the political front there were great hopes for our research institutions to help the United States maintain hegemony through military technological advancements, creating urgency to rally computer scientists behind this endeavor. It is interesting to note that the fall of the Soviet Union in 1989 put a halt to Star Wars ending its justification as a race against the Soviets.

What started as a competition against the Soviet Union resulted in the creation of the Internet. As early as 1957 the USSR launched Sputnik, the first earth satellite, causing the United States to form the Advanced Research Projects Agency (ARPA). Its mission was to work with the Department of Defense to help them expedite collaboration among scientific centers across the nation (Yurkanon, 2001). At the same time, Leonard Kleinrock completed his doctoral book at MIT on queuing theory in communication networks, and soon became a UCLA professor involved in the first Internet connection (Computer History Museum, 2006a). By 1969 four networking nodes had been created and Charley Kline attempted the first inter-computer communication supervised at UCLA by Leonard Kleinrock (Zakon, 2011). By the 1970s the Advanced Research Agency Network (ARPANET) had been established for use on projects in universities and research laboratories (Tomlinson, n.d.).

In the 1980s, the ARPANET was making great strides with the National Science Foundation (NSF) advised via congressional hearings to make supercomputers available to US scientists. By 1984, the NSF issued a request for proposals to establish supercomputer centers providing access to the entire US research community, regardless of discipline and location, and a new division of Advanced Scientific Computing was created with a $200 million budget over five years (Computer History Museum, 2006b). This resulted in readjustment from a restricted and defensive node system to an open, growing rhizomatic organism. While MIT was involved in this endeavor, Turkle's attention was not on studying the impact of network interactions. However, science fiction writers and filmmakers were already exploring the subject. Their suspicions played out in contemporary fiction, called cyberpunk.

In entertainment, cyberpunk culture was on the rise. The genre reflects a very different perspective of technology from the neoliberal establishment's optimistic push for expansion into the fabric of US culture and commerce. It articulated a growing uncertainty about technology, and as described by Douglas Kellner, cyberpunk culture "embraces technology which is used for individual's own purposes (although often against the purposes and interests of established institutions and usages)" (2003a, p. 302). As noted by Steve Jones (1995) in his article "Hyper-Punk: Cyber-punk and information technology," cyberpunk literature situates the future in the present and consists of societies in a high information state. He theorized, "the parallels we draw between machines and living things strongly color our understanding of the world... Now, information is central to biology—life is thought of as a genetic code, and like a machine code is available for editing" (p. 89). For Bruce Bethke (2004), cyberpunk is a fictional warning about "the science of controlling human functions and of electronic, mechanical and biological control systems designed to replace them" (Bethke, 2004). The technology of this genre is characterized by what he describes to be ultratechnology, where technology is used to create genetic mixes: machines that think like humans and humans that think like machines. Cyberpunk literature served as a warning against technology's potential dangers (Kellner, 2003a). This genre appears in landmark films such as *Blade Runner* and *Tron*, as well as in sci-fi literature such as William Gibson's *Neuromancer*.

Blade Runner (De Lauzirika & Deeley, 1982), based on the Philip K. Dick Novel *Why do androids dream of electric sheep?* (Dick, 1996), was unique for its depiction of a bleak, urban, Asian American future demonstrating a strong contrast to the 1950s and 1960s plastic pop sci-fi like the *Star Trek* TV Series (Roddenberry, 1966) and the popular film *Barbarella* (Di Laurentis, 1968). Directed by Ridley Scott, Deckard, a blade runner (aka bounty hunter) played by Harrison Ford, has to track down and kill four rogue cyborgs called Replicants. Through this process the viewer comes to question the definition of humanity and the line between authentic and inauthentic. The viewer is also introduced to the idea that the world can exist without clear distinctions between humans, machines, and altered states of being. Most interesting is the Replicants' superhuman qualities and the film's interrogation of the aging process and mortality, a theme we see often throughout the 1980s and 1990s. Nietzsche's ubermensch ([1883–1885]2012) can be used to better understand these cyborgs, as they are more physically and psychologically evolved than humans. Replicants represent complex machines that question their own metaphysical condition in their quest for freedom and to resolve their mortality. Although they transcend humanity, they still seek to become more like their weaker human makers. This film reflects the reality that at the time humans were pushing the boundaries of their own limitations through computer technology, yet cyberpunk artifacts reveal an opposite dynamic to illustrate the dangers this quest represents.

The original *Tron* (Kushner, 1982), directed by Steven Lisberger, depicts the hero Kevin Flynn, played by Jeff Bridges, as a software engineer and hacker who becomes trapped inside a computer's hardware and must fight for his life and freedom from this oppressive environment. Although the film was made with computer graphics limited to modest techniques resulting in a rather simplistic look, it is hailed as a milestone in the computer animation industry. Ironically, a film whose content is skeptical of technology utilized some of the most advanced technology of the time. Simultaneously, William Gibson was publishing his groundbreaking sci-fi book *Neuromancer* ([1984]2004), in which his protagonist, Henry Case, is a drug addict and cyberspace hacker who must use his hacking skills to save his life.

Each of these cultural works depict a rather grim view of technology overcoming humans and the latter having to use their unique qualities of logic and reasoning to escape impending doom. Like several past inventions that changed society, such as the printing press, telephone, and television, people's uncertainty and anxiety about contemporary computer technological advancements are reflected in the cyberpunk current. The genre is an interesting juxtaposition to the neoliberal push for idealizing technology as a path to a more open, free, liberated, and prosperous future.

Counter to the cyberpunk movement, Turkle's early 1980s book celebrated technology's social influences and potential for a better life and society. Although these writings are at odds with the film and literature at that time, they are consistent with the political, military, scientific, and MIT supported ideology that technology will protect and transform society for the better. Interestingly, sci-fi writers seemed to be more capable of deciphering the real and imagined abuses of computer technology.

Life on the Screen: Utopia in the Making

A decade later, Turkle's seminal book *Life on the screen: Identity in the age of the Internet* (1997) was published. It is an evolution from her first book as it relies less on empirical research and more on individual interviews to prove larger theoretical points. Whereas *The second self* looked at involvement with computers, this book extends to the early stages of cyberspace. Society viewed through Turkle's lens is one where virtualization enables marginalized groups to be more in control of their lives. She also credits computer technology with expanding diversity by aiding in opening up a "closed" modernist society to becoming a more "open" postmodern society, where a multitude of expressions are encouraged. Furthermore, she expands some of the ethical and moral challenges computer technology is posing to one's sense of what it means to be human, including conceptions of aliveness, spirituality, and God. These are some important findings given the fact, Turkle argues, that we have crossed into postmodernity, evidenced by her identity arguments.

What I appreciate most about this book is the mapping from modern to postmodern identity. She recognizes that society is no longer operating in a modernist frame where identities are stable, life is tangible and hierarchical, and the depth of meaning is to be minded. Rather, it is recognized that cyberspace was decentering and multiplying identity, creating shifting realities and meanings that are more surface and varied. Most concerning is the celebratory outlook on the current and imminent downside to cyberspace. Other than discussing the issue of virtual rape, she stops short of musing about the impact corporations and neoliberal ideology may have in and around this new environment. She does not preview corporate and political control and probing into citizen's cyberlife. Additionally, her observatory stance lacks a moral position on this issue.

One of Turkle's most salient points about identity in light of multiuser virtual environments like MUDs and MOOs is the fact that these cyber environments allow participants to more fully explore different aspects of themselves including the ability to play with their identity and try out new ones. Although identity scholars like Sheldon Stryker (1980) argue that our identities correlate with the roles we play in society, Turkle's observation opens up the idea that identity in cyberspace extends beyond the roles we play in society to include imagined roles conjured up in cyber environments. This is an important point given that up to this time the only identity play available was trying on different aspects of self in real life (RL) with much higher stakes, where certain types of identity play simply was not possible or extremely difficult (e.g., gender swapping).

By the early 1990s, the broader public was given access to the World Wide Web with the first web browser, created by Tim Burners-Lee, released in 1991 (Wall, 2013). At the time, computer connections were still very slow using modems and dial-up. Furthermore, the websites one encountered imitated print newspapers with webpages structured like newspaper front pages. Additionally, the ARPANET was disbanded and rapidly morphed into the Internet. Mosaic, the precursor to Netscape, was created, the WWW was released, and the Internet exploded. As outlined by the Computer History Museum, "what had been doubling each year, now doubles in three months. What began as an ARPA experiment has, in the span of just 30 years, become part of the world's popular culture" (2006b). Turkle was on the cutting edge with her exploration of these early Internet communities.

Life on the screen was published during the Clinton years, a time of economic high. The national debt of the Reagan years had been turned into a surplus and the country was experiencing an economic boom (Clinton, 2005). This was also the era of the dot com bubble, epitomizing society's obsession with the Web's potential to become the new "gold rush" of the time. The Clinton administration widely supported technological growth by keeping cyberspace free of trade barriers and a series of bilateral agreements on intellectual property, high tech products, services, and other sectors. For the Clinton administration, such technological policies were the building blocks of the "new economy" (National Archives and Records Administration, 2000).

Socially, the median family income increased, unemployment was at its lowest level in more than 30 years, and there were 7 million fewer people living in poverty (National Archives and Records Administration, 2000). This led to a time of social optimism and hope in a future in which the technology sector was an integral part despite its unrealized potential. Additionally, the administration was committed to doing what it could to narrow, or close, the Digital Divide by tripling the funds for Community Technology Centers, which provided access to computers and the Internet to low-income urban and rural neighborhoods. President Clinton also challenged the private sector to develop new business models for low-cost computers and Internet access to make universal access at home affordable for all Americans. Subsequently, by the end of the 1990s, 95 percent of public schools and 63 percent of American classrooms were connected to the Internet (National Archives and Records Administration, 2000). It was through these and other measures that Clinton was to fulfill his larger mission: to manage the nation's transition from the industrial age to the information age (Klein, 2003). Turkle's work during this transitional time reflects this optimism with cyberspace being an emancipatory agent, where machines and humans are becoming more alike than different, and where people are provoked to consider postmodern ideas about the instability of meaning and the lack of universal and knowable truths.

The technological high was also seen in cutting edge research with MIT switching its focus from the military to corporations. In the early 1990s, MIT received a $2.65 million dollar grant from Hewlett Packard to support research for improving the ways in which humans interact with computers (Moy, 1993). In 1995 MIT's media lab announced its newest project "Things that Think," referring to their mission to embed computing into common objects that are first and foremost something other than a computer or telecommunication device (Hsu, 1995). Additionally, the director at the time, Nicholas Negroponte, recognized that the media lab was a way for corporations to outsource their basic research. In a 1995 interview with the *Tech*, MIT's school newspaper, Negroponte states, "so from the corporate point of view, we are basically presenting ourselves and they see us, I believe, in this way—as a place where they can, at very low cost, still keep their finger in basic research into applications" (Hsu, 1995, p. 15). It is interesting to note that Turkle's writing does not foresee the commodification of identity to come nor higher education's role in this practice.

The hit film *Terminator 2: Judgment Day* (Austin & Rack, 1991) was released in 1991. In line with MIT's "Things that Think" initiative, it depicts cyborgs, machines with human qualities, that are capable of controlling humanity. The terminator protagonist, who had been the antagonist in the first *Terminator* film, played by Arnold Schwarzenegger, is sent from the future to prevent judgment day when machines release an atomic bomb and begin to exterminate humanity continuing the association of technological advancement with the decline of society as we know it. *Terminator 2* is interesting also because it marks one of the first times a digital effects character, liquid cyborg, is presented to the public. Extending technology advancement to biology, Steven Spielberg's popular film *Jurassic Park* (Kennedy & Molen, 1993) centers around biotechnology's ability to recreate the past in the form of dinosaur cloning. What starts out in the film as a marvel of biotechnological advancement soon turns into a nightmare as the dinosaur theme park breaks down and humans are terrorized by their own invention. In light of this critical view of the human–technology relationship, Turkle's writing at this time seems even more optimistic about this relationship. This aligns her work with the hegemonic narrative of the 1990s that technology promises a future filled with promises and unimaginable possibilities to release human potential.

Simulation and Its Discontents: The Onset of Disenchantment

Through most of the new millennium's first decade, the George W. Bush administration expanded the Clinton administration's support mechanisms for technology by acknowledging that school connectivity is not enough. As Bush outlined, "behind every wire and machine must be a teacher and a student who know how to use that technology to help develop a child's mind, skills and character" (Robelen, 2000, p. 1). The focus shifted from the number of schools that are wired to what children are learning within those wired environments. By the time Turkle's third book, *Simulation and its discontents* (2009), was published Barack Obama had just won the presidency and the country was going through ideological shifts on many fronts. One of the most striking aspects of Obama's campaign was his ability to connect with the population and fundraise through new media. He was the trailblazer for a wave of modernized campaign strategies and a legitimizer of technology as a cultural centerpiece.

Turkle outlines virtualization's contested terrain within science, design, and architecture and weighs the benefits and disadvantages of simulation. Most interesting is her account of the transformation professional identities are undergoing in light of technology. One of those changes includes an increased comfort level with opacity presented through software. For Turkle, young professionals are not concerned with understanding how a particular software arrives at an answer nor do they question whether it can be incorrect rather they accept the software "answers" as truth. It is noted that industry specific software programs have even reshaped minimum qualifications in fields such as architecture, where the ability to hand-draw architectural plans is no longer required. Furthermore, her findings start to unpack ideological divisions along generational lines spanning the fields of engineering, architecture, and the life sciences. It is at this point that Turkle's writing begins to show some uncertainty in her adoration of technology's impact on society.

This period is marked by economic troubles beginning with the weight of the continuous "wars on terror" and a sluggish economy, which soon becomes a major economic meltdown, followed by general panic and questioning of capitalism's ultimate outcome. By 2009, Obama tries to quell the mayhem by providing hope for a new approach to politics and works to achieve a renewed economy through bipartisanship. Unfortunately, the country became politically polarized, and a united opposition of conservative Republicans, who were prodded by the populist movement called the Tea Party, fiercely fought Obama's dream of a "new deal." Ironically, during the same time technology reached a critical mass with the explosion of social networking sites fueled by the same optimistic youth who were instrumental in voting Obama into office. These new phenomena provided a glimmer of optimism at this critical time. Not only were people able to share their lives in a novel, instantaneous, and interactive fashion, they were also able to use these tools to organize themselves for further social changes, serving as a precursor to the 2011 Arab Spring (Kellner, 2012a).

On the education front, the administration acknowledged technology to be a promising tool when it comes to teaching and learning. A new national center for advancing learning technologies called *Digital Promise* was launched to harness the efforts of stakeholders from educators to entrepreneurs to spur research and development by the adoption of breakthrough technologies. This initiative is designed to help transform the way teachers teach and students learn (Fact Sheet: Digital Promise Initiative, 2011). However, it ultimately results in a greater push toward standardization in the form of curriculum control, testing, and uses of big data techniques to assess students, teachers, and entire schools;

this problem is elaborated on in chapter 5. By 2009, Web 2.0 implemented more interactive graphic interfaces and the Internet was in full swing. Its high bandwidth capacity, earning it the nickname the super highway, helps expand technology's reach to become our new "other." We moved from largely one-way communication to two- way transactional communication that could cut across space and time, enabling geographically separated families, friends, and colleagues to build and maintain relationships in unprecedented ways. Thus, our reach was broadened to bring geographically dispersed people in our lives closer as a collective entity; everyone can follow each other's lives in a global sharing experience. This participatory environment enables us to project our "other" digital self, market ourselves to our inner circle, and maintain whatever composite image we wish to present. In this third book, Turkle does not expand her discussion to include more facets of identity as they are formed and presented across social networking sites such as these. This is especially surprising given that *Life on the screen* was consumed with the precursor to social networking, that is, MUDs.

At this time, not only are our machines increasingly fundamental to our lives, but also in the wake of the Iraq and Afghanistan invasions, the world witnessed the acceleration of unmanned drones turning war into a high stakes video game. These wars also precipitated the acceleration of humans merging with technology. The US military continues to spend a great deal of money advancing the creation of new, emergent technologies to enhance human capacities during warfare and to replace and replicate lost human body parts, creating some of the first cyborgs. In 2004, the MIT media lab's biomechatronics group received $7.2 million in funding from the department of Veterans Affairs to create what scientists hope to be "biohybrid" limbs that will use regenerated tissue, lengthened bone, titanium prosthetics, and implantable sensors allowing an amputee to use nerves and brain signals to move limbs ("Research aims to restore amputee limb function," 2004). These realities point to the fact that the real and the virtual as well as the biological and the machine are becoming less distinct.

Films of the new millennium such as *The Matrix* (Silver & Cracchiolo, 1999), *A.I. Artificial Intelligence* (Kennedy et al., 2001), and *Minority Report* (De Bont et al., 2002) depict technology being pushed to the point that viewers are provoked to reconsider human-ity. *The Matrix* presents life as simulation with machines using peo-ple as an energy source for "the matrix," a mechanism that enables them to live in a simulated world. Neo, the main character played by Keanu Reeves, is a computer hacker who attempts to overturn the machine's enslavement of humanity. Likewise, Steven Spielberg *A.I. Artificial Intelligence* is the story of a robotic boy who longs to be human and secure the love of his human mother. Although he looks human, he is able to overcome humanity's weakness by demonstrating deeper levels of empathy and ultimately surviving death. The film takes the ubermensch theme to the next level when the boy in the end is presented as the only survivor of civilization and the repository of humanity's memory. Finally, *Minority Report* presents a world where technology enables criminals to be caught before they actually commit a crime by creating a police state where everyone is a potential target. A problem ensues when one of the officers in this special unit is accused and strives to prove his inno-cence. This film shows that no matter how fail-safe a technology is presented to be, it is still subject to manipulation and malfunction. It also shows the enslavement of a group of people, clairvoyants called Precogs, who help the political establishment keep control of society.

Turkle's early work is consistent with these films in that it pres-ents cyberspace as a place to explore identity based on an emerging set of rules, which are beyond those in RL. Although she does not push the argument to the point of transcendence and overcoming death, her books present a path to this eventual state. I will expand on the ubermensch concept in relation to technology and the digi-tal world in chapter 3.

Alone Together: Approaching Dystopia

It is interesting that at a time when there is wide support of technol-ogy Sherry Turkle's most recent work, *Alone together* (2012a), takes a giant step back from her perspectives in *Second self* and *Life on the screen*. She argues that technological immersion and sociable robots, robots that she indicates have been introduced in Japan as social companions to the elderly, are creating a culture of isolation and obligation.

Alone together contains observations that digital immersion has created a new contradiction: We are both newly free and newly tethered. For Turkle multitasking has extended to multilifing where we now inhabit worlds of partial attention with little time for the important identity act of self-reflection. She points out a couple of modern-day dichotomies: technology has enabled us to be closer than ever but it has also isolated us; we are craving authenticity in our online interactions but increasingly find ourselves and others engaging in and accepting digital in-authenticity. Most surprising is Turkle's shift from technophilia to technophobia by concluding that the Internet has given us a new way NOT to think, and that the world of instantaneous communication has stifled the space needed to consider complicated problems. In the tradition of Erving Goffman, Turkle notes that when we are socializing online and creating our online avatars or profiles, we are giving a "performance" of us. This is also consistent with postmodern theorist Guy Debord's notion of *Society of the spectacle* (2004); he argued that modern society has a myriad superficial and manufactured distractions including "the obvious degradation of being into having... and from having into appearing" (sec. 17) that keeps society focused on the commodity, in this case the commodification of the self, at the expense of thinking more deeply about social life. Thus, for Debord, the "falsification of social life" (sec. 68) impacts our wants, desires, values, our very existence.

What I appreciate most about Turkle's book is her ability to take a step back from her earlier infatuation with technology's potential to explore an alternative perspective. Interestingly, many of her criticisms are consistent with the postmodern way of being that she valorized in *Life on the screen*. It would have been helpful to see an articulation of the line between a positive versus a negative postmodern state. Additionally, her perspective in this book could use more balance between that of young and older perspectives; technology's positive and negative impact; complete immersion and complete disconnection; and freedom versus control. Perhaps Turkle had such high hopes for technology that those hopes were dashed as she witnessed less empowerment and liberation and more control, an issue explored further in chapter 4.

On the technology front, the popularity of cloud computing moves the locus of data control from the individual to the corporate sponsor who in turn becomes the ultimate keeper of our data. By the 2010s, digital mobility devices take a central position and their miniaturization along with the plethora and sophistication of mobile applications (known as apps) become the main vehicle by which we infuse RL with virtual life (VL). It is this very mobility that Turkle is most critical of. Nevertheless, it is undeniable that the waves of devices, such as iPhone (est. 2007), Droid (est. 2009), iPad (est. 2010), iPhone 5 (est. 2012), Droid Razr HD (est. 2012), and iPad Mini (est. 2012), are marking an evolution from the desktop of the 1980s, the laptop of the 1990s, then crossing into mobility of the late 2000s, to the full mobile computers that they are by the early 2010s.

The Obama administration is in full swing and recognizes that technology is an essential ingredient of economic growth and job creation. It follows the guiding principle that technology, such as high-speed broadband Internet access, fourth generation (4G) wireless networks, new health care information technology, and a modernized electrical grid, is critical to America's long-term prosperity and competitiveness ("Technology | Guiding Principles," 2011). However, the country does not experience economic growth and feels beaten down by the continuous prosperity of large corporations in the wake of a massive government bailout. The crisis was used as a means to cut staff, reduce salaries, and obliterate pensions and health benefits while making record profits. It is the beginning of a new decade's class warfare in the United States.

On the social front, the persistent economic crisis has created a time of polarity, fragmentation, disparity, and a general mood of gloom. Turkle seems to reflect this mood in her writings by switching her stance from computers and the Internet being a place of self-discovery to a place lacking meaningful self-reflection. In contrast, technology continues to be embedded in everyone's life from social networking to increasingly smarter phones. Although Turkle highlights some of the negative aspects emerging as we become more reliant on our technology, she does not provide much of a solution outside of suggesting that we take a mindful step back from these devices. Theorizing ways of understanding are especially needed given the fact that the information and technology revolutions are entering a new phase, in the sense that they are becoming increasingly embedded in our culture. Thus, society needs theoretical tools to differentiate between individual agency and manufactured agency.

At MIT, the year 2000 marks the end of founder and idea man Nicholas Negroponte's leadership, and the transition of MIT's Media Lab to the corporate leadership mentality of Frank Moss, whose 25-year business background includes running software, computer, and life sciences companies (Weisman, 2006). In his interview with the *Tech*, Moss indicated that the media lab may conduct more research into projects of interest to its corporate sponsors, such as sociable robotics research to build machines that can interact with people on human terms (Weisman, 2006). In 2011, the media lab changed hands once again to that of businessman Joichi Ito, whose vision for the lab is to work on areas of education in a more connected and global environment (McQueen, 2011). Additionally, his plan is to balance long-term thinking characteristic of large corporations with the agility of short-term thinking associated with Silicon Valley start-ups, a refocusing from the venture capital approach of his predecessor.

During the 2000s, films like *Transformers* (Murphy et al., 2007) and *Avatar* (Landau et al., 2009) reveal a new narrative where humans and machines are more similar than different and their relationship becomes collaborative. Both films reflect a movement to a more postmodern way of thinking about humanity's coevolution and collaboration with technology. On one hand, in *Transformers* Autobots are hyperreal, larger than life robots with abilities and powers beyond any modern-day human made machine. On the other hand, they are representative of a classic American icon with personalities and a sense of morality. There is a mystical bond between man and machine that enables them to join forces to fight a mutual enemy. Likewise, in *Avatar*'s world, biology enables hybridization at the cellular level where human DNA is spliced with the DNA of Pandora's indigenous, the Na'vi. Human minds reside in Na'vi bodies with both human and *other* physical characteristics, completely melding to create a new identity. While inhabiting the body of their avatar, human drivers are able to roam the world around them, free from the constraints of their earthly life. It is a place where interspecies communication and relationships are possible. It is also a place where a paraplegic war torn veteran can once again experience the sensation of his limbs and the joy of living. This is a step beyond the current MIT work on prosthetic limbs, an aspect of technology Turkle doesn't grapple with ("Research aims to restore amputee limb function," 2004). Turkle should have expanded her definition of cyborgs to include this group of people as opposed to limiting her definition to people who carry or wear smartphones.

The new millennium's second decade introduces technology stardom: an embrace and glorification of the tech world within society's cultural psyche. The film *Social Network* (Rudin et al., 2010) illustrates this point by turning the birth of Facebook into a heroic endeavor. Programmers are identified as geeks in the movie; here a term previously pejorative is turned into a superlative. Technical prowess is depicted by showing the programmer immersed in an epic battle while wearing headphones as a protective shield from the outside world, commonly referred to as being "wired in." Being wired in is not an assembly line automaton but rather a modern-day warrior. This point is further illustrated through the film *Inception* (Thomas & Golberg, 2010): participants are wired into a machine that immerses their psyche with access to manipulating someone's dreams. Interestingly, Turkle shows being wired as analogous to the loss of human agency and control; yet as we see in modern films, being wired is also viewed as a liberating and desirable state, a step toward a heroic superhuman state of being.

Now that Turkle's work has been summarized and contextualized, I will outline several themes critical to virtual culture: identity; authenticity and digital conformity; surveillance and self censorship; gender, race, and class; and schooling. This will be accomplished by first summarizing Turkle's stance on each theme, then mapping areas of appreciation and concern, and concluding with implications.

Mapping Identity

One of the main themes across Turkle's writings is what computers do to us individually. *Life on the screen* perhaps does the most thorough job addressing the shift in our identity from a modern sense of hierarchy and depth to a postmodern identity that is multiple, fragmented, de-centered, surface, and simulated. This is one stance she does not step back from across her writings. Interestingly in

Alone together she uses the very criteria of postmodern identity hailed in 1995 to build a case that technology[1] is doing more harm to us than good and is trapping us in cyberspace as a way of life. Another point made across her work, as discussed earlier in this chapter, is that once we own a computer, we enter into a social relationship with our machine.

Turkle's observation that computers and humans interact transactionally is an important one. She argues that we interact with our computers but they also interact with us. In Turkle's view, this relationship has shifted from a positive one where identity exploration is possible and new meanings are gleaned about culture and society to identities that are fragmented, preoccupied by the task of managing multiple selves and multiple lives, overwhelmed by continual navigation of shifting surfaces, and increasingly comfortable with the virtual over the real. Subsequently, she argues, identity has become superficial with no time to reflect and with individuals who use their online selves as a laboratory for identity projection based on a prototype of who they want to be. Although I appreciate Turkle's observation, I am not in agreement that this relationship has soured because I see its pervasive and addictive qualities. Few people would be willing to give up this relationship given the fact that in the midst of this cultural change machines became more intelligent and we become more reliant on them. Therefore, we perceive that we reap more personal and social rewards from interacting through our computers than its associated costs. The price of breaking this complex addiction is to be off the grid and disengage from society at large as well as from our very identities. The rebooting of society through some of these social movements is characteristic of the post-cyberpunk movement, which will be discussed in chapter 3.

It would be helpful if Turkle were a bit more balanced with her stance across books, as she swings sharply from technophilia to technophobia. In *Life on the screen* very little time is spent on exploring the negative side of online communities, programming, hacking, and proprietary software. Additionally, in *Alone together* an analysis of the reasons for her conclusion that people are so immersed in technology that they could no longer think or interact meaningfully is missing. One unexplored explanation for some people's unfettered use of technology lies in our schools. As discussed earlier in this chapter, each US presidential administration since Clinton has had a vision and agenda for how to integrate technology into our classrooms and educate our society in light of this cultural phenomena; however, technology has outpaced our ability to respond leaving schools far behind in educating the public on how to handle these devices on a philosophical, socio-emotional, and relational levels rather than on the purely material level. The neoliberal education agenda that has spanned administrations since Clinton supports short-term learning initiatives at the expense of deeper societal improvements related to digital online culture. The Bush administration's *No Child Left Behind* and the Obama administration's *Race to the Top* and *Digital Promise* initiatives are perfect examples of a pattern that reflects a corporate culture of favoring quick results at low costs in the form of privatization, teacher deskilling, and reward and punishment mechanisms tied to positivist results, which is certainly why Obama's *Digital Promise* is a bipartisan endeavor.

Turkle makes another interesting observation about identity: "We make our technologies and in turn our technologies shape us" (2012a, p. 263), and simulation not only demands immersion but also creates a self that prefers simulation. Within these simulated environments, Turkle grapples with the issue of authenticity observing that young adults have an implicit understanding and tolerance for people who enhance online their projection of self. Although her findings are interesting, Turkle stops short of providing a deeper philosophical and social analysis. For instance enhancing an online profile relates to Jean Beaudrillard's notion of simulacra (1994): one's cleansed projection of self as communicated by a user profile is a simulacra of one's real self. Like Baudrillard's comparison of Disneyland's main street with a real American small town main street, the online profile is a vision of the person that has been altered to be a more perfected version of the real. This idea is further complicated by the fact that the perfected real is a projection of one's perception and thus part of one's identity. These findings provoke thoughts about the value of what it means to be authentic, which can be found in the imperfection. Our strengths as individuals lie in our essence and with that essence comes our individual quirks and weaknesses along with our strengths, ultimately endearing us to others. Stripped of these idiosyncrasies we become an empty shell of simulated perfection. Turkle's findings call into question whether an online profile is projecting identity as an empty shell and if so causes us to question what should be done about it. For instance, should our schools teach us how to "read" these profiles like we are taught to read the media? Should schools train students in the ethical use of the Internet including truth and honesty in one's self-portrayal? Difficult questions like these need further theorizing, which will be addressed in chapter 5.

Another way to look at Turkle's concerns in *Alone together* is to examine the multiplicity of values, meanings, and messages that are gathered from virtual communities, and to explore the various ways in which users decode these communities according to their own subject positions. Life on the screen is often polymorphous, containing multiple meanings in need of deeper exploration. Although Turkle's work is multiperspectival in many ways, it falls short in this area. According to Douglas Kellner (2011), a multiperspectival approach combines qualitative and quantitative, hermeneutical and critical, semiotic and structural, as well as the various critical theories to get at the full range of meanings. Unfortunately, Turkle's range of meanings lacks a fully rounded multiperspectival edge. Her interpretation should lend more time to looking at alternative perspectives such as how these tools are used and perceived across generational lines. This would help to corroborate the general belief that there is a deep divide across generations related to many technological issues.

Turkle's writing often implicitly refers to one of Marshall McLuhan's most useful axioms where he argues media is both a source of extension and amputation. Although not mutually exclusive to each view, extension articulates the positive aspects of these inventions, whereas amputation focuses on what is lost as a result of new technology. Applying this theory to Turkle's work, we see its usefulness more clearly. Virtualization has broadened our presentation of self and our abilities to share and to explore aspects of ourselves. However, it has also reduced our privacy, our old methods of connecting with people, old ways of thinking, and our means to escape from work. For Turkle, it has expanded postmodern identity and contracted modern identity, magnified our social relationships and brain power, and simultaneously shrunk them. I believe it has further augmented our humanity by enabling us to overcome several human limitations, a point explored in chapter 3, and it has decreased our civil liberties, a point discussed in chapter 4.

Authenticity and Digital Conformity

For Turkle, social media asks us to represent ourselves in simplified ways and then, via our online audience, pressures us to conform to these simplifications. Although she does not elaborate on the reason for being represented in simplified ways, it calls to question whether these simplifications are due to technical limitations: limitations imposed by the programmer as a choice, or the limitations of the users themselves trying to navigate social media tools, or a combination of these. From the fact that she argues that social media profiles present our edited life and then ponders, "if where we live informs who we become, in simulation, where do we live and what do we live for?" (2012, p. 277), it appears that she is basing this conclusion on the content of a profile rather than the novel and unpredictable interactions within these social media environments.

Turkle also posits that screen communication started as a mode of freedom and a laboratory for self-exploration but has now become a place to hide, where one can reflect, retype, and edit. Subsequently, more people are finding something as simple as the telephone conversation and the face to face conversation to be uncomfortable communication channels due to their spontaneity. Furthermore, she argues that technology has evolved to the point where people use it as an excuse not to deal with people in real time. I would also argue, they use it as a free pass from doing identity work in the areas of dialogue management, socially appropriate self-disclosure, and development of refined rhetorical styles. Digital, text-based communication does not require a sender to focus on both the message being sent and the nuances of the receiver, such as nonverbal cues of understanding (e.g., head nod), anxiety (e.g., affect displays—fidgeting with one's hair), or leave taking behavior (e.g., diminished eye contact, stepping away as one finishes a point). Likewise, socially appropriate self-disclosure occurs when one is able to consider the relationship with the sender, the amount of reciprocity from the receiver, and the larger social context in which the communication is occurring. Face to face identity work is important in our self-definition as it is through acts like social comparison and modeling that we shape who we are; a point Turkle does not engage. It would be helpful if Turkle had analyzed whether these are the same, different, or changed practices in the virtual.

Turkle does not see people as active theory-makers and meaning-makers. Rather, she argues people get caught up in technology to the point that they are led by its demands and influenced by its worlds at a low level of consciousness. In other words, people are not as strong as technology's pull. However, in social media environments, people can use video to present themselves in seemingly authentic ways. It should be considered that these environments still provide a lot of room for people to play with their presentation of self via camera angles, lighting, makeup, and in some cases costuming. Another point to consider is how our definition of authentic may be morphing as we come to accept social media environments as part of our lives. Turkle does not seem to see that it is an intensifying two-way relationship between technology and its users with each pulling and pushing the other.

Surveillance and Self-Censorship

It is refreshing to see Turkle develop her critical edge in *Alone together*. One of her most important observations is on privacy and civil liberties. She aptly notes that high school students do not really understand the rules of online surveillance. Turkle found that they do not know whether they are being watched or not. If they are being watched who is doing the watching and why? Is surveillance provoked or routine? Is it illegal? They lack understanding about the terms of service for Facebook or Gmail, for example, and they do not know what protections they are entitled to. I would argue this is not just true of high school students; Turkle should have included the population at large while making this point. The young differ in this area in their acceptance of just having to "be careful" online and their assumptions that if young people create an online company like Facebook or Google, then these companies can be trusted to be composed of ethical people. This is consistent with the attitude of the early computer culture, where open source, free access, open sharing, and goodwill (Stallman, 2010) are valued over proprietary communities that would like to profit from each new development.

Another interesting point Turkle mentions is the fact that young people do not know what else to do but to supply information. Their belief is that if they want to use the programs, what choice do they have? Turkle uncovers that there is a sense of resignation and impotence at the thought of online privacy. Like sheep following the lead of these proprietary companies, people provide personal information hoping for the best. This is in strong contrast to the hackers: modern-day Robin Hoods who work against these various practices and are hailed as heroic by this younger generation, which ironically abides by opaque software regulations. Our neoliberal education system should be held accountable for both creating a population unable to critically function within these environments and for failing to implement a plan that addresses this shortfall.

Turkle draws the analogy that cyberspace creates a warm cocoon where users feel secure and subsequently feel they are operating in a private space. The reality is the fact that the Internet is very public, always leaving a trace, and can be harnessed against its users. In some instances, we become the instruments of our own surveillance by providing the information and imposing a form of self-censorship on our actions, without proof that we are being watched. Turkle does not make suggestions for addressing this such as the role the education system in general and schooling in particular should play in helping to protect our citizenry from such infringements.

Another recurring theme unique to Tukle's work is that of virtual spaces as "objects to think with," which means they are vehicles by which we think of ourselves and of society. For example, Turkle points to virtual spaces like the MUDs of the 1990s as evocative objects that we use to think about identity and postmodern ideas. Turkle's work is interesting for the extent to which she maps computer culture's psychological and philosophical impact on human identity. However, she does not extend her analysis to include technology as an evocative object to think about race, class, deeper aspects of gender, social class, and its implications for schooling.

Limits on Gender, Race, and Class

Although Turkle does present plenty of female perspectives in her interviews and case studies, her discussion of gender issues is limited to that of programming preferences along gender lines, gender swapping in virtual environments as an opportunity to explore conflicts raised by one's biological gender, and virtual rape. Missing from this body of work is an expanded engagement of gender inequality in both RL and VL. For instance, Turkle argues that the nonhierarchical nature of simulated experiences makes the environment more welcoming for women, yet does not broaden her analysis to include how virtual environments can be objects-to-think-with about the social conditions, discourses, control, power, and struggles that impact women in these environments.

This point is illustrated by the fact that even today there are a disproportionate amount of men who program and who are part of the hacker culture, where control and access are at the heart of the group's work. This includes the creators of tools such as My Space, Facebook, and Twitter as well as creators of video games. As Turkle pointed out in *Second self*, "A computer program is a reflection of its programmer's mind. If you are the one who wrote it, then working with it can mean getting to know yourself differently" (2005, p. 24). If we follow this argument's logic, then those who use any given computer program get to know a little about the way its programmer thinks. It seems that culturally we are more aware of how men think in these contexts than women.

Another gender issue Turkle reveals is the problem of psychological or symbolic rape of MUD characters akin to RL rape. Deeper discussion is needed on how this shakes out across gender lines. In Turkle's case studies, it is the male MUD participants who are the perpetrators by taking forced control of another female MUD character through hacking or the creation of phantoms that masquerade as another player's character. In Turkle's summary, the debate demonstrates that although rape is an unsettled issue among the community, some players feel it is done in the spirit of "fun" without RL harm and should continue. Others feel the mind is an extension of the body and a psychological rape is akin to a real rape and this practice should be banned. In Turkle's limited sample, it appears male players share the position of accepting rape whereas female players oppose it; however, Turkle does not specify whether men or women controlled the victimized avatars. Furthermore, she does not explore cases of virtual rape applied to men. In cyberspace, a platform originally designed for freedom and egalitarian ideals, we find even the early inhabitants of the 1990s extend RL issues of patriarchy and female oppression into these communities.

The birth of Facebook, a worldwide social networking phenomena demonstrates the continued objectification of women. It was initially started via a system of comparing Harvard sorority girls to one another and rating which of them is "hotter" (Mezrich, 2010), illustrating the use of virtual communities as perpetuating female oppression. In this case, it took women, who through their intellectual prowess were admitted into Ivy League universities like Harvard, and reduced them to sex objects. Likewise, it implicates the men who were purportedly educated enough to know better proving that even virtual communities are battlegrounds for dominant, deeply ingrained, hegemonic views of women. This is a sociological and psychological area of cyberculture that needs attention. Unfortunately, even in Tukle's most recent book, *Alone together,* she does not explore this point.

Another oversight is Turkle's almost nonexistent discussion of race. Her work is devoid of analysis on how racial stereotypes and prejudices are treated in virtual environments or how virtual environments can be evocative objects-to-think-with about race. Some questions that need further considering are: Since users are now behind a screen, does that make digital online culture post-racial? If not, how does racial domination and hegemony manifest itself in digital online culture? How do the perspectives of these environments vary along racial lines? Whose perspectives are most represented in digital environments?

Finally, Turkle's work would benefit from contextualizing her findings within broader class related social conditions. Before proceeding on these points, I want to point out the limitations of Turkle's sample as it relates to class. Although Turkle makes some thoughtful observations, in the 1980s and 1990s, her subjects were mainly composed of privileged elementary school students as well as MIT students, who at the time had rather unique access to participate in early online communities like MUDs and MOOs. Furthermore, her sample sizes and demographic makeup are not always clearly revealed. This fact certainly does not negate her observations; however, had Turkle addressed the limitations of her sample's representativeness, the reader would better situate her conclusions' generalizability and overall limits. As Harvard Professor Martha Stone Wiske observes in her review of *Second self*, "the description of her methods are sparse... We do not learn much about the settings she studied, the way she collected and analyzed her information, the nature of her sample, the representativeness of the subjects she chose to quote, or the range of other issues and styles her subjects raised" (1985, p. 239). One thing we do know about her sample is many of them are from privileged communities. For example, her elementary students learn in computer rich schools that at the time of her writing were unique for their access to computers and online environments as well as for the level of training they received in how to program, use, and interact with technology.

Considering that Turkle's conclusions are not objective truth but rather a particular point of view, she does not address the class differential in the access, training, use, and creation of virtual environments. How does class influence one's biases in terms of what is done online, how one's identity is framed, and how one's identity is edited and presented to others? How does truth and authenticity versus simulation and fakery play out across class lines? For example, in *Alone together* Turkle finds that there is an implicit understanding that friends "enhance" their online profiles. This is not taken as an affront to truth but rather as a fact of simulation and another example of interreality culture. How do unwritten norms such as this manifest across socioeconomic strata? How are those from lower socioeconomic classes oppressed or empowered in virtual environments? Is there any correlation between class, gender, race, and cyberbullying?

Empowerment through Schooling

Turkle makes several interesting and thought provoking observations about schooling in light of technology; however, at the heart of these observations is the generational gap reflected in Turkle's writing. Just like those who came of age in the 1960s, a time in American history of great social and political change, today's generation is growing up wired with a very different outlook on society and identities; yet Turkle fails to acknowledge these differences.

Turkle seems most disenchanted about the fact that expectations have changed regarding technological transparency. Schools and children have moved away from learning how to program computers, which is a great disappointment to Turkle as she argues that programming is a way to understand the computer's power and to gain control over it. Turkle sees programming as a form of empowerment and as she notes, "the Macintosh and its 'double clicking' was emblematic of disempowerment, both technical and political... it made technology opaque and therefore a bad object to think with for thinking about society" (1997, p. 44). She expresses great concern over our tendency to replace programming with out of the box use of software, video game playing, blogging, and online chatting.

Although there is value in learning how to program a computer for the practical and thinking skills it imparts, Turkle's suggestion is problematic. Technology has become increasingly more complex and programming languages and skills have evolved rapidly over the last 30 years. Perhaps an epistemology of suspicion is a better position here over a solution that involves turning every student into a programmer. Rather, we should consider inculcating the student population to adopt the thinking skills of a programmer without programming. This includes the logical thought process dear to the "solutionists" who view everything as a problem solving equation that can be resolved through logic. This recommendation is not to suggest that all problems should be resolved through machine-like logic but highlights that such thinking is needed in a world where we are fusing with machines whose core function is based on such logic.

It is no surprise that Turkle argues programming is at the heart of computer literacy, yet her view is emblematic of a belief that humans should be the masters of their machines over the reality that humans should be psychologically preparing for the impending human–machine merger. Such human–machine fusion negates a dominant–subordinate dimension and suggests an egalitarian one where their difference no longer bears meaning. This point on the human–machine relationship is true as well for interreality culture, and one observation Turkle makes regarding this relationship is evident when she notes, "when it comes to human relations, simulation gets us into trouble. Online, in virtual places, simulation turns us into its creatures" (2012a, pp. 287–288). The word "creatures" exposes Turkle's view that humans and computer technology are settling into a subject–object relationship where humans hold a weaker position. Surprisingly, Turkle's only suggestion for remedying her concern is for users to master the machine via programming and then to also take an intentional step back from it. Given her level of concern, it is surprising that Turkle does not provide solutions by provoking readers to consider the role schooling might play in remedying some of these perceived problems.

Another point Turkle makes in particular about students' uses of technology in the learning process is that children thrive when allowed to tinker via trial and error. Such tinkering is also referred to as bricolage that, as Claude Lévi-Strauss detailed, involves a do-it-yourself mentality (1966). Although Turkle's presentation of this point refers back to mastery over the machine, I argue this is an important point to consider given that it connotes coevolution and collaboration with machines. The machines are driving a change to learning habits, as direct instruction combined with reading a textbook simply does not work in today's environment. In turn, students are embracing the new methods technology offers and employing it in unimagined ways at the service of their own curiosity to learn.

Unlike Turkle, I argue that schooling should begin its transformation with training in how to think about technology in terms of its pervasiveness and its fusion with the population. A critical theory of technology for schooling[2] is needed to provide schooling with additional tools for addressing the fact that the lines are blurring between RL and VL as well as humans and machines. This includes helping teachers and students to read digital online culture's embedded ideology, political economy, subtle forms of control and oppression as well as the treatment of race, class, gender, and socioeconomic status. Such a theory could also be employed to help students prepare to think about the integration of simulation and technology with their culture so that they maintain control over their life choices.

Turkle's work makes important headway in understanding the current changes we are undergoing as a society, a culture, and as individuals. It is to her detriment that she is unable to recognize the reality that mergers are underway. Thus, we need more scholarly theorizing on how to navigate digital online culture and understand its integration into our lives, along with its potential strengths and weaknesses.

As evidenced by this analysis, there is urgency for a critical theory of technology for schooling that better helps to explain and predict the ways in which we are constructing our own understandings of culture, life, and identity. We should look more carefully at the qualitative changes in behavior occurring in the course of our development alongside technology's development. Finally, further exploration is needed in the area of symbols and meaning making in terms of the kinds of meanings that are being created through our habitual interaction with the objects and simulated worlds. In the next chapter, I delve deeper into deconstructing VL–RL and human–machine distinctions by exploring the issue of identity change in light of the virtual.

3

Down the Rabbit Hole:
Identity and Societal Mutation

Identity: A Definition

We are all to one degree or another mesmerized by the new world that computer technology and cyberspace has opened up. Like Lewis Carroll's Alice, we popped down this rabbit hole never considering to what extent it would affect our lives. As Carroll so aptly noted:

> When the rabbit actually took a watch out of its waistcoat-pocket, and looked at it, and then hurried on, Alice started to her feet, for it flashed across her mind that she had never before seen a rabbit with either a waistcoat-pocket, or a watch to take out of it, and burning with curiosity, she ran across the field after it, and was just in time to see it pop down a large rabbit-hole under the hedge...In another moment down went Alice after it, never once considering how in the world she was to get out again. ("Alice's Adventures in Wonderland," Carroll, [1865]2009)

Today, we are traversing down our own rabbit hole and are on a path that is fundamentally changing our identities and culture.

In this chapter, I take you on a tour down the cyber hole to explore identity within the context of virtualization and digital online culture. Throughout, I examine identity using multiple social science perspectives including psychology, sociology, communication studies, and cultural studies while addressing identity in terms of how it is shaped by new media and the new culture surrounding it. I do not explore identity from the perspective of child development or psychoanalysis. Likewise, I do not grapple with identity as it is portrayed by premodernity epochs such as the Romantics. In addition to building upon constructivist psychology (see chapter 1), I also build upon Herbert Blumer's symbolic interactionism asserting that the life and action of people evolve in line with the changes taking place in their world of objects (1986).

Several contemporary scholars agree that our identities are in a constant state of flux with experiences, relationships, and culture feeding into who we are and who we are becoming (Best & Kellner, 1991; Gergen, 1991; Giddens, 1991; Stryker, 1980; Turkle, 1997). Our identities include what Stryker and Burke (2000) call cognitive schemes understood as our internally stored information and meanings that serve as frameworks for interpreting experiences. Thus, I recognize identity as a concept composed of a complex set of characteristics influencing the way we live out our lives. Some of these characteristics include self-reflexivity, worldviews, and the varying roles we play, each of which I will briefly explain.

It is important to note that these characteristics are not mutually exclusive nor are they immutable over a lifetime. Expanding on Anthony Giddens' (1991) definition, "self identity...is something that has to be routinely created and sustained in the reflexive activities of the individual" (p. 52). I include self reflexivity as one characteristic of identity especially as it relates to self-presentation and impression management; however, identity does not operate in a vacuum and there are other agents of change that may consciously or unconsciously influence it, such as the reactions others have to us, our use of and interaction with inanimate objects, cultural norms and rules, as well as the social roles we play; social roles being expectations attached to positions occupied in networks of relationships (Stryker & Burke, 2000).

Worldviews include the lens through which one interprets and understands the world, positions oneself in it, and interacts with others. Each is influenced by culture, past experience, daily habits, and communication. Best and Kellner (2001) speak to the idea of positioning oneself, noting that different people use different maps to make sense of the world and deploy a variety of ideas, models, and theories to organize their experiences. Giddens clarifies that "perspective" is constructed by interacting with the outside world.

He argues that a person's identity is in their capacity to keep a particular narrative going by continually integrating events that occur in the external world and then sorting them into an ongoing story about the self (p. 54). Although the fundamentals of identity formation have not changed as a result of the information revolution, this chapter employs constructivism to examine the narratives, tools, practices, norms, and habits of virtual life (VL), real life (RL), humans, and their machines as they relate to identity formation in the twenty-first century.

As I grapple with the idea of contemporary identity, I take into account current trends, both technological and social, and at times examine identity as it was understood during modernity and postmodernity to acknowledge elements that are still preserved, changed, and created within the digital age. We will begin with one pivotal factor impacting our interpretative process: The shifts in our identities through changing perceptions.

Digital Online Culture and the Establishment of the "Self"

As George Herbert Mead's seminal identity work (1967) suggests, there is an aspect of the "self" that is shaped by the attitudes of our surrounding culture. A salient part of today's attitudes is grounded in society's changing worldviews and multiple outlets of self-presentation. An understanding of this movement begins with mapping an inescapable part of digital online culture, celebrity culture and going viral, explained by social psychologist Charles Cooley's theory of the looking glass self.

Cooley uses the mirror (i.e., glass) as a metaphor and argues that just as we see our face and body in a mirror, and are interested in them because they are ours, and pleased with them according to whether or not they conform to what we would like them to be, we perceive how others interpret our "appearance, manners, aims, deeds, character, friends, and so on and are variously affected by it" ([1902]2012, p. 152). Cooley outlines three principle components of this theory including the imagination of our appearance to the other person, the imagination of the judgment of that appearance, and some sort of self-feeling, such as pride or mortification. Thus, we are ashamed to seem evasive in the presence of a straightforward person, cowardly in the presence of a brave one, gross in the eyes of a refined one, and so on (p. 152). For Cooley, the thing that moves us to self-pride or shame is not a simplistic mechanical reflection of ourselves but rather the imagined effect of our reflection on another's mind. Today more than ever we have a glimpse into other people's minds via social media and reality show programming.

Cooley also talks of hero-worship, the admiration of those we perceive to be above us. The act of hero-worship is said to help shape our sense of self in childhood and in adulthood to give us a sense of youth. As Cooley stated, "to admire, to expand one's self, to forget the rut, to have a sense of newness and life and hope, is to feel young at any time of life. Whilst we converse with what is above us we do not grow old but grow young; and that is what hero-worship means. To have no heroes is to have no aspiration, to live on the momentum of the past, to be thrown back upon routine, sensuality, and the narrow self" (p. 280). Most interesting is Cooley's observation that when it comes to hero-worship we never truly see a person in an objective sense, rather we use a few visible traits to stimulate our imagination to construct a personal idea we hold in the mind (p. 281). Cooley's work provides some grounding for today's cultural obsession with the elements of celebrity, going "viral," and media spectacle, which are all modern-day forms of hero-worship.

The rise of celebrity culture has reached an apex of adoration highlighting a shift from the modernist idea that celebrities are somehow unlike the layperson due to their born traits of looks, talent, and intellect to today's celebrity population, partially made up of ordinary people often acting outrageously in quite mundane situations. This is a result of various factors, including reality show producers using creative casting, dramatic editing, and careful selection of footage, that influence the viewer's perception thus producing a population fascinated with a manufactured form of celebrity (Rojek, 2001; Turner, 2004).

One of the genre's pioneers is arguably MTV's "The Real World," which brought together a group of young 20-something adults to live together; their everyday interactions were filmed, edited, and supplemented by clips from "off camera" participant interviews all packaged for dramatic effect and ultimately public consumption

(Curnutt, 2009). The genre has given birth to reality shows centered on just about any interest. It is no surprise that soon enough the noncelebrity became famous not for any given accomplishment or talent but because of their lack of restraint and allowing a camera to follow their every move (Turner, 2006). The reality-celebrity uprising is also fueled by society's changing news preferences. Today's competitive news outlets contain not just traditional news but also cable news, blogging, and Internet news. This creates a 24 hour cycle where there is a frenzy to be the first to fill air space, pushing networks to use some of the tabloids' fodder and subsequently broadened the media spectrum for celebrity news (Turner, 2010). Under these cultural conditions, going viral often presents itself as a genuine artifact of news, information, or even entertainment and is widely disseminated via classic and new media; yet the extent to which this "news" has been force fed under the umbrella of news frenzy should be questioned. Today, reality-celebrities often go viral despite the fact that the public often complains about the vacuity of the genre, yet at the same time continues to watch, discuss, and generally consume it, and by doing so expand its reach. Society's reality show love affair inevitably impacts self-view and behavior by providing us with models for what we should be proud of, mortified by, and generally strive for.

As the *New York Times* journalist David Carr observes, today, being interesting is the key to going viral (2012), and for the reality genre, the definition of "being interesting" involves unabashed displays of over the top personalities, idiosyncratic habits and customs, and often unconventional dress, hair, and overall styling. It also includes relentless, ultrahyped, media exposure. Kevin Kelly, executive editor of *Wired* magazine, notes that in today's world "attention is the currency" (2007). Going viral appeals to the feelings accompanying Cooley's hero-worship by providing the public with aspirations and celebrities including reality "stars" to be used as a basis for building personal ideals. On a psychological level, going viral is a path to becoming our own hero, and if the ordinary citizens of reality TV can do it, the rest of the public often feels they too can and many of them have (Trebay, 2012). On a material level, going viral is enabled by the radical change in our new media tools. These tools are encompassed in the term Web 2.0 and their accompanying high bandwidth allowing individuals to easily record, edit, upload, and view images and videos without the filter of big media corporations. The dissemination and diffusion of these images gives people an outlet for self-expression and an opportunity for others to freely access a talent pool. In a Freirean twist, individuals engage in a manufactured mass exercise to publish photos, videos, and the like to show their individualism to the world. In doing so, they are conforming to a larger capitalist driven trend to publish personal artifacts of a viral nature in the hope of boosting their sense of self by attaining celebrity status. This modern-day presentations of self are manufactured through the absorption of celebrity culture and presentational media.

The public is also exposed to a more insidious form of going viral, media spectacle, which Kellner (2012a) describes as a dominant form in which news and information, politics, war, entertainment, sports, and scandals are presented to the public. For Kellner, media spectacle refers to "media constructs and events which disrupt ordinary and habitual flows of information, and which become popular stories capturing the media and the public's attention, and circulating through broadcasting networks, the Internet, social networking, and other new media and communication technologies. In a global networked society, media spectacles proliferate instantaneously, become virtual and viral and in some cases becomes tools of socio-political transformation, while other media spectacles become mere moments of media hype and tabloidized sensationalism" (p. 1).

Media spectacles are also fed by news outlets moving from being reporters of the news to becoming commentators of the buzz emanating from digital online culture. They collect artifacts from the blog sphere, forums, chat rooms, YouTube videos, and a plethora of Web based sharing sites. These artifacts, presented as the echo of the entire public rather than the edited representation of a few, are selected based on spectacle criteria rather than sound journalism. Web based sharing environments are becoming a key component of societal change; their multitudinous, chaotic, and unfiltered nature provides raw material that intersects and sometimes conflicts with the organized, filtered, and scripted traditional form of news in either print, radio, or television. They are becoming active agents in shifting our perception of the world in part by the methods of acquisition and of diffusion that new media tools offer.

New Tools, New Lens

Marshall McLuhan ([1964]1994) articulated the fact that new technologies shape our identities by providing us with a different perception of the world. For instance, those with access to the global repository of information that is provided via the Web come to perceive the acquisition of knowledge differently, in the sense that it is accessible, easily obtained, and abundant. Furthermore, computer technology is influencing culture through changes to our language, as we now hear the name Google, a website, used as a verb "just Google it," and further illustrated through the Sapir–Whorf hypothesis, a theory that language, written or spoken, strongly influences or fully determines worldview (Kay & Kempton, 1984). This is also in line with George Lakoff's work on cognitive frames or using language to unconsciously conjure up thoughts to evoke an image or other kinds of knowledge. As happened with Richard Nixon during the Watergate scandal when he was accused of being a crook. When addressing the nation on TV, he stated: "I am not a crook" and everyone thought about him as a crook. (Lakoff, 2004). In the case of the information revolution, we have words like "Millennials" to conjure up a profile of youth as computer savvy.

Not only are new words being introduced to our lexicon but also communication is now morphing into forms specific to our media tools, which appears in the form of abbreviated bursts to satisfy tweets and texts.[1] These new tribal dialects are creating a codified and unique form of communication unified around common interests and tools. For each software and application there is a specific method of interaction. Around the globe, this is creating virtual cohesiveness between fellow users, and in many cases, trumping the social divisions of race, class, gender, and nationality. It is as if participants constitute an independent tribe assembled by a common interest such as those who connect about learning multiple languages (Leland, 2012) or those who form communities around an obsession for Air Jordan Tennis Shoes, dictatorships in Africa, or US politics.

With Herbert Blumer's (1986) notion of symbolic interactionism in mind, I will briefly discuss our changing world of objects and our psychological relationships with them. Humans with their biases and varying perspectives built machines and software, yet this is seldom at the forefront of users' minds. Database designer Michael Christie (2004) notes that the decisions (i.e., political and technical) and or controversies surrounding the design of a database become invisible once the interface is put into place. For Christie, the interface obscures by the illusion of objectivity, when in reality a database design often focuses on particular viewpoints at the expense of others. Furthermore, he notes, information architecture reflects a politics of knowledge and somehow enacts it. This point was acknowledged by Ted Nelson back in 1974 when he wrote, "People talk about the 'depersonalization' of computers. I want to emphasize the personalization of computers—that individuals design them, their programs, and languages, each with his or her own obsessions. So more than any book for beginners, this one stresses the personal contributions of individuals, and the wide ranging disagreements of a field which to many in the outside world seemed 'objective' and 'scientific'" (1987, p. 4). The reality is we are not highly conscious of programmers' and designers' impact on our tools and therefore on the shaping of our identities.

The ways in which we think about our machines often go unnoticed, yet as affordance theory demonstrates (J. J. Gibson, 1977), unexpected aspects of machines connect with us on a low level of consciousness. Don Norman's affordance work in his influential book *The psychology of everyday things* (1988) describes how we learn to use everyday things by the information available from the appearance of objects. Norman stresses the importance of "natural design" so that the artifact signals the user without requiring the user to be conscious of it. Such an artifact is created in ways that allow for users to intuitively know how to operate the device. In order for an artifact to be naturally mapped, it must take advantage of analogies and cultural standards that lead to immediate understanding. As Reeves and Nass (1996) found, user interface personality is actually communicated in several ways: error message language, user prompts, navigation options, choices for type font, and layout.

Apple, the maker of the iconic Mac computers, iPad, and iPhone, serves as an apt example of a company that has embedded standpoints into their product design by mapping them for easy handling and intuitive navigation. Jonathan Ive, senior vice president of industrial design, describes his first impression of a Mac computer,

"I was struck by the care taken with the whole user experience. I had a sense of connection via the object with the designers" (Ive, 2007). In a 1998 CNN interview, Ive shared that when designing the iMac he wanted to redefine a computer's form while making sure people could recognize it as a computer. Although he was going to step out of the "beige box" design that computers had been known for, he also recognized that by just looking at it, people should intuitively understand how to use it (i.e., that they could type documents, send email, and run applications). Another goal of the iMac redesign was to make it less exclusive and more accessible by adding a handle; as Ives notes, "while its primary function is obviously associated with making the product easy to move, a compelling part of its function is the immediate connection it makes with the user by unambiguously referencing the hand. That reference represents, at some level, an understanding beyond the iMac's core function. Seeing an object with a handle, you instantly understand aspects of its physical nature—I can touch it, move it, it's not too precious" (Ive, 2007). The machine becomes an active agent in identity formation and actions by teaching people how to handle and use it through its design. Design's impact on our behavior doesn't stop there, as it also influences the role computers play in our lives.

A current example of the specific and integral role computers and software are taking in our day-to-day lives can be found in Siri (Kittlaus et al., 2011), an application designed by Apple to be a digital personal assistant. Technically, Siri is a speech recognition and interpretation interface described also as a knowledge navigator. Siri's design is both verbal and visual as it understands and responds with natural speech, visually presents relevant material per the user's command, as well as sends messages and much more. It is unlike traditional voice recognition software in that it asks users questions if it needs more information to complete a task. Siri's true uniqueness, however, comes from its ability to utilize the cloud (i.e., servers accessible via the Web) where a powerful artificial intelligence algorithm analyzes words so that the more they are used the more it learns, and gradually becomes more adept at interpreting vocal commands (Daw, 2011). As an emergent technology, Siri expands its abilities as other humans feed it data, and thus all who use it contribute toward strengthening it. Siri is just one example of the level at which technology is being positioned to become indispensable to our lives. Its ability to assimilate our personal needs into its functionality gives the psychological impression that it completes us.

The impact of technological tools on our selfhood is echoed throughout Turkle's work. As she observes during an interview, "we often deny the power of our creations on us" (Coutu, 2003, p. 3). Perhaps what is most unsettling for Turkle and others is the fact that everyday life is becoming more difficult to predict and conceptualize. The modernist belief that the truth about people can be understood via a thorough examination of the details of life (Gergen, 1991) is being trumped by fact that we are developing ever shifting unpredictable and subsequently un-theorized ways of collaborating with technology. Confirming Turkle's belief that control is being transferred to technological invention, we may not always be aware of our technological devices, but one unintended consequence of their very existence is the impact they have on our behavior toward them and others.

As the new media tools we use become a part of our identity, they turn emotional because they are imprinted on us (Coutu, 2003; Norman, 1988; Reeves & Nass, 1996). These tools and their interfaces are loaded with cultural and historical associations holding a powerful appeal to our subconscious. Take for example the work of Shin Mizukochi (2009) who studies the pervasiveness of smartphone use as it relates to Japanese identity. His research agenda is focused on the extent to which Japanese youth are attached to their phones on a socio-emotional level, as the phones contain personal and emotional artifacts such as photos and a saved history of exchanged personal messages. This is further evidenced by the personalization of phones in the form of fancy covers, decorative straps, and even dangling charms (Baron & Ling, 2007). This point is corroborated within the constructivist psychology framework that argues perceptions are affected by the tool used. Just as the reality a physicist sees is affected by whether a phenomenon is looked at with the naked eye, an X-ray, or a telescope, our identities are shaped by the use of technological artifacts (Katz, 1981). For mobile societies, smartphones initiate a relationship with their users. This relationship in turn influences the way users perceive and interact with the world. Thus, identity in this arena is consistently in flux and adaptable to multiple modes of interaction including human–machine.

To hold on to modern notions of identity as static, regimented, and rather predictable is to deny who people are today.

The affordances of social networking sites are of particular interest for the psychological and practical impact they have on shaping our expectations and behaviors. In the act of inviting users to share their inner thoughts with their list of "friends," they find themselves addressing a forum of people without a sense of what this really means. This new form of distributive sharing is a result of how social networking sites function; as a program they establish rules of how the user will operate within the boundaries of their defined environment. We, as users, allow these environments to mediate our interactions without thinking about the implications of this distribution process, and soon enough our thoughts have an extended diffusion, sometimes worldwide.[2] As we type, we get familiar with the ease of the process and every random thought seems to become part of a larger dissemination.

Social networks not only influence the communication sent to others, they also filter the communication received from others. This filter comes from programs with established restrictions such as Twitter, with the maximum length of a tweet at 140 characters setting limits that require the user to adapt to this format and inadvertently create a new language to accommodate this form of communication, as discussed earlier. On one hand, users are prodded to consistently interact with others by being encouraged to post thoughts, images, videos, and links to other sites visible to their circle of friends, giving them a public medium. On the other hand, these sites give the false sense of being tailored to its users individually, with which comes a perception of uniqueness. Through this process, users are naturally functioning in a new psychological paradigm where they see everything coming to them personally, and at the same time every one of their thoughts is dispatched to a forum of people; all of which is happening with little time for reflection. Our perceptions are further impacted by the capabilities of today's new media.

Portability, Fragmentation, and Hybridization

Imagine if Alice is able to carry the magical Wonderland back to her home in England while maintaining relationships in both environments. This is the scenario in which we are now living, and Alice's worlds have become not only mobile but also portable, enabling her to simultaneously interact in both worlds. Portability allows a more complex state of simultaneity and fragmentation. One way to understand fragmentation is through the work of Fredric Jameson, who described it to be the emergence of the multiple in new and unexpected ways, unrelated strings of events, types of discourse, modes of classification and compartments of reality (1991). The portability and fragmentation of digital online culture enable us to bring along and interact in our individual worlds as we live out our daily lives, not only creating a population that is comfortable with both portability and fragmentation, but also helping to prepare the population for what is to come. As discussed by journalist Juliette Barbara in a recent article in *Forbes*, "in the future, what we now call 'gadgets' are built into every moment. Technology isn't a separate entity that needs to be turned off and on. It blends into our environments and moves with us. It knows where we are at all times because it's already there" (Barbara, 2013, p. 2). Those who participate in digital online culture today are currently being prepared for a new world in the making.

Portability is also fostered by our infrastructure with Web-enabled coffee shops, airports, and even cities offering opportunities for fragmentation. In the past, we were only able to activate a given portion of our identity within a singular context and interacting between two contexts was limited by location such as with the land line telephone; however, portability enables us to move between and among multiple identities across multiple contexts sharing visually, textually, and graphically at the same moment in time. These tools are directly contributing to digital online culture by creating a society of users more adept at its navigation, and who expect it to happen even while interacting face to face with others. Some scholars argue that this contributes to the degradation of identity. Kenneth Gergen notes that we are now playing "such a variety of roles that the very concept of authentic self with knowable characteristics recedes from view" (1991, p. 7). Likewise Turkle posits that "even a simple cell phone brings us into the world of continual partial attention" (2012a, p. 161). Portability and fragmentation certainly have their weakness; however, I would like to explore an alternative interpretation.

We now inhabit spaces populated with individuals who have adapted to a highly complex environment. Just as one trains the mind and hands to type on a keyboard without having to think much about the process, a person whose life has been consumed with portability is invariably developing the cognitive and physical abilities to function dexterously. When one is living this reality it is a "normal" state of being. Take for instance a recent *New York Times* article reporting on the evolving expectations of Web users. It was found that users' expectations for speed are increasing faster than the infrastructure. With four out of five online users clicking away if a video stalls while loading, mobile service providers are scrambling to build a network architecture for the kind of speed users now expect (Lohr, 2012). Just as our technology pushes us to expand our identities and actions, we push our technology to further enhance our identities by extending beyond what is currently possible. Through such transactions, we are incrementally becoming hybridized with technology.

Hybridization, characterized by human–machine fusion, became especially noticeable with the advent of Bluetooth, a short range wireless network. Suddenly, we started to see people walking in public, apparently talking to themselves, enveloped in invisible communication between wearable devices such as an earpiece and its smartphone. Today, hybridization is going further with more advanced technologies enabling fusion between our own reality and the virtual, for example, the new abilities of facial recognition software. Such software enables advertisers to determine the age range, sex, and attention level of a passerby, so that ads can be tailored to their specific demographics (N. Singer, 2011). As noted by Alessandro Acquisti, an associate professor of information technology and public policy at Carnegie Mellon: "It's a future where anonymity can no longer be taken for granted—even when we are in a public space surrounded by strangers" (N. Singer, 2011, p. 2). Technology is becoming so embedded in our culture that we often do not have a choice about interacting with it because it interacts with us. As we progress deeper down the rabbit hole, another upshot of portability becomes apparent: multiplicity and parallelity.

From Multiplicity to Parallelity

The postmodern idea of multiplicity is often used to analyze and theorize identity change in the light of a computer mediated world. Kenneth Gergen (1991) argues that social saturation through new media capabilities enables "multiple and disparate potentials for being" (p. 69). Likewise, Sherry Turkle (1997) posits that in simulation identity can be fluid, easily moving through multiple identities (pp. 49, 231). Best and Kellner (2001) observe that technology enables identities to expand and multiply (p. 8). Michel Foucault's notion of heterotopias further clarifies the idea of multiplicity. For Foucault (1986), heterotopias constitute a mixed or joint experience analogous to looking into a mirror. When one looks into a mirror he sees himself in an unreal, virtual space. His reflection projects himself "over there where I am not" (p. 4). The mirror is an utopia in that it enables one to see oneself where one is absent. Foucault notes: "The mirror functions as a heterotopia in this respect: it makes this place that I occupy at the moment when I look at myself in the glass at once absolutely real, connected with all the space that surrounds it, and absolutely unreal, since in order to be perceived it has to pass through this virtual point which is over there" (p. 4). The notion of the mirror can be seen throughout our cyber presentations of self. We now can see ourselves and others where we are technically absent, making identity both real and unreal. However, unlike a reflection in the mirror, what we project in cyberspace can be very different from what is projected in RL. So identity on the other side becomes a reflection of our desired selves cleansed as we pass through the cyberspace medium.

Multiplicity has expanded to include a simultaneous state of parallelity in which digital online culture participants are able to be in several places at the same time. Today, this is happening in numerous everyday contexts where individuals are present in real time while also maintaining a parallel cyberspace presence; its implications for identity are very real. US military use of what are now called RPAs (Remotely Piloted Aircraft, also referred to as drones) illustrate this point. Although those "deployed" in combat are not in imminent physical danger, they are exposed to the emotional trauma of being in a war zone. These pilots develop relationships with the troops on the ground via mobile phones and the Internet, work long grueling hours, and undergo a different kind of war zone stress from those on the ground, so they too are at high risk for posttraumatic stress disorder (Zucchino, 2012) just as if they were on location. Although these pilots are physically working in a command post located in the Nevada desert and at the end of their shift are able to go back to their civilian homes without fear of attack, they have been immersed all day in an actual war, creating relationships and connections and feeling its psychological effects. This demonstrates that a parallel RL–VL condition has physical and psychological repercussions on identity.

Parallelity often involves multitasking but is not limited to it. To be parallel is to maintain and seemingly enact multiple identities at the same time. What I refer to as parallelity, Turkle calls multilifing—both involve a constant state of partial attention. Although the idea of partial attention seems a negative practice, this is not necessarily the case. It has been used in computer science in the form of parallel processing involving computers simultaneously processing instructions to complete a task. Multiple processors multitask by sharing the work to be done, dividing the task into threads, and distributing them across numerous processors for completion. The interesting thing about parallel processing is that it is mainly accomplished by preemption, interrupting a given task temporarily to complete another one then resuming the original task. It time-shares the threads of the task between processors. This may seem like a simultaneous action but parallel processing is actually breaking a task into individual parts and thus fragmenting the processing. Parallel processing's appearance of simultaneity is a result of the speed at which it executes its tasks. Like these processors, our technological practices can arguably change our neural pathways to enable us to adeptly function under these new conditions. This pathway idea is supported by research on neuroplasticity (Fredrickson, 2013).

Our ability to quickly "parallel process" multiple, fragmented selves is best explained by the Stroop Effect, to which parallel processing has been frequently linked. It is a theory used by computer programmers and psychologists alike to explain a task's reaction time. To briefly summarize, John Ridley Stroop's study (1935) found that research subjects were able to name colors when the text color matched the color named (e.g., the word RED written in red ink), yet when the text color did not match the color named (e.g., the word RED written in blue ink) research subjects' reaction times slow down and are more prone to errors. Research done by Cohen et al. (1990) found that practice and pathway strength (i.e., a particular process is assumed to occur via a sequence of connected modules that form pathways) produces gradual, continuous increases in processing speed. Using this logic, individuals are becoming more proficient at multitasking as they become more practiced at it.

Although, partial attention is certainly an upshot of this new state of existence, there are technological advances designed to push the idea of parallelism to the next level. Each year new devices are released enabling humans to increase their processing speeds. The popularity of augmented reality is evidence of this. Not only is augmented reality easily accessible via smartphones, Google Glass streams real time information directly to eyewear eliminating the need to look down at a smartphone. With Google Glass, a user is able to navigate worlds, real or virtual, hands free and instantaneously, "it is very quick to learn and once the user is adept at navigation, it becomes second nature and almost indistinguishable to outside users" (Bilton, 2012, p. 1). Specifically, Google Glass enables users to monitor the world in real time and overlay information about locations, surrounding buildings, friends who might be nearby, and so on. What we see unfolding here is another example of the making of a new culture. An interreality culture that is multiple, parallel, and producing citizens who are adept at navigating these layered demands for their focus and attention. The questions to be answered are as follows: Who are we becoming in light of these capabilities? How we will continue to evolve in our relationships, gestures, norms, rules, and values as our devices enable us to more easily and fluidly move in and out of realities? Although answers to such questions are still to be determined, we do know that this new culture also includes an evolved hyperreality.

Hyperreality: A New Culture in the Making

In a post-cyberpunk era, technology is society (Person, 1998). The cyberpunk work of the 1980s was a fringe movement beginning among science fiction writers and spilling into the larger culture reflecting a general angst about computer technology. As discussed in chapter 2, at the time, computer technology was characterized by big, ominous supercomputers, fears of "big brother" watching, and a counter movement among hackers to subvert this system. Today, technology is infused into life. Kevin Kelley, executive editor of *Wired*, describes the world as being embedded with "Web-ness and connection...so that our environment...becomes the Web" (2007). A fact consistently cited by today's technology writers is the idea that we are adding something to our capabilities. Whether this is criticized or applauded, as technology evolves, we evolve along with it. We are adapting to today's significant technological innovations as we did to past ones. Electricity is largely taken for granted today, yet it changed our culture. The myriad equipment that surrounds us is powered by electricity in one form or another. As we switch on/off all kinds of devices all day long, they have transformed our sleep/wake cycles, our entertainment, our dependence on each other, and the rhythm of our lives. Computer technology, like our adaptation to electricity, is melding with our thinking and way of life.

Within this new culture in the making, technology is enveloping us creating a multitude of options. It is as if our brain is expanding too and is adding new sets of neurons and synapses all firing data at the same time. Such an overwhelming flow of communication creates further fragmentation as we race to perform tasks in synchronicity to fulfill a general desire to include every option possible. We often codify our rapid bursts of information into shorter and shorter bursts so that we can address all incoming demands. These bursts are accomplished through an exchange of tweets, texts, phone calls, as well as voice and gestural commands. Such cacophony becomes a well-orchestrated symphony that turns this technology mediated communication into an altered form of high context encoding and decoding, where the receiver is expected to fill in the gaps, read between the lines, and generally interpret for themselves the encoded communication.

Through miniaturization, mobility, and virtualization, our natural inclination is to function in parallelity, and with it comes a state of hyperreality. In the real, a highly contested term, we interact with tangible people and environments as well as their *representations*. Nicholas Oberly (2003), from the Chicago School of Media Theory, explains that hyperreality is not a static term and thus can be challenging to define. However, the two concepts most fundamental to understanding hyperreality are simulacrum over simulation. As outlined in Oberly's article, simulacrum is a copy with no original whereas simulation is characterized by a blending of reality and representation. Just as Alice's Wonderland is without a model, in our world, reality has no true definition. Following Baudrillard's theory, a hyperreal state is one of forgetting the "real." As Baudrillard and Evans further elaborate in their 1991 article "Simulacra and Science Fiction," the hyperreal is "not a question of parallel universes, or double universes or even of possible universes: not possible nor impossible, nor real nor unreal" (p. 311). Science fiction has traditionally played upon the double, artificial replication or imaginary duplication, yet the double has given way to the fact that "one is always already in the other world, another world which is not another, without mirrors or projections or utopias as means for reflection. The simulation is impassable, unsurpassable, checkmated, without exteriority. We can no longer move 'through the mirror' to the other side, as we could during the golden age of transcendence" (p. 312). We are living in a time when the tangible 'real' and hyperreal are homogenizing. Alice's Wonderland no longer exists just down the rabbit hole, it is now fused with her England. Perhaps this point is best illustrated through an analysis of contemporary film such as *Scott Pilgrim vs. the world* (Platt, 2010) and extending to the film *Sucker Punch* (Snyder, 2011).

Based on a graphic novels series by Bryan Lee O'Malley, *Scott Pilgrim vs. the world* is a superhero movie with Scott Pilgrim, played by Michael Cera, living a post–high school life as a band member and roommate courting Ramona Flowers (Mary Elizabeth Winstead) who must fight her seven ex-love interests in order to conquer her heart.

A distinguishing characteristic that separates *Scott Pilgrim vs. the world* from the plethora of superheroes movies such as, *X-Men* (Shuler-Donner & Winter, 2000), *Spider-Man* (Ziskin et al., 2002), and *Iron Man* (Arad et al., 2008) is how the world is portrayed. Instead of a realistic environment where superheroes are accepted as the norm, *Scott Pilgrim* offers an augmented reality where comic book graphics are embedded into life. Thus, blurring lines between a common, realistic environment and a hyperreal one where the main characters are naturally enhanced yet remain very pedestrian in their behavior and look. The characters in this story accept their augmented world as normal through their blasé attitude toward what would ordinarily be shocking or surprising conduct. A. O. Scott, film reviewer for the *New York Times*, calls it the "best video game movie ever" (2010). Director Edgar Wright is able to "collapse the distance between gamer and avatar not by throwing the player into the world of the game, but rather by bringing it to him. As a result, the line between fantasy and reality is not so much blurred as erased" (Platt, 2010, p. 1). As Betsy Sharkey of the *Los Angeles Times* describes: "That is the genius and difficulty of *Scott Pilgrim*; it both defies and, at its lower moments, meets expectations for this sort of film. Director of photography Bill Pope, who's no stranger to the conversion of graphic concepts to the big screen, having done *Darkman* and the last two *Spider-Man*, among others, keeps Scott's world on the ethereal, hyperrealized side whether or not he's in superhero mode" (2010). As Peter Bradshaw, film reviewer for the *Guardian*, points out: "Scott Pilgrim is an intriguing picture for being so exotic and eccentric, and for aligning itself with the style and structure of a videogame rather than a film: following not conventional narrative arcs, but a series of game-levels and flavoring this sequence, not with the usual dramatic reversals and character-development, but with an open-ended comic shtick" (2010, p. 1).

Consistent with Baudrillard's observation that we are already engaged in multiple worlds (1991), Scott Pilgrim takes our immersion into digital online culture in the form of video games and virtualization and gives us a glimpse into our coevolution with it. The film can be understood as a reflection of our current version of reality. Although we still have to logon to enter, this film visually illustrates the psychological melding and our increasing acceptance of the fact that boundaries are blurring. The film *Sucker Punch* also illustrates this point.

Although *Sucker Punch* garnered the scorn of film critics (Roeper, 2011; Scott, 2011; Sharkey, 2011), director Zack Snyder presents viewers with a world characterized by a pastiche of overlapping and blended realities. Three intertwined stories are presented so that the viewer does not accept any one of them as the only tangible reality, yet each of them is a possibility.

The first reality is presented as an account of the main character, Babydoll, played by Emily Browning, wrongfully committed to an insane asylum. This narrative is interrupted by introducing a second reality where the asylum is now presented as a brothel where girls are imprisoned and forced to put on burlesque shows in a swanky men's club. In turn, this reality transitions into a third one where our heroine is now a warrior fighting various entities such as samurais, World War 1–era zombie soldiers, fire-breathing dragons, and futuristic robots in phantasmic environments. These realities are reinforced with a highly stylized look and camera work to differentiate them. The use of filters shows a contrast between a depressing real world and warmer and colorful alternative worlds. Additionally, the change of the camera's motion and speed work in concert to give the feeling of a virtual ballet or dance where everything is in constant choreographed motion.

Throughout the film, Babydoll is made to look like a fragile, sexualized little girl only to reveal a warrior princess when escaping to another reality resembling a video game. As the *Los Angeles Times* film critic Betsy Sharkey writes, "the warrior princess leitmotif tracks back to Greek legend and has turned up in fiction and film ever since" (2011, p. 1), yet what is unique about Snyder's Babydoll is her superhuman attributes once she enters into a hyperreal world of characters. Most interesting is the mechanism script writers Zach Snyder and Steve Shibuya employ to blend multiple realities and demonstrate humanity's changing nature so that when Babydoll and her other female friends enter into what some critics describe as a fantasy world (Roeper, 2011; Sharkey, 2011), a world akin to immersion into virtualization, they become more than human. They are more moral, as evidenced by each task's goal to save the earth from some type of destruction even at the expense of personal loss. They fuse with technology to the point that they are neither human nor avatar but a new entity with physical and mental capabilities beyond ordinary humans.

As A. O. Scott of the *New York Times* describes: "Babydoll and company leap around like video-game avatars, following the instructions of a crinkly faced guru" (2011, p. 2). For Scott, the problem with a film that incorporates video game characteristics is that it struggles to overcome the "inherent tediousness of watching someone else play." For some this may be an apt observation, however, the film demonstrates the emergence of a new narrative. With virtualization, we enter into a world, often without references, that frees us from RL to become stronger, smarter, more capable, and even at times hold ourselves to higher moral standards than in our real lives.

Throughout the film, the viewer does not know with certainty which of the three realities is the real or whether they all work in concert to produce a new type of "real." What is clear, however, is in the hyperreal narrative, life can be fast forwarded or slowed down, it is far more exciting, and the stakes are often much higher. *Sucker Punch* further supports Baudrillard's point that we can no longer move through the real to the other side. Both RL and VL as well as the human–machine merger are blending to the point that our expectations and perceptions are shaded by both and we come to accept hyperreality as a natural state. The other side is coming to us and as it progresses we find our culture grappling with the very natural concerns that come with it.

Critiquing Identity

Before proceeding to the final thoughts in this chapter, the perspectives of several critics are worth analyzing (N. Carr, 2011; Gabler, 2011; Gergen, 1991; Turkle, 2012a). Each of their concerns center on the idea of inundation as it relates to the human–machine relationship. For Gabler information inundation is stifling thinking to the point where we are no longer motivated to do so. For Turkle, others inundate us via the World Wide Web and mobility to the point that relationships suffer. Gergen expresses concern over the inundation of the self through social saturation resulting in the fragmentation of identities to the point that they no longer exist, and finally, Carr argues that inundation is eroding our ability for deep thought and contemplation to the point where our very humanity is in question.

Neil Gabler's *New York Times* article "The Elusive Big Idea" (2011) argues that we now live in a post-idea world. For Grabler, one can understand post-idea by juxtaposing it with post-enlightenment with its style of thinking that no longer deploys the techniques of rational thought. In contrast, post-idea means that thinking is no longer done, regardless of style. Of the many factors contributing to this post-idea world, he highlights that public intellectual is eclipsed by the pundit in the mainstream media, substituting outrageousness for thoughtfulness. Grabler argues ideas are more difficult to express due to the rise of an increasingly visual culture, especially among the young. The biggest culprit for Gabler is the amount of information we now have access to via the Internet and we are inundated with so much information that we do not have time to process it even if we wanted to. The problem, for Grabler, is most people do not want to. Therefore, he asserts that living within Gresham's law in which trivial information pushes out significant information, we prefer knowing to thinking because it keeps us in the loop, connected to our friends and cohorts. We live in a world of information sharing via social networking sites, yet for Grabler, this is not the kind of information that generates ideas. These social sites serve as a distraction to thinking. Thus, thinkers and their ideas are victims of the information glut. The ideas of today's famous technologists like Steve Jobs changed the way we live but do not transform the way we think because their products are material and not ideational. Gabler ends on the pessimistic note that there is a future of information looming without people who actually think about it. Sherry Turkle is another skeptic who believes our changing world is causing us to develop habits of mind and behaviors that are detrimental to our culture.

As outlined in chapter 2, Turkle's most recent book *Alone Together* (2012a) reflects growing concern over our addiction to technology. For Turkle this results in neglected relationships, kids longing for the attention of their technology absorbed parents; decreased personal contact, people preferring to text rather than talk; and no time left for self-reflection and meaningful thought, we are losing our ability to stay still and reflect. She also laments that the Internet has enabled us to avoid doing things we should do like apologize, make amends, and respect someone's privacy. The most disturbing part of Turkle's conclusions is her assertion that people are weak in the presence of technology. People experience anxiety because they are not as strong as technology's pull, and we conform to what technology wants (Turkle, 2012a, p. 242). Just as Turkle expresses concern over technology's influence, we see in Gergen's writings a concern over technology's natural tendency to flood our sense of selfhood.

Indeed Kenneth Gergen's outlook is not much brighter than Turkles'. He argues that the degree of complexity added to our lives by technology is increasing to the point that our "ability to take a rational coherent stand on issues is impossible" (1991, p. 79). Furthermore, deep personal relationships are unattainable as we become more fragmented over an array of partial and circumscribed relationships. It is through the technologies of today that the number and variety of relationships in which we are engaged, frequency of contact, expressed intensity of relationships and endurance through time all are steadily increasing to the point of social saturation. For Gergen, the upshot of saturation is a sense of self that is manifold, competing, and multiphrenic in which "one swims in ever shifting, concatenating and contentious currents of being" (pp. 62, 79). Gergen also notes that the very concept of an authentic self with knowable characteristics recedes from view and "the fully saturated self becomes no self at all" (p. 7). Nicholas Carr's writing in many ways mirrors that of Gabler, Turkle, and Gergen.

Nicholas Carr uses a more balanced approach than the aforementioned authors yet is still a skeptic. Employing his skills as a columnist, he incorporates research grounded in neuroscience, media theory, and philosophy to support his point that our incessant work on the Web is rewiring our brains in ways that alter sustained concentration, deep thought, and memory. By the end of his book, *The shallows* (2011), he extends this argument to make a point similar to Gergen: "one of the greatest dangers we face as we automate the work of our minds is…a slow erosion of our humanness and our humanity" (p. 220). In his afterword to the paperback edition of the book, like Turkle, he calls for a rebellion against the future "our computer engineers and software programmers are scripting for us" (p. 224).

What seems to be reflected in these scholars' writings is the very natural concern about change. When change is fast and abrupt in our lives, it is often resisted; yet when people have time to psychologically process it, they tend to gradually accept details of the new situation and the reordering that comes with it (Bridges, 1991). Our ability to assimilate change can be compared to Kübler-Ross's grief cycle (Kübler-Ross, 1997), where we cycle through denial, anger, bargaining, depression, and acceptance. Gabler, Turkle, and Gergen collectively appear to be expressing longing for the way life used to be and in doing so are inherently denying that we are undergoing a major, rapid cultural metamorphosis that is affecting our way of thinking and doing things in general.

Although Carr is past the denial stage, he has yet to accept that today's net driven cultural change is not necessarily going to be as disastrous as he deduces. We see across these writings the natural tendency to compare what is new and partly unknown to what is known. Neil Gabler's concerns about our thinking abilities in light of technology assume that we remain static as our culture evolves around us. His observation that we have no time or desire to process information can be read as a lament for the way we used to process information. It is not that today we do not engage in the act of thinking, we are just in the process of training our minds and bodies on how to do so differently. I argue that high-tech societies are in the midst of developing a new set of thinking and life skills that have plunged us into a state of transition and not all of society has psychologically accepted this idea.[3] This is not to suggest that these changes should not be interrogated and critiqued only that the critiques should provide more multiperspectival analyses and should be geared toward solutions.

In addition to her book *Alone together*, Sherry Turkle has been on the lecture circuit urging people to not wholly forgo their technology devices but to take a mindful step back (Turkle, 2012b). In a recent *Ted Talk*, she argues: "What I am calling for here, now: reflection and, more than that, a conversation about where our current use of technology may be taking us, what it might be costing us…I am not suggesting that we turn away from our devices, just that we develop a more self-aware relationship with them, with each other and with our selves…start thinking of solitude as a good thing. Make room for it…create sacred spaces at home." The fundamental problem with Turkle's path is her urging people to take a premeditated and habitual step back, something I argue is unrealistic. Nicholas Carr mirrors this position by calling for a rebellion against the future.

A society immersed and in the midst of a transitional time simply cannot step back, it can only move forward. Ironically, Carr acknowledges a significant step back is highly unlikely even admitting that he himself cannot step back for too long. He acknowledges that he needed to silence his devices in order to complete his book, yet reveals that as he typed the closing chapter, he "backslid" by keeping his email running all the time, jacking back into his RSS feed, playing around with multiple new social networking sites, posting on his blog, and even purchasing new hardware that would enable him to stream information from the Web to his television and stereo. He closes with a tongue in cheek confession: "It's cool. I'm not sure I could live without it" (p. 200).

The recommendations of Turkle and Carr are misplaced in that we should be focusing on how to manage the change and embrace the future, as opposed to rebelling against it especially when one weighs the benefits computer technology brings against its liabilities. As Kevin Kelly notes, "it [technology] will just become more of the same thing but only better...it will become more ubiquitous in terms of filling our environment, and we will be in the middle of it" (2007). Technology is already more than ubiquitous, it seems to be in the passenger's seat and the ride is just beginning.

As today's technology continues to gain a stronger hold on us, it is within society's best interest to focus on one of its primary engines of progress, education. It is through modern schooling that we can stop denying, lamenting, trying to step back from change and instead work to contribute to our meaningful co-evolution. Understanding the change, a central goal of my work, is critical to knowing how to respond to it. On a final note, another way to think about identity change today is to look to the ideas of Friedrich Nietzsche.

Movement toward the Technomensch

Neitzsche's concept of the übermensch is so enduring that an entire volume of the Journal of Nietzsche Studies (Loeb, 2005) has been devoted to it. In his editorial foreword to this volume, Paul S. Loeb, notes that many influential observers outside of Nietzsche's world think we are entering an era that will fulfill Nietzsche's famous prophecy of a posthuman future (Best & Kellner, 2001). The goal of the volume's writers was to think about what the übermensch means in light of twenty-first century developments and debates. Subsequently, a theme consistent across the writings is that the übermensch involves man overcoming his condition (e.g., metaphysics, states of being, ideals).

I use Neitzsche's übermensch as a tool for analysis as I pull together the contemporary observations and developments contained in this chapter. As illustrated, society is in conflict over the changes virtualization and digital online culture poses to individual identities. Some scholars, artists and technocrats within wired societies are arguing that we are moving toward an übermensch state where technology allows us to transcend our human condition. Other scholars posit that we are rather becoming an untermensch state where technology is degrading humanity. I propose a third interpretation that we are adjusting to a technomensch state, a middle ground between these two opposites, where technology enables but not without limitations.

The technomensch is characterized by our human-machine co-evolution. As outlined, our sense of self is mediated through cyberspace, presentational media, Web 2.0 tools, smartphones, and a morphed news cycle. The Web and new media enables us to be more portable, fragmented, multiple, and hybridized. They are causing us to adapt to a culture where hyperreality is reality and we no longer live on the other side of the mirror as Foucault argues but rather the other side of the mirror no longer exists. As Baudrillard asserts, the mirror lives alongside us in parallelity. Technology increasingly complements human characteristics allowing for a new global, unrestricted dimension of being. In a fascinating expansion, identity can now be expressed through various mediums as we engage in diverse facets of self-exploration. We can transcend our mortality through our digital permanence and become virtually immortal, yet we still cannot escape many of the challenges and limitations of our physical condition including death. The main nature of our mind can soar by being one and multiple at the same time as our hybridized bodies still eventually plummet by the slow decay of our aging process, bringing us closer to the inevitable.

A final thought on the changes our culture and identity are going through as they relate to the technomensch: It can be viewed as an accidental evolution where each computer technology improvement in the form of miniaturization, hardware sharing, flexibility of software, and wireless bandwidth of data was initially focused on resolving individual problems. These improvements made possible the ability to remotely access and use software as well as store the end result; all bundled into distant servers and offered to users as a service recognized today as cloud computing. Although there are many definitions of the cloud, it is commonly understood as a metaphor for the Internet. I use the term to represent the current state of the World Wide Web where software, applications, and data are being stored, moved, and used across the network. This enables the expansion, enhancement, and hybridization of our identities.

It is through the cloud that we are also able to meet our highly individualized needs. We have turned into a society accustomed to personalization characterized by specific demands. We feed our requests with minute details to get our unique needs fulfilled. There is an expectation that if we search for a doctor, for example, we should be able to find one matching numerous criteria such as specialty, background, location, gender, language, or a combination of these. An assumption consistent with whatever the subject might be, and for the most part the cloud enables us to easily meet such expectations. As we use the Web to meet individualized needs, we globally project our identity by sharing our opinions through reviews, blogs, participation in virtual interest groups, and engaging in a constant exchange of ideas, pictures, and thoughts. We simultaneously feed the cloud and in doing so become part of an amalgam of all identities, self-organizing and enhanced through technology.

In contrast to this euphoria, economic and political forces are also part of this equation, generating immense wealth not seen since the industrial revolution. Fueled by a race for profit, the cloud provides society with an incredible engine of creativity by supporting startup companies that bring about new improvements and as well as encouraging the expansion of existing tech companies. This creative dynamic is dual, on one hand, it carries an altruistic, genuine energy that is open minded and groundbreaking in its approach. On the other hand, however, it embraces pure capitalism where profit is achieved in the most indirect and ethically questionable fashion. Nothing is off limits in today's wild-west mentality, such as poaching other companies for user data or mining it. This duality can be summarized as *friction*. It is through friction generated by both users and providers that the cloud subsists and expands. With it comes prosperity for various participating entities and privacy infringement for others. In chapter 4, I explain the concept of friction and explore some of digital online culture's multifaceted and often contradictory aspects.

4

Manufactured Consciousness and Social Domination

As we progress deeper down the cyber hole, the 1999 film *The Matrix* comes to mind. As Neo is about to enter a more conscious state through taking a truth pill, he is warned:

> You take the blue pill and the story ends. You wake in your bed and you believe whatever you want to believe... You take the red pill and you stay in Wonderland and I show you how deep the rabbit-hole goes... Remember that all I am offering is the truth. Nothing more. (*The Matrix*, Silver and Cracchiolo, 1999)

The shifting of our identities in the shadow of technology's expansion comes at a cultural cost with great implications. For all the freedom of sharing, instant celebrity, and the multitude of access the Web offers, it requires that we surrender our privacy. That prized possession, vigilantly guarded through our laws and rights, yet under attack by corporate capitalism. This chapter employs the work of the Frankfurt School as an analytical tool to interrogate digital online culture and its impact on the balance of social control and domination within modern society. Furthermore, this chapter references Hans Magnus Enzensberger's (1975) notion of the consciousness industry, whereby he argued that radio, cinema, television, recording, advertising, and public relation are tools of manipulation and propaganda. He extends this group of communication mediums to include education, as he saw it as a fully industrialized system that is becoming a mass media product. For Enzensberger, the mind industry's main business is to "expand

and train our consciousness in order to exploit it" (p. 72). I would extend Enzensberger's mass communications definition to include cyberculture. Although it did not exist at the time of his writing, cyberspace has rapidly emerged as a dominant mass media tool with global reach that has taken the forefront as an instrument of manipulation in Enzensberger's list of culprits.

Drawing on Baudrillard's notion of simulacrum, I argue that our digital selves reflect our real life (RL) identities, yet in cyberspace, many of the rules and norms of the real do not apply. Our digital actions are often seen as separate from reality and mediated by an idealized view of the world where information and people are free and somehow distinct from RL. However, as I argued earlier, there is no longer a clear demarcation between reality and its online representation. The purpose of this chapter is to cull together several cultural factors involved in the commodification of our identities as part of the manufacturing of false consciousness. This is achieved by analyzing the normalization of freely exposing our personas, discussing some of its dangers and rewards, and demonstrating that the practice of social domination is very much alive within cyberspace. I further argue that part of our core values have been taken hostage by a neoliberal cyber agenda emerging from technology corporations. An agenda originally born out of academia is transformed into a tool of manipulation intended to turn the user's identity and interests into a commodity. I will use a multiperspectival approach to address a series of cultural dialectics related to this dynamic, and will articulate the manner in which digital online culture is reshaping hegemonic and counterhegemonic ideas to redefine core values.

Although several frameworks can be employed to help with this task, this chapter draws from constructivist and convergence approaches to pull together the different ways in which ideas, norms, identities, language, and other cultural practices work to create a social structure that enables and constrains individual agency (Jackson, 2011; Jenkins, 2008). It also draws on Tessa Morris-Suzuki's theory of information capitalism, which argues that the computer age has allowed for the unprecedented generation of and access to social knowledge, enabling corporations to expropriate it in the service of new market creation (1988). Subsequently, this chapter makes several arguments: corporate domination is at the heart of many popular Internet inventions; movement of information over the Web, which I call friction, is the main vehicle of personal exposure, big data, and the reason for the very existence of most tech companies; friction enables digital identity to be freely taken and willingly given away; there is a new cultural narrative emerging that trivializes loss of privacy; transparency and surveillance have become institutionalized and normalized in American culture; there are several transformative, yet fringe, counter movements fueled by technology that are working to swing us back to democratic ideals.

Friction in the Cloud

As society moves its commerce, socialization, and government services to the Web, myriad information is passing through computers and the Internet. With cloud computing, more and more personal information is being held on the servers of various organizations, such as private technology corporations or government agencies. At the heart of all this circulating data is what I call friction. Friction is the commodification of identities through the movement of personal data over the Web. It comes from user initiated Web activity that creates data in the first place, the manufacturing process of data transformation, and the market activity around its exchange. Consistent with today's capitalist production model, this vast quantity of data has become the raw material that feeds the cyberdata manufacturing process. Steps in the friction process are depicted in figure 4.1.

Information acquisition is the first step in the friction process, and in order to deconstruct this practice, I begin by clarifying what constitutes our information (aka data). Online data related to an individual is made up of several kinds of Web information. One source is through government administrative sites where information is kept about people based on records from a variety of agencies such as the DMV, social security, military, post office, voter registration, professions requiring government licensing, homes and property ownership, any interaction with law enforcement or the courts, and census material. The data is also acquired through several cultural practices including willingly giving personal information by sharing over the Web. The data is

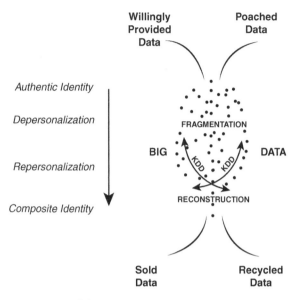

Figure 4.1   Friction model.

further procured through the poaching of personal information from entities like smartphone service providers, social networking sites, search engines, and Web browsers. It is worth noting that participation is often prodded by social network sites in the form of updates and requests for opinions such as "like," "review," and "comments." Data can additionally include the network of one's Facebook friends, Twitter posts, LinkedIn connections, search history and patterns, online shopping choices, photograph sharing, global positioning system (GPS) for geographical location tracking, and so on. Such information is often referred to as digital "breadcrumbs," and although they do not look like much individually, when added together they become significant. The data in figure 4.1 is initially depicted as a solid line analogous to the narrative of a person. This collection process forms a dataset kept in a virtual vault where massive amounts of information is stored commonly referred to as big data.

At the center of big data is the practice of Knowledge Discovery in Databases (KDD), the nontrivial extraction of implicit, previously unknown, and potentially useful information from data (Vedder, 1999). The KDD process begins by cleaning up the dataset through a preprocessing stage where the data is "depersonalized" and unusable data (also called noise) is removed. During this phase, the narrative is fragmented into singular markers represented in the figure by individual dots. The data is then organized in the transformation phase, where it is converted from one type to another (i.e. changing nominal to numerical) in preparation for analysis. The analysis step of the KDD process, known as data mining, is a repetitive, iterative process where specialized analytical methods (i.e., classification, regression, and clustering) are employed for pattern discovery and extraction (Fayyad et al., 1996). The last step in this process is the production of knowledge. This knowledge becomes a data product consisting of the reconstitution of our digital online self based on partial information, which is then sold for marketing purposes and (or) recycled back into the data vault for further data mining.

My critique of the friction process is consistent with the Frankfurt School's Marxist critique of the capitalist production model's role in the legitimation and mystification of social reality. I argue that the digital age has not changed the manufacturing of false consciousness and social domination rather it provides a context where new tools covered in a mask of freedom, equality, and liberation are used to further manipulate and sometimes suppress members of society. Enzensberger's critique of immaterial exploitation supports this point: any given "product" becomes more and more abstract, and the industry depends less and less on selling it to customers. He notes, "direct advertising and political propaganda is something nobody buys, rather, it is crammed down our throats" (1982, p. 9). Enzensberger's immaterial exploitation can be applied to friction where our perception of what part of ourselves we protect and what part of ourselves we project is becoming blurred. Instead of this choice being our decision, information capitalists are dictating what we need to keep private and what we need to share.

It is through hegemonic mystification that much of our personal data is willingly given, and in the name of entertainment leads us to become our own paparazzi, market researchers, publicists, and the like. It is no surprise that social media sites are developing relationships with corporations and unlike advertising companies, these sites do not have to figure out what their customers prefer because users share this information freely by way of simply using the site

(Guynn, 2012). The fact that a great majority of the cyber population willingly gives away their personal data is a result of several factors. The most significant of these is a new ideology infiltrating society via a young cultural intelligence force, one that I call high-tech capitalists, composed of but not limited to technologists like Mark Zuckerberg, Sergey Brin, and Larry Page, who are working to impart changed norms about privacy, transparency, and individuality. This is not surprising given the fact that dominant technology company leaders are pushing the idea that privacy is anachronistic, transparency is synonymous with digital living, and individuality is supreme. Take, for example, Facebook founder Mark Zuckerberg who believes privacy is no longer a social norm (Johnson, 2010) and Google CEO Eric Schmidt who argues, "if you have something that you do not want anyone to know, maybe you shouldn't be doing it" (Bartiromo, 2009). These attitudes represent a larger cultural struggle reflected in infamous hacker George Hotz's observation: "This is the struggle of our generation, the struggle between control of information and freedom of information" (Kushner, 2012, p. 7). The struggle today is over control of information by the individual versus the corporation as well as the appropriation of the "freedom of information" practices in service of capitalist ends.

As noted in chapter 2, Sherry Turkle found that most young people accept the idea of having to be careful online and inherently trust the founders of large tech companies to do the right thing. An attitudinal shift further corroborated by one of Facebook's advertising strategies involving turning customers' "likes" into endorsed advertisements to their friends. One Facebook user jokingly posted a "like" for a 55-gallon barrel of personal lubricant and then found that an advertisement with his face next to his endorsement had been sent to his collection of Facebook friends. Upon this discovery, he reacted, "I know the costs of using Facebook. It does not cost me money. It uses my personal information" (Sengupta, 2012). Another person who unwittingly became an advertisement via his Facebook endorsement commented: "It would be naïve...to count on an entirely free deal from Facebook" (Sengupta, 2012). Both reactions demonstrate an acceptance of privacy infringement and are what Facebook, other Internet companies, and even the government relies on. When Facebook was sued for what plaintiffs argued were unfair and deceptive practices in deploying users' names and pictures without consent, they used a freedom of the press argument stating that sponsored stories based on "likes" were actually "news" because all Facebook users were public figures to their friends (Sengupta, 2012). Baudrillard argued that language and ideology work together to structure perceptions and define a new real. I argue that within digital online culture, one way in which tech capitalists are manipulating social development is by making personal infringement justifiable through redefining the meaning of people's online interactions. Lakoff's theory on cognitive framing applies here (Lakoff and Wehling, 2012), as Facebook attempts to frame its users (i.e., the general public) as celebrities and by doing so change privacy rules designed to protect them.

Data Movement

Our false perception that personal data is safe in the hands of either high-tech capitalists or government agencies is being challenged by the two-way information flow between the private and public sectors. Not only is the government selling and supplying information to the private sector, but also the private sector is assisting the government in generating information about individuals (Singel, 2009; Solove, 2002). In essence, it is open season for buying, selling, and often poaching digital information from the global citizenry. This practice is not entirely new, since the 1970s the US government has been selling census data to marketers. Additionally, many states have a long held practice of selling public records to the highest bidder (Solove, 2002); however, today just about all government records are digitized, they can be pulled together for selling with the push of a button. In other words, the selling has expanded from census data to a wide variety of data types.

The US government has also been buying information about individuals from the private sector. One example of this can be found in the private company ChoicePoint, Inc., which holds a database of ten billion records and contracts with agencies such as the FBI and the IRS (Solove, 2002). Data about individuals is not limited to government agencies, it is also very important to corporations. The practice of mass quantification is so popular today it reportedly will leave no area untouched (e.g., academia, business, government) (Lohr, 2012). This trend toward quantification is no surprise given the fact that new media such as Google searches, Facebook posts, and Twitter messages make it possible to measure behavior and sentiment in fine detail. Such tools are contributing to society making decisions based on data analysis rather than on experience and intuition. We see here an erosion of what has traditionally been an important part of the decision making process, the subjective quality of perspectives grounded in unique characteristics.

Much of the motivation behind today's new forms of data collection and analysis can be traced back to the political economy of advertising. Since the advent of television, a prime time 30-second advertisement spot was considered the most effective way to expose a large audience to a product ("Internet Advertising: The online ad attack," 2005; "Internet Advertising: The ultimate marketing machine," 2006). By the early 1990s, the Internet, initially an ad-free zone, rivaled television viewership. At the same time, Internet companies were running out of venture capital and looking for ways to turn a profit without compromising their values of keeping Web products *open* and *free*. Tech companies and advertisers teamed up to explore mutually beneficial ways to collaborate. As companies shifted some of their advertising budgets to the Web, they saw a medium they could turn into a space full of banners and pop-up ads. In the 1990s, 55 percent of all online ads were formatted as banners, 37 percent were sponsorships, and 8 percent were hyperlinks, interstitials (full screen ads that run in their entirety between two content pages), and pop-ups (ads that appear in a separate window on top of content that is already on the user's screen) (Rodgers & Thorson, 2000). Pop-ups were also followed by a more egregious advertising method called adware or spyware software programs that run in the background even when the original file-sharing software is not operating and sometimes quietly uploading information about the Web surfer's habits (Wilson, 2004), a first step toward surveillance discussed later in this chapter.

By the late 1990s, Internet advertising's interactivity became a salient feature that differentiates it from other advertising medium by enabling users to participate in the persuasive process in the form of choosing to click on a banner or not, searching for an advertising website, or selecting pages to look at. Most importantly advertisers recognized that Web advertising could be personalized to the consumer, referring to him by name, or indicating that she is known for a particular interest (Rodgers & Thorson, 2000), illustrating the next step in the relationship of a consumer to society via products theorized in Herbert Marcuse's *One-dimensional man* ([1964]1991). For Marcuse: "The people recognize themselves in their commodities; they find their soul in their automobile, hi-fi set, split-level home, kitchen equipment... And as these beneficial products become available to more individuals in more social classes, the indoctrination they carry ceases to be publicity; it becomes a way of life... the so-called equalization of class distinctions reveals its ideological functions" (pp. 8, 9, 12). Its ideological function, Marcuse argues, is the shared vision to preserve the establishment. I draw on this point to highlight that today the customization of products psychologically seduces the consumer to believe that the artifacts of digital online culture, including advertisements, websites, and mobile phones, have been made specifically for them, and through this uniqueness consumers transcend themselves to another social strata. The psychological seduction of these new commodities anchors social control in "the new needs which it has produced" (p. 9). I argue the manufactured "need" for today's digital culture commodities laid the framework for the giving, taking, and selling of identity. The need of public consent on the part of tech-capitalists seems to come from a desire to adhere to the specter of a real democracy, when in fact what they are really seeking is a passive population that marches to the beat of their drums. This point is consistent with Enzensberger's position that self-appointed elites who run modern societies must try to control people's minds to secure their positions (1982).

A turning point in users' digital identity becoming a commodity began in 1996. Internet entrepreneur Bill Gross created Idealab, a company at the heart of the paid search or pay per click advertising practice. Gross' idea was the inspiration for Google's AdWords, which involves placing advertising links next to relevant search results and charging only for clicks with the added twist that advertisers could bid for keywords in an online auction. AdWords led to the creation of another Google product, AdSense, a system that goes beyond search results pages and places advertising links on the webpages of newspapers and other publishers that sign up to be part of Google's network. Both approaches are contextual in that they are relevant to the webpage's content and the advertiser pays only when a Web surfer clicks ("Internet Advertising: The ulti-mate marketing machine," 2006). All of this collective clicking and searching has also created unprecedented datasets rich for analysis and hegemonic use.

Companies routinely use Web analytics, a field concerned with collecting, analyzing, and interpreting Web metrics (i.e., informa-tion about how website visitors use the site), to improve the qual-ity of their websites (Phippen et al., 2004; Weischedel & Huizingh, 2006), and help companies to market products. Before the Internet, corporations had to rely on other methods of market research such as surveys, interviews, general tabulations (e.g., count of grocery stores in a given area), and limited government statistics (Larson, 1994; Lockley, 1950). Although these methods are a form of pri-vacy infringement, they still maintained a degree of anonymity (Lockley, 1950).

The newfound abilities of companies to gather and analyze data from these massive Web-enabled datasets attracted large technol-ogy companies, such as IBM, Microsoft, Oracle, and SAP, to invest in business intelligence and analytics software. Thereby paving the way for bringing more advanced and accessible data mining products to the market. One of the most well-known analytics companies is the SAS corporation, a private analytics software and services company specializing in helping corporations "gain predic-tive insights" and "seize new opportunities" ("Business Analytics and Business Intelligence Software," 2012). It is no surprise that big datasets equate to big business, as they are one method of achiev-ing market and social domination. Corporations and governmen-tal agencies, large and small, are the beneficiaries of this process as it redefines customers' identities through depersonalization and repersonalization.

One way to understand this practice is through the work of Holland (1998), who maintains that the identity production process is influenced by the "positions" offered to us in different "figured worlds" or environments in which we operate that are socially and culturally constructed. For Holland, when people are positioned they are no longer actively engaged in their own identity forma-tion but rather are relegated to a position of accepting, rejecting, or negotiating the identities being offered to them. In my view, within the context of high-tech capitalism, individual agency is further suppressed, as our identities are not even presented to us for comment before being presented to the world on our behalf. To further understand this practice, a multiperspectival approach offers the ability to shift the point of view and highlight the important points of the process through different lenses. Thus, I begin with the user's perspective, as the depersonalization process is centered on who we are as individuals. Then, the product's perspective is used, as repersonalization is focused on marketing the "product" to its potential "customers." Here a product ranges from a shampoo sold by a corporation, a checking account introduced by a bank, or even a list of "suspects" identified by the government.

Depersonalization and Repersonalization

It is important to note that personal data like DNA is composed of specific markers. As these markers disassociate from our authentic identities, they are considered to be benign, singular, anonymous information bits. At first glance, this seems rather harmless as it uses data that has been depersonalized from the individual it was originally linked to and then added to a general dataset to be analyzed. But any one of these little bits defines us sociologically and in a multiple, parallel, and fragmented world grounds our authenticity, our original identity. Nevertheless, this is a pragmatic part of the KDD process, as depersonalized data is not protected under US privacy laws and norms. So, in the name of "privacy," obvious indications of an individual's identity such as name and social security number are removed. In essence, our data is depersonalized when dumped into big data vaults and combined with other peoples' information, and after the KDD process, it resurfaces as data analytics. However, even without official markers, it is possible to zero in on a singular individual via unique characteristics and behaviors. Thus, people can be identified using combinations of unconventional markers such as zip code or an Internet Protocol address (IP address), a unique number that identifies a user's modem or point of entry into cyberspace. The noteworthy part of this process is that the final data product is repurposed back to users on an individual level in the form of practices and policies that impact their lives such as credit scoring, medical data health risks predictions, and direct marketing (Vedder, 1999).

The data mining process is built on the ability to run algorithms on a significant number of organized data to extract knowledge. The more data the better, as a single variable analysis has little worth, while, the accumulated quantity of data from multiple users strengthens the predictive quality. Here, the product perspective takes center stage as it guides the process by defining parameters of what constitutes the "perfect customer." The goal is to match-make between the product and its suitors, the targeted users, who have been profiled through pattern recognition. Thus, at the heart of repersonalization is the creation of the perfect customer.

KDD is further implicated in this reality as the post-KDD data product is our digital online self, reconstructed based on partial information constituted by combinations of our disparate online actions mixed with the bits and pieces we leave around cyber-space. Further exacerbating the problem, these bits are pulled away from a variety of contexts crucial to their meaning. We may be surprised to find our data mined selves to be very different from who we understand ourselves to be thereby problematizing iden-tity by abstracting us into composite sketches of a person who fits corporate marketing needs. As noted by Leah Lievrouw, UCLA Information Studies Professor, "no matter how extensive informa-tion about a person may be, it is never a complete or full picture of a person's life. Judgments made on this basis of such partial and out of context information can have major unintended consequences"; also "data from divergent sources and contexts can be combined inappropriately, so that negative and incriminating conclusions can be drawn, even if they are not justified" (Wyer, 2012).

Depersonalization and repersonalization articulate a complete commodification of the citizen whereby identities are collectively sold to corporations to satiate the need for new customers. This demand has been accentuated by the micro-segmentation of mar-kets reflecting a push for companies to secure a consumer base for their wares during an especially volatile economic time, thus pushing corporations to be increasingly more reliant on the KDD process. The aforementioned identity commodification process is parallel to any number of futuristic dystopian films such as *The Matrix* (Silver & Cracchiolo, 1999) or *Soylent Green* (Seltzer & Thacher, 1973), in which human beings are in essence both the literal food of the system and the consumers of this food, that is, we are becoming both the producer and consumers of our own identities.

An example of composite identity sketches can be seen through corporate use of predictive analytics, subsets of marketing departments devoted to discovering hidden patterns and trends (i.e., KDD) setting up "the golden age of behavioral research" as noted by Eric Siegel, the chairman of the Predictive Analytics World conference (Duhigg, 2012). Their work is not limited to understanding consumers' shopping habits but extends to unpacking customers' personal lives. In his *New York Times* article titled "How Companies Learn Your Secrets," columnist Charles Duhigg (2012) outlines a fairly new role statisticians play in mapping the intersection between data and human behavior. The ability of corporations to analyze data at fine-grained levels was the highlight in Duhigg's uncovering of how Target determines whether customers are expecting a baby, a time when couples are most flexible in their brand loyalties. Sending a coupon or catalogue before a baby is born happens to be one of the best times to incite a consumer to begin spending in new ways. It is through friction that companies like Target can analyze conscious and unconscious patterns via datasets and algorithms revolutionizing what they know about shoppers and markedly changing how precisely they can sell to them.

Staying within its legal bounds, it turns out that Target is able to use 25 products that when analyzed together, allow researchers to assign each shopper a pregnancy prediction score. An estimated due date could also be calculated within a small window so that Target is able to send deals and offers timed to very specific stages of a shopper's pregnancy and subsequent brand loyalty vulnerability. Andrew Pole, a Target statistician, notes: "even if you're following the law, you can do things where people get queasy" (Duhigg, 2012). In essence, just as in the film *Minority Report* (De Bont et al., 2002) where Precogs are able to see a near future event before it happens. It could be argued that corporations are using big data to move toward their utopian marketing ideal of sales predictability. Through this, a guaranteed consumer would be created, a captive citizen stripped of individual agency.

Target certainly is not alone in its advanced data analysis and there is an even darker side to the practice with some discriminatory social costs. Numerous current events attest to the fact that companies take data without overtly asking for it, as evidenced by the widely reported practice of smartphone providers and web application companies who help themselves to users' personal information (Perlroth & Bilton, 2012; Yin, 2011). Taking user data without permission is not limited to smartphones, as it continues to be a widely used practice across the Web. Taking information is disguised as an acceptable practice when that information is in digital form. Once a personalized sketch of us is composed based on this tacitly acquired data, no matter how inaccurate, we can be stereotyped thereby further exacerbating social inequalities such as discriminatory practices around employment, credit and insurance eligibility, banking practices, and other denied opportunities (Andrews, 2012; Danna & Gandy, 2002). The Web has not helped to solve critical theorists' critique of false boundaries and hierarchies that are constructed to justify domination of one group over another. Although marketing departments have traditionally used everything from census data, audience test groups, surveys, and other tools (i.e., Neilson box) in a search to understand and predict audience preferences, unique today is the level of specificity these companies can tap into. Two especially egregious practices related to repersonalization are *weblining* and *firing the customer.*

The concept of weblining is based on the old practice of redlining where customers were discriminated against based on geographic location. Insurance companies literally drew a red line on a city map around neighborhoods the insurers presumed to represent unacceptable high insurance risks and charged those customers more for their insurance. Like redlining, weblining involves any number or exclusionary practices based on data mining including limiting choices in products or services, charging more for a product, or completely eliminating someone's access to opportunities. Unlike redlining where entire groups of anonymous people were blanketed under one discriminating umbrella, weblining is based on personal data about an individual to create a specialized customer profile and uses that profile to limit access and opportunities (Hernandez et al., 2001). Weblining occurs in the financial industry, for instance, when a customer is profiled to fall above some risk criterion level, and subsequently, he or she is unlikely to be told about lending programs and other credit offers (Danna & Gandy, 2002).

The practice of firing the customer is a more convoluted concept as it implies that individualized profiles are intertwined with data on health, education, loans, and credit history (Stepanek, 2000) leading to further discriminatory practices. Firing the customer involves providing disincentives to stay to certain customers such as a bank raising an undesirable customer's ATM fees while lowering the same fees for a desirable customer (Danna & Gandy, 2002; Peppers & Rogers, 1997).

I argue that weblining and firing the customer are another expression of the politics of representation in action, only the profiling of individuals is not limited to race, class, and gender. Rather, it has expanded to the funneling of products and opportunities to consumers most likely to afford and purchase them with the intent of furthering market access and magnifying economic impact while ignoring the subjective nature of people. Interestingly enough, even if the method of funneling and/or denying products is based on a form of discrimination, there is still a product for everyone regardless of how economically disadvantaged they may be. The KDD process combined with the repersonalization of identity and our changing norms about privacy have worked to pave the way for another form of hegemonic manipulation involving democratic societies under surveillance.

Surveillance, Politics, and Political Economy

Rather than a formal declaration of war, the erosion of our privacy has happened slowly beginning with adware and spyware, described earlier in this chapter, and more recently in the name of national security to find those hiding in plain sight. This occurred with two goals in mind: to search for individual suspects and to cast a net in the hope of finding just the right mix of information to thwart the next terrorist attack. Interestingly, before the September 11, 2001 terrorist attack on the United States, Robins and Webster (1999) recognized that surveillance and intelligence procedures had become central to the state, and in the name of security "state surveillance has become a pandemic, and even normative, feature

of modern society" (pp. 162–163). The turn of the millennium terrorist threat provided one of the best justifications for further eroding citizens' civil liberties and getting people to accept surveillance
as part of American cultural life.[1]

To better understand American's general acceptance of surveillance, I will briefly revisit my earlier discussion on the larger cultural
narrative about transparency. First, we are a culture in transition
with a population of youth who have become accustomed to the
idea of transparency to the point where they believe privacy is not
critical (Thuraisingham, 2002; Turkle, 2012a). Privacy is linked to
civil liberties considering that a stranger cannot open postal mail
without committing a federal offense, yet email is shareable and
unprotected. Digital online culture with its tools, practices, and
values has been particularly important in reproducing this new
privacy belief. The popularity of openly sharing one's thoughts and
life in general through a combination of mobile computing, via
smartphones, social networks, and the tendency to use one's time
to consume such artifacts has been working to change perceptions.
The transparency trend has not just stopped at online sharing, it
has led to changing views on surveillance solidified through the
cultural outlets of news, politics, television, films, and other texts.
This is evident in the role news entities take in helping politicians
to "sell" the nation's need for an ever expanding public safety infrastructure including widespread surveillance and data collection
(Jackson, 2011).

It is no surprise that over a decade after the first major terrorist attack on US soil, we are as deep as ever in the security and
surveillance business in the name of counterterrorism efforts, as
indicated by the Transportation Security Administration (TSA)
practices, reminiscent of a totalitarian state. Two of the most recent
US advancements[2] are the relaxing of restrictions on how counterterrorism analysts retrieve, store, and search information gathered
by government agencies for purposes other than national security threats (Savage, 2012). The new guidelines allow the National
Counterterrorism Center to hold, for up to five years, private information about Americans when there is no suspicion that they are
tied to terrorism. The guidelines also result in the Center making
more copies of entire databases and data mining them. Instead of
focusing on specific individuals, there is an increased reliance on

casting a wide net, listening to phone conversations, and capturing massive amounts of the general population's emails. Second is the running of KDD style algorithms to pinpoint possible terrorist behaviors. Although the US government cites the genuine need for changes to better thwart terrorist attacks by correlating existing intelligence intercepts and communications in order to analyze and detect threat patterns over time, many states have not used their shared intelligence and databases to detect terrorists (Priest & Arkin, 2011). Rather, such databases have been used to collect, store, and analyze information on thousands of US citizens and residents. In the PBS documentary *Are We Safer?* (2011), reporters Dana Priest and William Arkin's investigation reveals an Orwellian moment when several nonviolent US activists groups, one even consisting of several nuns, have been unjustifiably targeted by these enhanced and coordinated surveillance programs.

A notable awakening of how deep the surveillance goes is evident in the Edward Snowden case: a former analyst at a private company contracted by the National Security Association (NSA) called Dell to run KDD on classified surveillance data. Edward Snowden exposed how the NSA spied on US citizens and foreign diplomatic figures by sending a trove of documents to two major newspapers, the *Guardian* (UK) and the *Washington Post*. In doing so, he revealed to the world the breadth and depth of US surveillance in the wake of the 2001 terrorist attacks (Andrews et al., 2014). He also stirred global debates among both the highest echelons of governments and citizens over NSA's practices.

Another perhaps even more startling surveillance development is the increasing popularity of drones. As the editor and chief of *Wired*, Chris Anderson, argues we are now entering the drone age. Popularized by their military application in the post-9/11 Iraq and Afghanistan wars, drone use has been promoted domestically by the US State Department to post Predator and Reaper mission clips on YouTube in the name of "enlightening" US enemies (Thompson, 2009). With over 10 million views, such videos, coined "drone porn" for the controversial aspect they represent, are consistent with the society of spectacle introduced by Guy Debord in his book *The society of the spectacle* ([1967]2004) and further explored by Douglas Kellner in his book *Media spectacle* (2003b). These videos show how citizens are desensitized from basic human rights by the captivating spectacle of surveillance followed by the tracking and killing of human beings. As Debord notes: "But a critique that grasps the spectacle's essential character reveals it to be a visible negation of life — a negation that has taken on a visible form (2004, sec. 10). The denatured aspects of the drone images, where a black and white simplistic visual accompanied by technical audio presents humans as mere distant ghostly figures, further corroborates the negation of life. Following Debord and Kellner, these military "snuff films" draw on the societal taboo associated with pornography where the viewer senses it is wrong but still consumes the spectacle. Furthermore, these spectacles are pushing for drone acceptance in the eyes of the public; Kellner notes: "As military activity itself becomes increasingly dependent on computer simulation, the line between gaming and killing, simulation and military action, blurs, and military spectacle becomes a familiar part of everyday life" (2003b, p. 10). The widespread consumption of drone porn as military spectacle combined with the winding down of two US led wars paved the way to bring the drones back home with the troops.

The US decision to open up national airspace to unmanned aerial vehicles (UAVs) for commercial, scientific, law-enforcement, and public safety uses[3] (Paumgarten, 2012) passed through congress without much fanfare or debate. Such congressional harmony has been attributed by critics to collusion between drone manufacturers, faced with declining military budgets, and law enforcement agencies. I would add to this point that it was also the result of marketing efforts to garner drone acceptance by the general public, as described previously. The domestic application of drones was further made possible by their miniaturization through the development of small-scale types that can be controlled locally and launched by hand like a model airplane or cell phone with wings. Drone supporters' attitudes reflect the new cultural ideas about privacy in that they believe the era of privacy ended a while ago and a few aerial shots in addition to all the other surveillance we are under (cell phones, city cameras, the Internet) is not going to change things much.

Like most technologies, the future use of drones is not all good or all bad but does take a strong step toward becoming what the American Civil Liberties Union calls a "surveillance society" where our every move is recorded, tracked, and scrutinized. The combined efforts of dominant forces such as the US military, large tech firms, government agencies, and other nontech companies to garner widespread cultural acceptance of surveillance are eroding our long held cultural values of individuality, anonymity, and privacy. One of many ways this is achieved is through reframing perceptions about the affordances of drones.

The rhetoric for using drones at home is focused on benign applications such as search and rescue operations, fire-fighting, catching criminals, inspecting pipelines, and even possibly delivering packages. Some argue that like the Internet, which started for military use, drones could be used for personal fun and enhancement like having a personal robo-videographer to log footage of one's vacations, sporting events, or other life activities (Anderson, 2012) taking the idea of personal celebrity to the next level where individualized drones become our personal paparazzo helping us to create our own reality show to be shared with our followers.[4] Embedded within this discussion is the potential of drones to be another provider of pseudo-reality in the form of spectacles, as depicted in the popular film *The Hunger Games* (Jacobson & Kilik, 2012) where the young characters' gladiator-style fight for survival is televised as a public spectacle.

Although drones can be used for entertainment and the larger public good, as with all potentially good things, there are a few additional caveats. First, US privacy laws are not strong enough to ensure that this technology will be used responsibly and consistently with democratic values (Stanley & Crump, 2011). A drone's affordances have not been fully realized especially when monitoring civilian lives. Drones have the potential to give someone, law enforcement or criminals, the ability to subjugate, aggress, or even assassinate unwitting citizens (Paumgarten, 2012). Another downfall is the use of drones to spy without due process, leading to a police state or even a state whose own citizens watch each other. We have a potentially dangerous mix considering the combination of widespread drone use, data mining, and individual profiling all potentially feeding a high-tech military industrial complex.

The US economy has an interest in keeping the citizenry complicit with surveillance and transparency. Following the 9/11 attacks, a multitude of businesses have flourished from the emergence of a concerted antiterrorist effort. Governmental institutions such as the Department of Homeland Security, the CIA, the NSA, and the Department of Defense (DoD) have extended their reach by opening up myriad careers in the counterterrorism industry: Private security firms supply screening services; pharmaceutical firms provide vaccines in preparation for bioterrorism; and drone manufacturers continue to adapt their aircraft to meet both military and nonmilitary demands. It becomes clear that there is a strong financial interest from a variety of stakeholders in maintaining widespread acceptance of the war on terrorism (Jackson, 2011) including surveillance. Thus, we have a renewed military industrial complex including a national safety market legitimized through selling a discourse of public fear.

This same argument can be made for transparency acceptance. As mentioned earlier in this chapter, it is through friction that tech companies such as Google, Facebook, and Twitter are able to serve what Lievrouw (2011) has identified as their real customers, corporations. The same corporations who have been in the data mining business are now in the surveillance business.

It is within this context that we must consider that American government and commerce have an interest in upholding transparency to facilitate surveillance. Broadly applying a social exchange framework (Emerson, 1976), we can see the story is not entirely one-sided. The public values the fact that the World Wide Web is "free" and has allowed it to transform our lives making them more manageable and fun in many ways; however, the tradeoff is we share a little slice of who we are through seemingly benign micro-acts like clicking the "accept" button, posting a video to share, or commenting on someone's blog post. These micro-acts translate into cumulative macro-intrusions into our personal lives, which for a growing number of cyber citizens results in costs that they perceive as not outweighing the rewards of participation.

Countersurveillance

As articulated through this chapter, today's culture is being redefined through a change in its normative practices from privacy to transparency, anonymity to celebrity, and surveillance to security, all representing modern-day dialectics in a battle over social control. In the midst of this struggle, there are several fairly power-ful counterhegemonic forces responding in the form of activist and alternative movements (Lievrouw, 2011). I will limit my analysis to cyber activism and varying types of journalism (alternative, par-ticipatory, and activist).

I argue that cyber activism is an action against the individual-istic trend that today's neoliberal tech-capitalist practices are pro-moting. As discussed in chapter 3, the combination of today's social networks, search engines, and other Web 2.0 tools have enabled the personalization of the user's account into a glorification of individ-uality; a complex term used here to describe a circumscribed envi-ronment with a manufactured egocentric user at its center. There are a variety of rogue cyber activist groups pushing back against the social and personal dangers looming from tech-capitalism run-ning free. Often times, such counter reactions emerge through an amorphous identity largely organized through and shielded by the Web.

One of the most well-known counterhegemonic computing enti-ties is Anonymous, a leaderless cyber group, often inaccurately characterized by the media as "global cyber warriors," "cyber vigi-lantes," and "online activists," which according to scholar Gabriella Coleman (2011) illustrates the broader media's misunderstand-ing of them. Anonymous is the product of the digital world. Like other digital online activist groups, their membership is fluid, politics evolve organically, and their activities involve a combina-tion of "feral tricksterism" and expert online organizing (Coleman, 2011). Consistent with Coleman, I characterize Anonymous as a new form of cyber activists since their main points of differentia-tion from other cyber activist groups are their notion of Lulz[5] and their amorphous form, which, in my view, does not negate their activism. Some of the societal critiques they are known for are their attacks against several hegemonic forces. One of them, Operation Changology, was an attack on the Church of Scientology's Internet censorship. Another, Operation Payback, was a campaign that par-alyzed the websites of companies that opposed WikiLeaks in the name of free speech. They also have been involved in the Occupy Movement, to name a few (Coleman, 2011; Olson, 2012).

There are many parallels between cyber activist groups like Anonymous and first generation hackers. One of the main similarities is their belief in digital utopianism, viewing computing as a force of social transformation. Anther includes anti-authoritarianism, devotion to the preservation of open access to information, and finally their trademark pranks. They differ from first generation hackers, who intended to demonstrate the skill of the programmer/engineer rather than to disrupt or damage a system per se (Lievrouw, 2011). Today's generation of hacker-activists,[6] however, will interrupt and damage systems as well as physically take to the streets in their pursuit of social transformation. It is no surprise that Anonymous chose a Guy Fawkes mask as their symbol given that this mask represents disobedience, dating back to England's 1605 gunpowder plot and most recently popularized by the film *V for Vendetta* (Silver et al., 2006).

In this film, its hero, who wears a Guy Fawkes masque, is called "V" and uses unorthodox means to fight against a totalitarian regime. Another notable classic activist film *Spartacus* (Lewis, 1960) illustrates the rogue revolt of gladiator slaves against the Roman Empire. Most interesting about these two films are their closing scenes: unification and solidarity are championed in *V for Vendetta*, each citizen donning a Guy Fawkes mask and likewise in *Spartacus*, through each slave claiming to be their leader in the famous line "I am Spartacus." Like the antagonists in these films, today's cyber activists illustrate the ability of people to unify the population within digital online culture. They organize and collectively, yet anonymously, challenge formal, codified, and political aspects of society in unique and effective ways. Of course, Anonymous is only one of many such groups. In the same trickster spirit, the Pirate Bay, a Swedish BitTorrent site, responded to the use of drones on civilians by announcing its plans to load their servers onto drones and have them be permanently airborne to protect them from law enforcement (Paumgarten, 2012), illustrating new activist groups are often part of strong political and cultural critiques.

While cyber activists' ideals may be utopian, it could be argued that their form is not. In order to fight the neoliberal cyber agenda, it would appear the work of these groups would be better served if they were to stop diluting it with their prankster tone and actions. However, another way to look at this is that their pranks are what differentiates them and may have even helped them to stay under the establishment's radar. It could also be argued that another problem they may have to eventually resolve is their lack of a definitive leader to guide the group. Activism without clear leadership can become diluted to the point that it loses its meaning, as we saw happen with the Occupy Movement.

Another perspective on this is that it is precisely because they do not have a "Julian Assange" poster figure that the news and government agencies have been left to reinvent a narrative every time these amorphous groups take action. Despite these problems, cyber activist groups are gaining voice and influence across digital and mainstream culture. Another struggle at the crossroads of false consciousness, social domination, and new media is in the area of journalism.

Corporate Journalism and New Media

Democratic governance requires an active and informed citizenry to ensure fair and equitable participation and is largely achieved through societal tools that help to facilitate these ends. One of the most long-standing and respected industries for this purpose is the press. Journalists and news outlets are charged with the task of providing the public with fair and neutral coverage of social, political, and world events so that society can engage in meaningful debate on these topics. This responsibility was confirmed by both the First Amendment guarantee of "Freedom of the Press" and the Federal Communications Commission (FCC) mandate of news divisions in broadcast corporations to devote time to "public service" traditionally appearing in the form of a nightly news summation.

Another noteworthy FCC mandate was the "Fairness Doctrine" requiring broadcast networks to present controversial issues in a fair and balanced fashion. In the midst of 1980s conservative deregulation, however, the "Fairness Doctrine" was slowly eliminated and as recently as August 2011 the FCC formally removed the language that implemented the doctrine. Another upshot of deregulation is partial control of the nation's airwaves moved from the public domain, subject to government regulation, to giant news conglomerates paving the way for the rise in corporate journalism, where entrepreneurs who own and control media broadcasting hold unprecedented media power. This transformation became more pronounced after the success of CNN, created in 1980, as a full time cable news source, which was followed over 15 years later by the creation of MSNBC in 1996 and Fox News, the same year. Soon, all were fighting for viewership in a shrinking market when the Internet entered the game bringing with it a plethora of bloggers and alternative news sites. Although this explosion of spontaneous reporting challenged journalism's "public service" ethos, it did not obliterate corporate journalism.

Media conglomerates are now able to use their massive media outlets to promote their own interests, agenda, politicians, and policies (Kellner, 2012a; McChesney, 2014). This is significant because it is through journalistic practices that dominant ideologies are upheld and citizens come to accept hegemony as either natural or the product of common sense (Gitlin, [1980]2003). One example of this is outlined in Douglas Kellner's article, "The Murdoch media empire and the spectacle of scandal" (2012b). In essence, the Murdoch media empire, now under scrutiny by several governments, chose to align programming with a conservative political party. They also colluded with police departments and other public service entities at the expense of ordinary citizens and even celebrated members of society such as Britain's royal family. Communications scholar Robert McChesney characterizes Murdoch's business model of "tabloid journalism" to include journalism designed to attract viewers by replacing professional reporting with pontifications. Subsequently, his media outlets have dubious records of fairness, accuracy, and integrity (2014). The exposure of Murdoch's business practices is consistent with the public's general disillusion of what used to be a sacred cow in democratic societies: A free, ethical press operating for the benefit of the public as opposed to corporate profits.

The general lack of confidence in traditional news can be further attributed to the phenomenal propaganda manipulation witnessed during the Iraq war. It started with the widespread failure of the press to challenge the Bush administration's rush to war (Papandrea, 2007), then was further amplified with the "embedded journalist" position offered to the press by the government. This could be seen as a repercussion of how the Vietnam War was covered with gruesome pictures and vivid reports of a failed military operation. Raw and emotional coverage was considered influential in ending that conflict. It is known that further wars such as Grenada and the first Iraq war were off limits to the press, but the "off limits" practice was not a solution as the news coverage was still nonsupportive of the operations. The solution of placing news teams in the midst of the troops can be considered a factor in the biased coverage the war received and the spectacle of combat. Given the fact that reporters were sharing a foxhole with fellow "soldiers," it is difficult to criticize those on whom your life depends. Viewers could now follow, in the comfort of their homes, the war adventures of their favorite journalist as part of the larger military spectacle, unfolding daily like an episodic TV series.

A strong and pervasive perception that the news is biased and packaged has prompted networks to reshape their format into two parts. On one hand, news sources began to rely on pundits, and on the other, they became aggregators of alternative news models. As Raymond Williams (1977) notes, hegemony "does not just passively exist as a form of dominance. It has continually to be renewed, recreated, defended and modified" (p. 112). In the midst of media privatization, news stations across broadcast networks have employed the use of pundits or experts hired to give their opinions on the news for the purpose Williams outlines (Hopmann & Stromback, 2010). In a race for viewership, many televised news programs conflate professional reporting with the opinion of these pundits to the point that the two are indistinguishable. They also engage in cost saving measures that seriously limit news perspectives through aggregation practices such as pulling news and comments from social networks, blogs, and so on. Additionally, in an attempt to stay solvent, more local news stations are sharing news sources such as video feeds, helicopters, and even the scripts written for their nightly news anchors across local stations resulting in the numbers of editorial voices being drastically reduced in a given market (Stelter, 2012). The recent practice of using sponsored content further illustrates this point (Vega, 2013). In a quest to find new ways of marketing to potential online customers and for publishers to find new revenue sources, advertisers are now sponsoring or creating content that looks like traditional editorial content making it even more difficult for readers to differentiate journalism from advertising.

Given these practices, it is of little surprise that cable networks began to support comedic synthesis of news organizations' biases and blunders. Together these entities have systematically critiqued mainstream news sources and simultaneously provided an alternative news outlet. Thus, journalism is not limited anymore to what I argue has been pseudo-professional restrictions on objectivity. One of the most influential news sources today is Comedy Central's *The Daily Show with Jon Stewart*, an alternative form of journalism. The show has steadily risen to be the preferred method of news consumption among 18–34 year olds (Feldman, 2007). Traditional journalists hold *The Daily Show* both in reverence and contempt as they struggle with the limitations of being a "real" journalist with professional ethics to uphold as opposed to a faux journalist or comedians who are held to a much different standard. Most interesting is the idea that alternative news sources have challenged the very ethic that is supposed to differentiate journalists from the rest, objectivity.

Since the early 1900s, the field of journalism has anchored its trustworthiness and believability on the notion of objectivity, and it is through this value that journalists contend that news, as opposed to other media genres, provides factual and thus trustworthy accounts of events (Feldman, 2007). Alternative news sources have proven that objectivity is a myth, something that never was and simply cannot be achieved. Even at the dawn of the 1960s televised news commentators, the "most trusted man in America" at the time, Walter Cronkite, was biased in his reporting. As noted by his biographer Douglas Brinkley, some of Cronkite's dispatches during the liberation of Europe were deliberately misleading about Allied progress (Menand, 2012). This is not limited to Cronkite. Another respected journalist, Dan Rather, had his professional credibility challenged in his 2004 firing from CBS over his inaccurate reporting of George W. Bush's military record (Cook, 2005). Such events attest to the mythical aspect of objectivity where news is mystified to serve as filtered information, cleaned up, scrubbed, and fed to a sheltered consumer society.

Alternative news outlets do not claim to be objective, rather much of their popularity rests on the fact that they are unabashedly biased. As noted by Mark Baard's (2004) *Wired* article on blogging, the blogsphere is a form of journalism that is free of editors and centralized authority and clear about their biases, yet if viewers subscribe to 2–3 blogs, they are able to see a story from multiple perspectives. This is likely provided that the multiple blogs an individual is reading present different views; otherwise, it becomes a bias echo chamber. As noted in Eli Pariser's work on filter bubbles where he argues that news feeds over the Web (i.e., through Yahoo, Google, Facebook) use algorithms to personalize news to the point that they show us what they think we want to see as opposed to what we need to see. Thereby creating a bubble of information that does not challenge us or make us feel the slightest bit uncomfortable (Pariser, 2011). Despite the reality of filter bubbles, the blogsphere has been overtaken by the "Twitter generation."

Twitter's short-burst format enables citizens to participate in political and social changes at a level of immediacy never conceived of before. The Arab Spring of 2011, a wave of demonstrations and protests that even toppled governments in several Arab countries, was attributed to citizens' use of Twitter as a journalistic tool. Many of these Arab states limited access to journalists and the international community (Aday et al., 2012), and some areas were simply too dangerous for traditional journalists to enter. This led to an explosion of blogs, videos, and Twitter feeds devoted to debunking Egyptian government propaganda, creating alternative propaganda of their own, and generally bearing witness to events as they unfolded (Aday et al., 2012). The unprecedented move by Twitter to delay a critical network upgrade because of the role it was playing as a communication tool during Iran's 2009 postelection protests foreshadowed what was to come during the Arab Spring. Subsequently, when the uprising hit Egypt, their government swiftly moved to shut down its Internet connections and cellphone services, with the cooperation of international firms, to try to quell the protesters (Richtel, 2011). This act ultimately forced Egyptian citizens to take to the streets in mass numbers further energizing the crowd against the government, thereby legitimizing Web 2.0 tools as modes of resistance and mobilization.

Wikileaks is another form of activist journalism causing celebration and ire. As a nonprofit, global, free press journalism organization, it uses virtual spaces to circumvent traditional hegemonic information control by publishing documents, images, and videos that governments and other institutions regard as confidential.

This organization has a pattern of releasing information related to corruption, malfeasance, and ineptitude by corporations, governments, and individuals (Benkler, 2011). The activist characteristic of Wikileaks comes from the fact that the news they distribute via traditional media outlets are neither altered nor edited. Rather, it is raw news with the exception of occasional blacked out names on some of their released documents to protect sources or if the news could endanger the people mentioned. The US forty-seventh Vice President Joe Biden referred to Wikileaks founder Julian Assange as a "high-tech terrorist" whereas others see him and his organization as going against the grain of political and corporate control to provide the public with a form of what Assange has called "scientific journalism," a journalism that can be verified and checked to avoid the power imbalance we have today, where gatekeepers control and monitor what is released and limit the public's ability to check corporate news "facts" leading to abuse (Khatchadourian, 2010). Assange's notoriety demonstrates that the hegemonic forces are paying him a great deal of attention in order to neutralize him, and through Assange, neutralize Wikileaks.

Society's move away from traditional journalism represents a swing back to creating an informed and opinionated citizenry capable of meaningful debate. Most interesting about alternative journalism is its facilitation of social justice. Alternative outlets allow cyber citizens to access perspectives that are less male, less bourgeois, and less dominated by the market, and ultimately fosters more active and inclusive forms of citizenship (Harcup, 2011). It is through digital online culture that we are witnessing a major push back against gate keeping, unitary perspectives, and political and corporate control. Alternative journalism has proven to be a strong step toward a more socially balanced method of informing the citizenry. However, it should be noted that this is not a panacea, as the media, including alternative journalism, is still in a battle over hegemony. Forces have co-opted alternative sources to further their dominance evidenced by the selling of the *Huffington Post* to the AOL corporation and the fact that despite its "alternative rhetoric," the *Daily Show with Jon Stewart* is a Comedy Central program, owned by MTV, which in turn is owned by the Viacom conglomerate: a wolf in "alternative" sheep's clothing.

Fighting Seduction

There are several important points to be drawn from this analysis. The struggle against oppression and for a more socially just society extends into digital online culture. For the multitude of freedoms cyberspace affords us, there are issues of social control, domination, and manipulation utterly embedded within each online activity we engage in no matter how seemingly benign.

I have established that for tech companies to flourish they need a citizenry actively engaged in digital friction, for without friction they cease to exist. Their agenda is capitalist, which is often presented as inextricably bound with democracy and the realities of cyberspace life, yet in reality is often at odds with the democratic and cyber ideals of openness, fairness, and equality. Companies now want to "own every waking moment" (Streitfeld, 2012) through building a device, selling it to consumers, selling them the content to play on it, and then using that content for their own monetary benefit, direct (i.e., monthly dues) or indirect (i.e., AdSense). The beauty behind this dynamic is that users fill databases with personal information to the point that they bind themselves to the company that manages their account. I argue that the addictive quality of these tools isn't necessarily due to users' natural craving for more interaction, but rather it is fostered through a crescendo of requests for user action bordering on harassment (i.e., friction) that can reach compulsion. The tech company's actions in this instance are analogous to an intravenous drip that slowly delivers a constant flow of data (Streitfeld, 2012); however, in this scenario, the intravenous drip flows both ways. Just as digital online identities are tied to the devices we commit to such as the Mac/PC divide (Turkle, 1997), our identities are slated to expand to the particular digital ecosystem to which one commits and pour one's life into.

It is critical that Internet citizens are not seduced into thinking the Internet is completely open, free, and egalitarian. They must be trained to recognize there are several covert battles going on in relation to cultural norms and practices mixed with long held basic rights. As our world is redefined through discourse around changing ideas of privacy and transparency, we should keep in mind the need for consciousness about what constitutes a true democracy. An arena where social justice battles continue to take place is within the education of the citizenry along with the mechanics behind how cyberspace, including large tech capitalist companies, are not always in line with democratic ideals. For democracy to flourish, we need a well-informed and engaged citizenry, otherwise we will continue on the path where the control for our digital selves is contested terrain; a battle over social domination. The citizenry can only remain free from what Debord described to be one of the main forms of societal distraction and stupefaction, "the spectacle is the moment when the commodity has attained the total occupation of social life. The relation to the commodity is not only visible, but one no longer sees anything but it: the world one sees is its world" ([1967]2004, sec. 42), through rigorous training in media literacy, the mechanics of hegemony, consciousness, and choice. This naturally leads to the responsibility of schools. In the next chapter I interrogate past and current responses of schools to the information revolution.

5

Virtualization and Neoliberal Restructuring of Education

As I have worked to unravel the contrast between real life (RL) and virtual life (VL) in the midst of the information revolution, I have demonstrated that the line between the two is becoming less distinguishable. Also, I have identified how the current burgeoning of inventions, both in hardware and in software, are pushing technology's integration with the human body to the point where they will be intertwined. Whether or not one thinks it is valid to call this a merger, a fusion, or the like, the reality is that we are witnessing an expansion of human abilities through technology. Thus, I see a need to prepare the citizenry, and more specifically the younger generations, for this upcoming state of being. In the midst of these unstable realities, students need to be psychologically grounded to help them effectively function in this changing world. As Sherry Turkle so aptly noted, "we are ill prepared for the new psychological world we are creating" (Coutu, 2003, p. 3). Guidance should come from a curricular and pedagogical path that provides the tools to appreciate, respond to, question, and anticipate the present as well as the next evolution of technological advancements. A critical theory of technology for schooling would provide such a framework, a concept I discuss in chapter 6. First, however, I summarize my observations about the relationship among users' digital objects, identities, and knowledge acquisition. I then map schooling's past and current responses to virtualization. From there, I interrogate the use of virtual schooling as part of a larger neoliberal agenda to privatize schooling at the expense of human development. Finally, I move toward an alternative solution that upholds the ideals posited by critical theorists Kellner, Giroux, and Jenkins.

As I embark on this task, it is critical to remind the reader that I write this with a globalized, digitized, and more or less connected society in mind. According to Kellner, "in a globalized world it is important to project normative visions for education and social transformation that could be used to criticize and reconstruct education in a variety of contexts" (2005, p. 59). I am critically aware that all over the world, there are some societies who struggle for basic school necessities let alone technological access. Given their historical, political, and economic contexts, the issues I discuss here may be realized, adopted, and thought about according to one's own unique circumstances. Nevertheless, the time is overdue to articulate how schooling systems could live out their present and future realities. As I work toward a critical theory of technology for schooling, I draw on the historical and synoptic work of several critical theorists: Douglas Kellner, Henry Giroux, and Henry Jenkins.

Douglas Kellner (2005) articulates a critical theory of education as a normative and even utopian dimension that attempts to articulate how education and life construct alternatives to what currently is:

> A critical theory of education must be rooted in a critical theory of society that conceptualizes the specific features of actually existing capitalist societies, and their relations of domination and subordination, contradictions and openings for progressive social change, and transformative practices that will create what the theory projects as a better life and society. A critical theory signifies a way of seeing and conceptualizing, a constructing of categories, making connections, mapping and engaging in the practice of theory-construction, and relating theory to practice. (Kellner, 2005, pp. 58–59)

I also utilize the work of Henry Giroux who argues that a theory of schooling should engage the hidden curriculum or the unstated norms, values, and beliefs embedded in and transmitted to students through the underlying rules that structure the routines and social relationships in school and classroom life (Hudson, 1999). For Giroux, "the essence of the hidden curriculum would be to establish in the development of a theory of schooling concerned with both reproduction and transformation; at the core of such a theory would be the imperative to link approaches to human consciousness and action to forms of structural analysis that explore how the latter interpenetrate each other rather than appear as separate pedagogical concerns" (1981, pp. 295–296). Finally, I draw on the work of media scholar Henry Jenkins who writes that "access to participatory culture functions as a new form of the hidden curriculum, shaping which youths will succeed and which will be left behind as they enter school and the workplace" (2009, p. xii). Jenkins continues, "educators must work together to ensure that all young Americans have access to the skills and experiences needed to become full participants, can articulate their understanding of how media shapes perceptions, and are socialized into the emerging ethical standards that should shape their practices as media makers and participants in online communities" (p. xiii).

Invariably technology will bring about new forms of schooling just as it has reverberated through most sectors. As discussed in chapter 1, postmodernists advocate that humans are coevolving with technology to create novel configurations of the population. Although, schooling is bound with a rapidly changing society, it is often slow to change. However, it will soon find it does not have a choice in the matter, as our machines and tools in concert with their users will demand and require it.

Schooling can learn from postmodernism to allow new ways of thinking about its core function. Postmodernism brought about ideas related to bricolage and opened another social lens, which can now be used to pave the way for schooling's own transition to occur. As indicated in chapter 2, Turkle observed that in light of technology users are provoked to consider postmodern ideas about the instability of meaning and the lack of universal and knowable truths. It is time for schooling to acknowledge that its own legitimacy is in the midst of being challenged.

In the United States, policy makers are looking to schooling as means of taking a stronger step into the future, as seen in the launch of *Digital Promise*, a national center for advancing learning technologies discussed in chapter 2. Largely missing from these national discussions is the voice of intellectuals who theorize, outside of corporate and government interests, and represent an independent position that utilizes a critical eye and robust critique.

In order to clarify my analysis, I will explicate my preference for the term schooling over education and users over students. My analysis employs the term schooling over education to provide a more nuanced understanding of the methods by which we achieve the ideals of education. In conceptualizing schooling, I especially draw on Kellner's synthesis of classical ideals of education where the process of schooling "develops pedagogic practices that allow for the greatest release of human potential and cultivation of citizens who will produce a just society, and counter education contrived to fit students into the existing social system and reduce schooling to an instrument of social reproduction" (2005, p. 54). I also draw on Giroux's ideas of structural analysis, human consciousness, and individual agency as a means of both reproduction and transformation. I would like to also highlight that my suggestions for schooling are to help mitigate the effects of neoliberal agendas for social reproduction in the digital age.

Both in and out of school, teachers, students, and administrators are all technology practitioners, therefore I will not be discussing teachers and students experiences with technology as mutually exclusive. Although I recognize that generational differences exist related to comfort and skill levels, it should be acknowledged that soon enough today's users, who possess disparate orientations to technology, will eventually be replaced by users who have been born into a technology-saturated world. The generational gap between these newcomers and their elders will be even more pronounced, yet the gap will begin to diminish along with the natural workforce turnover. However, such generational discrepancies will still persevere, as technology will invariably take new turns that will continue to result in various forms of generational handicaps. Therefore, in this chapter, I will extend the discussion of altered identities to include all "schooling users" including students, teachers, and administrators.

Another population to consider is those who merge with technology, in essence cyborgs. This idea broadens users to include those who could hold various positions within the human machine merger. In chapter 6, I use the term "altered being" to refer to those who have begun their own merger with technology in the form of wearable and embedded devices. Such people could eventually extend to a portion of the schooling population who are fully fused with cyber electronics to the point where they will be identified as "machines."

Intelligent Learning Companions: Swiss Army Knife

Digital objects surrounding modern life have drastically changed identities. With the expansion of the Web into the middle class American home, which quickly shifted from bulky desktop computers to mobile technology, the personal computer device's relationship with humanity became increasingly influential. Through design, messages (verbal and nonverbal), and graphic user interfaces, designers and programmers are able to create a symbiosis between users, their machines, and software. This is true even when a machine or software is obsolete, as the user will often defend it against all logic. Thus, these objects hold the power to effect users' attitudes and behaviors in ways they suggest (Diana, 2013; Fogg, 2003). Personal computers are also treated in many ways like fellow humans (Reeves & Nass, 1996). A relationship that began to deepen with the explosion of the World Wide Web and the miniaturization of the personal computer, which quickly evolved into the smartphone and tablet computer. This reality combined with the expansion of software complexity has empowered digital practices with populations now possessing intelligent objects that accompany them in living their daily lives. Even the name "smartphone" for a mobile device could have been called an "enhanced cell phone," yet the current name humanizes the device to the extent of projecting its affordances to the human psyche (J. J. Gibson, 1977; Norman, 1988). Technology now participates in how humans acquire knowledge, which can be understood from two overlapping perspectives: the user and the machine.

Although there are many ways to be a user, in every user there is a learner. Technology is reshaping learning identities regardless of whether ones' practices are toward formal or informal ends (i.e., work or play). Already, several changes in learning identity among frequent users have been documented. The Web has enabled them to be their own personal reference librarians by requiring them to navigate through confusing, often complex information spaces

(J. S. Brown, 2002). This has led to new styles of collaborative and playful learning as seen in discovery based skill building through video gaming (J. S. Brown, 2002; Johnson, 2006; Tapscott, 1999). It is no surprise that high-tech users have demonstrated an aversion to learning by reading a manual or listening to linear instructions. Instead, they learn by intuition, by working with others from around the country and the globe, as well as by virtualized exploration in the form of tinkering. This is evident in everything from entertainment, such as video gamers who arguably develop an intuition for how the game works rather than learning the rules, to those looking to You Tube to help them solve everyday problems (Foege, 2013). In these virtualized contexts, proficiency is achieved through thinking tactically, developing hypotheses and strategies, making subtle judgments based on little information, recognizing abstract patterns, and the constant awareness of multiple variables as they change throughout the quest (Bissell, 2008; Gee, 2005). It also involves the ability to learn through informal, collaborative, and participatory means.

Subsequently, a shift in reasoning practices is occurring from deductive and abstract to the more inductive and intuitive use of bricolage, a concept discussed in chapter 2. This often results in understandings that are largely socially constructed and shared. In doing so, learners take on new roles as members of a particular community of practice where learning becomes a part of both action and knowledge creation (J. S. Brown, 2002; Tapscott, 1999; Wenger, 1999).

Machines are also playing an integral role in the classroom. A growing majority of learners now arrive at school with virtualization in their pockets in the form of a personal Swiss Army Knife of the digital age: A full-time digital teaching and learning companion in the shape of their Web enabled, multipurpose, portable devices. Digital companions are turning students into more savvy learners. In simultaneity with a given classroom lesson, these devices provide students with near instantaneous answers to any number of enquiries at the time when their curiosity is piqued. Most interesting is the fact that many of these enquiries are not mandated by teachers but can be inspired by the machine itself through automated text messages, proposed enquiries based on previous searches, GPS positions, and other past behavioral patterns. Machines are becoming active agents in knowledge construction by offering an ongoing stream of information in the form of symbols and codes all of which are to be stored, processed, and used in the knowledge acquisition process. The symbol and code interpretation process is inextricably bound with identity, as the self is built out of experiences and interactions, which in turn impact interpretations. The interpretative process progresses us toward our own truths, which may vary depending on which virtual standpoint is adopted (see chapter 3).

Digital companions are portals to virtualization where there is an ongoing, global, general, and specific flow of information most often available to users anytime anywhere. Learning has been freed from the time, place, and access constraints of traditional schools, opening the door to people and documents that would have proven too difficult in the past. A renowned professor may be near impossible to reach in person or by telephone yet with surprising speed will respond to an email. Documents confined to specialized libraries in specific geographic locations have now been set free, accessible within minutes. With this radical change in the learner's access to information, symbols, and codes, it is no surprise that the knowledge construction process will also adapt to this multilayered, global, instantaneous, and simultaneous exchange environment.

While knowledge construction is an innate part of humanity, society has deemed schooling as the dedicated environment for its acquisition and dissemination. Changes in users' learning identities and knowledge acquisition processes have resulted in traditional forms of pedagogy and curriculum falling behind leaving an ever growing disconnect between schooling and students (Welch, 1998). Traditional forms of pedagogy that rely on memorization, lecture formats, and hard copies of printed material face challenges from the global information society, including virtual pedagogies, which allows students to access information (whether in formal courses or not), share knowledge, pose questions, and seek advice from individuals (not necessarily academics) worldwide. The work of linguist James Paul Gee and literacy expert Elisabeth Hayes (2011) illustrates some of these nuances when they outline the reality that schools present content without the modern methods, practices, and controversies necessary for evaluating that knowledge. They further maintain that a considerable amount of important knowledge today is produced outside of academic institutions and most distinctively in popular culture activities using digital media. It is further acknowledged that the kind of learning happening in a digitally saturated world cannot happen in schools that are "remotely like we have known up to now." This is echoed by Ronald Goodenow (1996) who contends that the power of cyberspace cuts to the legitimacy and survival of what has traditionally worked for educators.

Adding to this problem is the fact that in the not too distant future, the knowledge acquisition process will be challenged once again as technology becomes embedded within the human body. Artificial intelligence and neuroscience specialists are making progress in their sustained quest to mimic human biology. A common theme running through the next generation of digital tools and software is the mimicking of the way the brain absorbs information and learns from it as seen today with Apple's Siri (Kittlaus et al., 2011), an emergent technology discussed in chapter 3 that gets more accurate as people feed it data. Another case is with Google's Street View, which employs machine vision to identify specific addresses (Markoff, 2012). Learning companions are only one of many technological innovations inspired by human biology. We are now moving toward appropriation of the human body in the form of physical electronics designed to change physiological performance.

Transient electronics, electronics that physically disappear over time, allow all types of human–technology mergers, bringing people a step closer to the idea of a cyborg state. Currently such technology is under study for its medical applications such as implantable diagnostic and therapeutic devices that resorb in the body to avoid adverse long-term effects (E. Brown, 2012; Hwang et al., 2012). As of the writing of this book, researchers are striving for human trials of transient devices (E. Brown, 2012) demonstrating that the population is quickly moving from external to internal technologies that are able to pass through people as needed. It is not too hard to imagine a future with transient learning technologies that will offer a more seamless fusion between users and their intelligent companion; at which point, the line between users and their devices will blur to the point that we fully enter into the fifth discontinuity,[1] as Best and Kellner theorized (2001). Additionally, artificial intelligence advancements continue to improve in the form of deep-learning programs, which resemble the neural connections in the brain (Markoff, 2012). It is not too hard to imagine that users will eventually be able to tap into their learning companions through thought processing (Bilton, 2013). This is just the beginning of what I understand to be the new psychological world Turkle refers to. Part of this new psychology is the reality that machines and users will interact with one another differently. Machines are programmed to exhibit uniformity in how they relate to users, despite the user, while users retain subjectivity in their responses to machines. This status quo changes when both sides merge, a point addressed in chapter 6.

The Virtualization of Schooling

In the midst of these technological advances, it should be recognized that schooling has made great efforts to address the digital age. Beginning in the 1990s, school districts across America responded to the Clinton administration's charge to ramp up technological competency among the nation's youth (Cuban, 2001). This resulted in schools pouring a great deal of their resources into the hardware, software, support staff, and training to get their campuses and teachers ready to meet the demands of the high-tech generation. By fall 2005, nearly 100 percent of public schools in the United States had some type of Internet access (i.e., library, administration) and 94 percent of classrooms within these schools had access. When compared to 1994, only 35 percent of public schools had Internet access and only 3 percent had Internet access in classrooms (Wells & Lewis, 2006). Within ten years, we see substantial and impressive actions taken by the government to set up American schools and classrooms to be fully operational for the digital age. These efforts have been hailed as important for moving schools into a position that better prepares youth for a knowledge-based global economy (Greenhow & Robelia, 2009).

Through the first decade of the new millennium, the meaningful integration of technology into America's classrooms has been recognized as important to schooling's progress (Carlson, 2005; Gray et al., 2010). In addition to policy makers' push for infrastructure, students also expected their education ecologies to include technology (Arafeh et al., 2002; Carlson, 2005; Jonas-Dwyer & Pospisil, 2004; Kennedy et al., 2008). Subsequently, schools across the nation have responded by supporting technology related professional development. In 2005, 83 percent of public schools with Internet access offered professional development on how to integrate the use of the Internet into the curriculum and 49 percent of schools had between 51 percent and 76 percent of their teachers attend (Wells & Lewis, 2006). A 2009 study revealed 78 percent of teachers found that independent learning prepared them (to a moderate or major extent) to make effective use of educational technology (Gray et al., 2010). These moves have increased educators' general computer competence but surprisingly have resulted in an increase in computer use in unexpected ways.

Teachers and college faculty confirm they use computers regularly to research and plan their classes (Cuban, 2001; Russell et al., 2003). However, when it comes to actually implementing, and I would argue addressing, technology in their classrooms, they either failed to do so all together or did so unevenly and infrequently (Cuban et al., 2001). Often times, when technology was used, it was in relation to low-level tasks such as navigating the newest software, developing isolated skills such as word processing, or creating flashy PowerPoint presentations. Educators stopped short of harnessing the essence of technology to help students grow intellectually (Cuban, 2001; Ertmer, 2005; Zhang, 2009).

Politically driven initiatives to wire all schools and train educators are a good first step, yet the capitalist intent behind them must be considered, which is to prepare workers for production in a radically changed world. These neoliberal ideals fail to capitalize on technology for the betterment of humanity and the community. Students are not taught to engage with technology as a cultural reality that both frees and suppresses work, leisure, education, professions, civil rights, and social justice.

A more radical change emanating from the digital revolution is national partnerships between K-12 public school districts and proprietary virtual schooling alternatives. Unfortunately, in their current state, they only complicate schooling's problems. The nation's largest private supplier of online public schools, K12 Inc., runs 54 taxpayer financed online schools in 33 states (Mathews, 2013). As of April 2014, it reported revenue of $235.2 million, increasing

7.9 percent year over year (Q3 2014 – K12 Inc. Earnings Conference Call, 2014). It should be noted that K12 Inc. is only one of many others including Connections Education, owned by Pearson, Kaplan formerly owned by the *Washington Post* and now owned by K12 Inc., and a multitude of much smaller operators (Layton & Brown, 2011). Virtual schools operate like charter schools, and they are funded by taxpayers, accredited, and "free" to students. The instruction in virtual schools is monitored, reviewed, and graded by credentialed teachers, yet a committee develops the curriculum. The most striking difference is that a parent, or other responsible adult, must agree to sign on as "learning coach" who spends two to five hours a day, depending on the grade level, to help facilitate their child's progress through daily lessons and also works to modify the pace and schedule according to the student's needs (How a K^{12} Online Education Works | K12, 2014).

Analyzed from educational entrepreneurs' perspectives, virtual schools are filling a gap in modern schooling by providing an educational model that is flexible, mobile, and provides choice and unconventional options regardless of students' geographic or economic circumstances. Furthermore, they provide students with what they believe to be greater individualization, and a more evolved educational experience that better prepares them to function in a new, networked society.

The virtual K-12 proprietary model has been broadly criticized for its aggressive advertising tactic, focus on profit, targeting of underprivileged students, unrealistic student to teacher ratios, lackluster academic performance, and most importantly its hidden agendas (Bottari, 2013; Cody, 2014; Fang, 2011; Mathews, 2013). Before I engage and extend some of these criticisms, it must be noted that similar phenomena is happening at the college level with the explosion of MOOCs, massive open online courses. Many believe MOOCs are the future of higher education while a growing group of academics view them as anathema to higher education's core values (An Open Letter From San Jose State U.'s Philosophy Department, 2013; Heller, 2013). Like K-12 virtual schooling, MOOCs are largely free, enroll massive numbers of students, and are proprietary; in 2012 two major MOOC producers, Coursera and Udacity, launched as for-profit companies (Heller, 2013). The dropout rates for both models are higher than traditional classes and the overall success rates lower. There are certainly valid explanations for these realities such as the fact that at the K-12 level virtual schools tend to attract struggling students. At the higher education level, they tend to attract lifelong learners and education dabblers, yet their flaws are much deeper than this. In order to deconstruct the complexity of virtual schooling, an understanding of conventional schooling and capitalist production is merited.

Schooling and Capitalist Production

The seminal writing of Samuel Bowles and Herbert Gintis in *Schooling in capitalist America: Educational reform and the contradictions of economic life* (1976) sheds some light on the relationship between schooling and capitalism. The main tenet of their theory is that capitalist production is also a form of social production achieved through the values schooling instills, such as learning for external versus internal rewards in the form of grades as opposed to personal fulfillment. They argue that education is even hostile to students' needs for personal development, and successful school reform cannot happen without questioning the basic structure of property and power in economic life. Additionally, an educational system can be egalitarian and liberating only when it prepares youth for full democratic participation in social life and with equal claim to the fruits of economic activity.

In order to understand education policy as Bowles and Gintis see it, one needs to look at the objectives of dominant classes, which are "the production of labor power and the reproduction of those institutions and social relationships, which facilitate the translation of labor power into profits" (Bowles & Gintis, 1976, p. 129). The virtual world in which parallel and simultaneous lives are lived is the latest arena where institutions and social relationships are being reproduced. Technology brings with it hope for new models of freedom and equality, yet this hope is quickly being co-opted by political, technological, and financial forces that seek to harness it for profit at the expense of freedom and equality.

The work of Carlos Alberto Torres (1989) sheds additional light on educational policy formation in capitalist states. His theoretical work on the political sociology of education argues that in order to understand education policy and practices, we must understand a theory of the state, including issues such as domination, power, rules, and political representation. For Torres, when one looks at the determinants of policy making, "one must also concretely identify the institutional apparatus of the State and who directly controls it" (1989, p. 86). In the case of the United States, there continues to be a rather longstanding tradition of neoliberal educational policies largely focused on quantifying the unquantifiable and using the results to shape education policy, practices, and even the learning process itself (Torres, 2005; VanHeertum & Torres, 2011). This continues to be corroborated by the various state and federal programs enforced during the last two presidential administrations, the Bush administration's No Child Left Behind legislation and the Obama administration's Race to the Top initiative. The recent practice of value added teacher evaluations and the continuation of standardized testing are not only neoliberal in their philosophy but also provide a great deal of big education data (Hancock, 2012). An even more egregious neoliberal coup is in the area of virtual schooling. I critique both virtual schooling and big data within education later in this chapter.

Each of these policies uses the façade that the programs are designed for the betterment of society, yet most of them are based on the capitalist ideals of positivism. Evidence based policy making is creeping into education culture through intense competition. It is manifested through the student learning outcome process, student evaluations, and other measures of "student success." In many cases, such assessments have been designed to crunch numbers that are then fed back to students, instructors, departments, districts, and states as measures of their competence. Results become a reward and punishment mechanism that impacts the institution in the form of ranking, funding, and autonomy. Unfortunately, the common core standards movement does not mitigate this problem, as it too has come under scrutiny for its reliance on standardized testing results as a measure of teacher performance and student learning (Rich, 2014; A. Singer, 2014). The crunching and dissemination of all this data is pushed further through unit planning and accreditation requirements. As in the manufacturing process of goods and services, education uses knowledge discovered in data to make predictions and discrimination about teacher competence, student learning, and fiscal efficiency. Today, this analysis process is focused on the political economy of big data, tomorrow it may be cloud based real time data feeds (Hardy, 2012), which could quite rapidly undermine education's legitimacy.

Neoliberal Restructuring of Teacher/Student Identity

When schooling shifts from the public domain of the state and citizenship to the private domain of the market and consumerism, students and educators are left with rushed and standardized curriculum, rote memorization, and uniform teaching styles. This happens at the expense of the humanity of teaching and learning and the advancement of human development including educating for virtualized democracy. Schooling that upholds its ethical ideals by allowing for the development of the whole person as a socially responsible citizen is becoming a thing of the past. As John Dewey observed, "A curriculum which acknowledges the social responsibilities of education must present situations where problems are relevant to the problems of living together, and where observation and information are calculated to develop social insight and interest" (2009, p. 126). Thus necessitating schooling that avoids conformity and values the Deweyan ideal that education should be transformative. Dewey's progressive educational model precludes learners to be treated as automatons by allowing them to develop their individuality, "but the voice of nature now speaks for the diversity of individual talent and for the need of free development of individuality in all its variety" (p. 61). Neoliberalism leaves little room for students to openly and freely realize Dewey's vision. Rather, the thinking, values, and practices of users are being manufactured, similar to what Bowles and Gintis theorized, and consistent with Torres, to benefit those in power by maintaining classical forms of inequity and oppression. Today, neoliberalism is evident in several realities including decentralization and privatization, deskilling of the teaching profession, likening the student to a customer, and relying on big data.

Decentralization and Privatization.

In the name of modernization and digital disruption, virtual schooling has further enabled neoliberalism to open education as a new territory for entrepreneurs to monetize. Under the mask of technological modernization discourse, proprietary online schools including MOOCS are really after US education dollars. They entice enrollees through the appeal of a progressive paradigm with a broader array of course choices and an original pedagogical format. The United States spends around $500 billion a year on the entire education sector, including colleges, representing nearly 9 percent of US gross domestic product (A. Singer, 2012). A major player in the race for these funds is Pearson Education, the British multinational conglomerate. As of May 2014 Pearson Education has taken over teacher certification in New York (A. Singer, 2014) and will also administer tests aligned to the common core standards, a contract described as being of "unprecedented scale" in the US testing arena[2] (Cavanagh, 2014).

It is no surprise that even media companies including Amplify, the educational arm of Rupert Murdoch's News Corp as well as NBC Learn, a subsidiary of NBC Universal whose parent companies are Comcast and General Electric, have also jumped into the education arena. Virtual schooling is the next sector to be mined by mega corporations looking to diversify and expand revenues (Quillen, 2011). As Steven Pines, the executive director of the Educational Industry Association, aptly notes, "Teaching and learning is a huge enterprise that is federally, state and locally funded" (Quillen, 2011). The madness around mining these dollars from education has been compared to what happened with the Wall Street hysteria around US housing. We must not forget that the citizenry were the real losers in this crisis while the Wall Street executives were left unscathed and in some cases even received huge bonuses (Quinn, 2009). This could repeat itself with students in a looming education crisis.

This situation has also attracted venture capitalists, investment bankers, and education entrepreneurs who have aggressively worked for years "at converting the K-12 education system into a cash cow for Wall Street" (Fang, 2011, p. 3). We are in the midst of an educational frenzy to privatize American compulsory education. The battle is how to solve the agreed upon problem of low graduation rates and test scores. Neoliberals are "selling" virtual schools as the answer, but these schools have no given track record that they are able to make significant improvements in these areas (Fang, 2011; Huerta et al., 2014). Venture capitalists

are utilizing strong education tech lobbyists, education philanthropists, and politicians to create legislation to allow them to
more easily tap this money (Fang, 2011; Glass, 2009; Saul, 2011).
Politicians pushing for the expansion of virtual schools, and
in the case of Florida the mandatory requirement that all high
school students take at least one online class to graduate, are
financially supported by tech conglomerates such as Microsoft,
Blackboard, and Dell as well as the virtual schools themselves
such as K12 Inc., Person (which owns Connections Education),
and APEX Learning (Fang, 2011). Most notably, these corporations directly fund Jeb Bush's, governor of Florida, Foundation
for Excellence in Education. It is of little surprise that Bush is
vigorously passing favorable virtual schooling legislation (Fang,
2011; Mencimer, 2011). Problems with the privatization of education are numerous, and they include decentralization, curriculum control, deskilling the teaching profession, student-customer
models, and poor student performance (Cottom, 2014).

Educational decentralization or the transfer of decision-making
authority and policy responsibilities from central to lower administrative tiers is associated with different meanings (Hanson, 1997;
McNamara, 2007). This analysis, however, utilizes McNamara's
notion of privatization as a form of decentralization wherein
"private actors are given complete authority over administrative
matters" (2007, p. 63). The ideology behind decentralization is
explained in Martin Carnoy's work, which posits that those critical
of public education look at it as a form of public bureaucracy that
is too distant from local users to be responsive and as a monopoly
that lacks the competition needed to promote efficiency and quality. As a result, they frame the argument to convince the public that
government bureaucracy tends to produce poor quality education.
Carnoy further explains that by decentralizing the management of
schooling, limiting the role of the state, and increasing the level of
competition, market ideology suggests it is possible for education to
achieve larger gains in efficiency and deliver cost effective services
while at the same time attracting private capital and resource flows
(McNamara, 2007). Virtual schooling applies this same logic to a
human development endeavor.

Decentralization in the context of virtual education exaggerates
inequalities. These new educational models further the unrelenting

agenda of manufacturing and monetizing students', teachers', and administrators' identities. Some hail decentralization as an equalizer of power as it shifts control from the center to the periphery. In the case of virtual schooling, it readjusts power from influential groups such as teachers' unions, school districts, state governors, and political parties to private corporations and investors who are more supportive of the neoliberal agenda (Hanson, 1997). Decentralization can break up national collective bargaining and reduce teacher power, which would result in declining salaries and deteriorating working conditions (Saul, 2011). Some have used decentralization to take power from teachers unions and transfer it to more supportive bodies, such as parent councils. As reported by Hanson (1997), Chile broke the power of the national teachers' union by municipalizing and privatizing education, thus making teachers the employees of municipal governments or private schools. Most decentralization strategies seek to transfer some degree of financial responsibility for education to either regional municipal governments or the private sector. This can take the form of using public funds to support private schools (i.e., vouchers) (Hanson, 1997). In the recent case of Pearson Publishing taking over the teacher credentialing process in New York, the role of the public professional, namely the master teacher and university mentor, is given over to a corporate employee less familiar with the given teacher's abilities and perhaps less qualified to evaluate the student (A. Singer, 2012).

Not unlike fortune 500 companies, virtual schools aggressively market to their customers (i.e., students and parents) (Kirkham, 2012; Toppo, 2012). In the case of elementary and high school students, virtual schools place banner ads that show up on websites for students seeking help coping with depression and Google ads that show up next to a search for "bullied at school." They also target kids through Facebook and television ads on Nickelodeon and Cartoon Network (Toppo, 2012). These are strategies similar to those at for-profit higher education institutions such as the Apollo Group, the largest for-profit higher education institution and owner of the University of Phoenix. They too target college students who are marginalized due to their lack of academic confidence and track record as well as those whose life circumstances push them to a less competitive and more flexible schooling model. These are the very students who are well positioned to receive financial support in the form of federal education grant monies.

Aside from aggressive marketing tactics, privatization results in curriculum control. In public schools, curriculum decisions at the macro level are shared among departments of education, school administrators, faculty, and parents. At the micro level, the delivery method along with a million nuanced decisions about what to teach, how to teach, and the sequencing of information are left to those most qualified to administer it, the teacher. Conversely, in online schools, curriculum decisions are created by other entities (e.g., committee, management, a subject specific "super star") and dictated to teachers and even professors. Most startling is the stifling of critical thinking. As one online instructor reported, when he questioned an online school's lack of critical literature on racism, sexism, and inequality, he was instructed to teach the curriculum as is and not force students to engage in controversial material (Cottom, 2014). Likewise, in an open letter to Harvard Professor Michael Sandel from the philosophy department at San Jose State University, which refused to pilot a MOOC class in Justice taught by Dr. Sandel, it is argued that using a purchased prepackaged course limits diversity in schools of thought and plurality of points of view, the heart of a liberal education (An Open Letter From San Jose State U.'s Philosophy Department, 2013). Equally important is that it represents a first step toward restructuring education to reduce costs and eliminate the need to pay skilled teachers and university professors. If teaching assistants could facilitate a given "expert's" material presented in video format and modules, then there is less need for hiring and compensating other experts. This is also true of the K-12 system with some virtual schools hiring $15/hour instructors to monitor 130 students at a time as they work on computers (Buchheit, 2014).

Deskilling the Teacher

The problem of deskilling the teacher is real. Deskilling is a term used to describe the daily experience of teachers who have been gradually losing control of their own labor (Wong, 2006). This problem is not unique to MOOCs and the university system, as Darcy Bedortha, a former K12 Inc. instructor, recounted that her interaction with students was reduced to answering technical questions, clarifying assignments, setting up courses, due dates, and pathways in connection to a pre-established and ever changing digital curriculum (Cody, 2014). As investigative reporter Lee Fang aptly explained in a public radio interview, avatars and parents replace teachers and students teach themselves (Lopate, 2011). Progressive ideas for the cultivation of society and personal identity via unorthodox notions of education is not necessarily new, as radical schooling ideas can be found in the philosophical eighteenth century writings of Jean-Jacques Rousseau ([1762]1979) and Mary Wollstonecraft ([1792]2012) as well as that of twentieth century theorists such as John Dewey ([1916]2009) and Paulo Freire ([1968]2000). Although products of their time, each philosopher recognized the value of teachers' autonomy and demonstrate strong support of teachers' competence to craft learning experiences tailored to student needs, maturity level, and motivation. An effective teacher's identity is composed of multiple areas of expertise. This individual is more than an educator; rather he/she is a psychologist, a liberator, a child development specialist, a content specialist, and an artist. It must be recognized that a teacher's role is unique in society. The teacher is an intellectual guide, a mentor who awakens the burgeoning minds of students. Deskilling removes this human element of teaching and reduces the teacher to an automaton.

Deskilling naturally bleeds into compensation structures. The pay of virtual schooling executives has bloated to almost unimaginable levels. The CEO of K12 Inc., Ron Packard, earned $16 million in compensation from 2008 to 2012 with almost all the money coming from US taxpayers (Bottari, 2013; Compensation Information for Ronald J. Packard, Chief Executive Officer of K12 INC, 2014). In comparison, the average salary of a US school principal is $96,000. To put it into perspective, the CEO of K12 Inc. earns roughly 600 times that of the average high school principal (School-Principal-Salary, 2014). Consistent with private industry, as the pay of executives skyrocket, the compensation scheme for workers, (i.e., teachers) is plummeting including student to teacher ratios in virtual classroom reaching up to 300 to 1, generating considerable profits at the expense of teaching and learning (Buchheit, 2014; Cody, 2014). The national average salary of a K12 virtual teacher is $38,833 (K12 Virtual Teacher Salary, 2014) and the average salary of a traditional K-12 teacher is in the range $41,000–$45,000 (Teacher Salary—Average K-12 Teacher Salaries, 2014). As one teacher, Cherie Ichinose, a proponent of online K-12 schooling noted, "at the end of the day, no matter what your teaching platform, you are still a teacher, responsible for encompassing all that this prestigious title represents" (2014). Education entrepreneurs would like to change this reality. In a recent Florida investigation, K12 Inc. was accused of trying to avoid paying the higher rate of certified teachers by using uncertified teachers (O'Connor, 2012). Furthermore, they were criticized for outsourcing essay grading to a company in India (Huerta et al., 2014). This would enable K12 Inc. to collect the same amount per student from state public school districts while increasing profits for shareholders (O'Connor, 2012). If education is now defined as a product with students as customers and teachers as service providers, we must question what happens to the student–teacher relationship. Market logic should not prevail when it comes to our educational future, as schooling is not a commercial product to monetize but rather an intrinsic value, a fiber of our democracy.

The issue of virtual school funding has drawn a great deal of legislative attention. There is no shortage of national policy debates over how to fund full-time virtual schools based on the cost differences between virtual and traditional brick-and-mortar schools. Despite the debate, no tangible action has been taken. As noted in the National Education Policy Center's 2014 (NEPC) report on virtual schools in the United States, "no state has implemented a comprehensive formula that directly ties actual costs and expenditures of operating virtual schools to funding allocations." Additionally, "no states have calculated funding by methodically determining costs for necessary components of effective and efficient virtual school models" (Huerta et al., 2014). In 2012–2013, the state of Florida created a single funding system for all online providers in which the portion of full-time equivalent (FTE) funding for online coursework was split between the home district and the virtual provider. The Florida Virtual School along with other providers of virtual schooling including K12 Inc. and Kaplan are aggressively lobbying for legislation that would allow virtual schools to compete for the same level of funding for their courses offerings as traditional schools (Huerta et al., 2014). They cited the loss of revenue and subsequently jobs as the major problems associated with split funding.

When education is developed toward market ends, students suffer. Given that K12 Inc. is the largest supplier of virtual schooling in the nation, it again serves as an apt example. It has come under scrutiny in several states for its ethically questionable cost cutting measures such as asking teachers to delete students' failing scores from records, and making false statements and omissions regarding the performance of students in their schools (Huerta et al., 2014). It has also been criticized for its vast lobbying efforts, hiring 153 lobbyists in 28 states in 2012–2013 and using public dollars to advertise its school operations, amounting to 21.5 million in the first eight months of 2012 (Huerta et al., 2014). Numerous reports confirm that students in virtual schools perform lower than their counterparts (Fang, 2011; Glass, 2009; Huerta et al., 2014; Saul, 2011). Comparisons across the following indicators: adequate yearly progress, state ratings, and on-time graduation rates, suggest that virtual schools are well behind brick-and-mortar schools. The findings also reveal that virtual schools operated by private Education Management Organizations (EMOs) underperform when compared to public virtual schools with no private EMO involvement. Virtual schools blame this difference on the assessments advocating that measures should assess student gains as opposed to non-scaled traditional tests (i.e., criterion referenced) (Q3 2014—K12 Inc. Earnings Conference Call, 2014). Both camps agree that more complete data is needed to fully assess the impact of virtual schooling on student success.

The NEPC's 2014 recommendations for policy makers include the following: to slow the growth of virtual schools; to develop new accountability structures; to establish geographic boundaries and manageable enrollment zones by implementing state-centered funding and accountability systems; to create guidelines and governance mechanisms to ensure that virtual schools do not prioritize profit over student performance. Furthermore it is suggested that virtual schools reduce student to teacher ratios; the federal National Center for Education Statistics identify full-time virtual schools in their datasets. Finally, it is proposed that state agencies ensure that virtual schools fully report data related to the population of students they serve and the teachers they employ (2014). Ironically, these are the same recommendations made in 2012 and 2013 (Miron & Urschel, 2012; Miron et al., 2013), and so far, it looks like lobbyists are winning the battle.

Student as Product and Consumer

Outside of the virtual school discussion, contemporary schooling is also implicated in keeping students in the object position as a result of the larger cultural shift to virtualization, the systematic loss of public funds, and their new reliance on corporations for capital. This is illustrated in several educational practices designed to save time and money often requiring teachers to use proprietary software and Web platforms to upload, store, and disseminate curriculum, syllabi, and course assignments. In doing so, students are also prompted to engage with these systems as part of functioning in the school environment. In higher education, this includes requiring students to use school accounts to register for classes, file paperwork, to more fully utilize the library services, and to access their individual class content such as grade books and study guides. From these requirements, I see two phenomena occurring, first that students are inculcated to become users from the start of their educational experience, and second a multiplying of collection mechanisms able to harvest personal education data. I see nothing inherently wrong with using technology to help institutions and students. However, the problem lies in the fact that students are left without training in how to become conscious virtualized actors and thinkers. Furthermore, it enables the collection of vital private teaching and learning data. Whether it is an elementary school, high school, community college, or tier one research university, schools are pushing teachers and students to become "users" while simultaneously using KDD (see chapter 3) as a form of evaluation, resource allocation, and so on.

Class warfare of a new kind is emerging with a divide between those trained to be technologically conscious and those subjected to virtualized manipulation. The class warfare I am referring to extends beyond the ability to crunch raw data. It includes subject–object positions as they relate to manipulators versus the manipulated through the cultural codes of digital online culture. As Manuel Castells notes:

> The new power lies in the codes of information and in the images of representation around which societies organize their institutions, and people build their lives, and decide their behavior. The sites of this power are people's minds. This is why power in the information age is at the same time identifiable and diffused. We know what it is, yet we cannot seize it because power is a function of an endless battle around the cultural codes of society. Whoever, or whatever, wins the battle of people's minds will rule. (2010, p. 425)

The cultural codes of digital online culture are a complex set of symbols, practices, and norms that influence values and behaviors. They can be found in practices of the open source movement, the symbols behind activist groups operating online such as Anonymous and Wikileaks, and the new norms around transparency. The same cultural codes are also used by corporations specifically tech capitalists to manipulate users for the betterment of the corporations themselves in the form of privacy infringement, targeted advertising, identity manipulation, and big data sets used to further control and monetize identity. Those whose minds are most vulnerable to the influence of these new artifacts are users who are not active agents in their creation and who are not trained to understand them. Those especially vulnerable are traditionally underserved groups such as the poor, ethnic minorities, and the undereducated, as they have historically been the groups to receive the lowest quality and quantity of education as well as have the least amount of technological cultural capital. In chapter 4, I outlined a friction model explaining the process of using big data to manufacture and ultimately commodify identity. When applied to teaching and learning under the neoliberal education venture capitalist's agenda, these become tangible products to be mined and monetized.

Current technology based educational reform models reflect the societal contradictions about how to best address these omnipresent technologies as they relate to educating people. Recent attempts to reimagine schooling in light of technology appear to be altruistic, yet when examined more carefully, they continue to be trapped in the neoliberal values of "knowledge production and training assisting in the maintenance and proliferation of a system premised on capitalist accumulation, profit maximization and market ethos spreading to all areas of political, economic, and social life" (Olmos et al., 2011). Beyond virtual schools at the compulsory level, this point is further illustrated through an analysis of two contemporary educational experiments, MOOCs and Khan Academy.

Big Data in Education

One of the fastest growing higher education movements today is crowdsourcing technology in massive open online courses (MOOCs), where elite universities across the United States are experimenting with offering free noncredit courses. Daphne Koller, cofounder of Coursera (Coursera | About Us, n.d.),[3] extols MOOCs for their potential to provide free of charge quality education to global citizens. A distinguishing feature of such courses is their massive enrollment of thousands of students across the globe. In a 2012 Ted Talk, Koller elaborates on how quality teaching and learning is achieved through harnessing technology to grade quizzes and papers. In this environment, concerns over the subjectivity of grading papers are addressed by using a modified form of the peer review process as a strategy for providing reproducible grades. Most interesting is Koller's point that "the data that we collect here is unique. You can collect every click, every homework submission, every forum post from tens of thousands of students. So you can turn the study of human learning from the hypothesis-driven mode to the data driven mode, a transformation that for example, has revolutionized biology" (2012). Two areas of immediate concern that I will explore further here are the use of students enrolled in these courses as a free labor force and the ability to capture personal learning data.

Although these courses have proven to be widely popular, are praised by technophiles like Thomas Friedman (2013), and the enrollment of the first such course taught by Stanford professor Sebastian Thurn attracted 160,000 students in 190 nations (Lewin, 2012), there is a down side to them. Christopher L. Eisgruber, Princeton's provost, noted that Princeton's primary goal in offering

MOOCs was to find ways to improve education at Princeton and thus will not offer a certificate program or credit for such courses because the college does not want to mislead the MOOC students into thinking these courses are equal to Princeton courses (Lewin, 2012). It is of little surprise that more and more elite universities are moving forward with MOOCs given the fact that they have much to gain at very little cost.

Crowdsourcing technology in large-scale online courses presents a new opportunity to apply KDD to the classroom. Supporters like Daphne Koller assert that information gleaned from "the crowd" can be used to help students by personalizing education and scaling high-quality tutoring via online engagement (Weld et al., 2012). Additionally, it has been argued that crowdsourcing combined with data mining provide students with several advantages. For example, different perspectives of students via rubrics and peer assessments can be combined to achieve a higher quality evaluation tool than that of a single instructor who typically has limited time and a single perspective (Weld et al., 2012). Algorithms can be employed to measure student competence on multiple dimensions including confusion detection, curriculum optimization, question routing, and other functions. The information gleaned can then help to match struggling students with peer tutors (Koller, 2012; Weld et al., 2012). These are certainly exciting possibilities; however, they should be balanced with consciousness about some potential problems.

Consistent with my arguments that under the paradigm of "free" users are paying in the form of giving their data (i.e., identities), which is then used to create a product for their consumption (see chapter 3), free online courses come at a cost. In the past, crowdsourcing was accomplished by paying participants as in the case of Amazon's Mechanical Turk (Amazon Mechanical Turk | Welcome, 2013), a crowdsourcing Internet marketplace for work that requires human intelligence. Free online courses provide a self-selected crowd of fairly skilled users[4] whose online participation in the form of discussions, comments, likes, and test performances are used freely to solve problems associated with large-scale online enrollments. Elite universities are not as benevolent as we would like to believe, as this information can also be used to track individual students' skills and abilities to help improve the university's system. Furthermore, it allows for an indelible record of students' learning processes that can be kept and potentially used in unforeseeable ways. Even more disturbing is that these students are also being used as free labor through the practice of peer review grading, which eliminates the need to pay experts for this service. Thus, free university classes are implicated in free labor and personal privacy infringement, the very practices that a college education is supposed to equip students against.

I would like to recognize that in theory MOOCs have a noble goal, which is to "establish education as a fundamental human right, where anyone around the world with the ability and motivation could get the skills that they need to make a better life for themselves, their families and their communities" (Koller, 2012). Unfortunately, there is already evidence of capitalist monetization of user data. The Chronicle of Higher Education reports that one revenue source for MOOCs is to sell its match making service to potential employers who, with the students' permission, will receive information about high-performing students, both in terms of grades and online "helpfulness" per their involvement in classroom chat areas (Young, 2012). Even though the system allows students to "opt-in" one student rightfully expressed concerns over opting in, yet not completing a class, which may reflect negatively to future employers. Another point to consider is that the MOOC match making services will inevitably contribute to the globalized poaching of talent. This has the potential to further place top tier universities at the service of tech corporations.

The larger question to consider is the role tech corporations are playing when it comes to societal power, domination, and control. These establishments have already reached their apex of revenue with most of them valued in the billions, yet they continue to push for more control of users via their data. It is of little surprise that they are now turning their attention to schooling. This can be seen through another tech reform model—Khan Academy—and the practice of flipping the classroom.

Data Centric Teaching and Learning, Khan Academy

Harvard graduate Sal Khan's free Web service, Khan Academy, has gone viral by building an online following of over four million students worldwide (Khan Academy | Learn almost anything for free, 2013). Khan Academy uses a rather simple online format, yet its students are made to feel like they are sitting next to a real time tutor working through a lesson specifically tailored to them. As I outlined in chapter 3, the Web is becoming more tailored to individuals as they come to expect specific and personalized service, a service that extends to one's learning environments. Individualization is also not surprising from a Rousseauean perspective, as it recognizes the inherent nature of the learning process. Furthermore, Khan Academy embraces the open source ethos with its nonprofit status and mission to provide a free world class education to anyone from anywhere. It even embraces the spirit of Silicon Valley startups who are allegedly and arguably driven not by profit but by the task at hand.

The national education system is in a scramble to maintain competitiveness in this technologically saturated society, as asserted most recently by the US secretary of Education, Arne Duncan, who called for an end to the printed textbook in the classroom (Lederman, 2012). It comes as no great surprise that Khan Academy software is now entering the education establishment as a pilot program in several Silicon Valley K-12 schools. Sal Khan maintains that his collection of videos does not provide a complete education on any one subject; however, these pilot classrooms are replacing textbooks and direct instruction with Khan academy videos. The term "flipping the classroom" is now used to describe this schooling experiment: The night before class students watch videos related to the next day's lesson. Students arrive at class ready to complete modules related to the previous night's video. Again, the role of the teacher in this scenario is reduced to that of a helper and facilitator rather than a skilled knowledge provider.

As Khan admits, his ideal is for students to use the academy for working at their own pace and for mastering subjects. The teacher is then able to focus direct instruction tailored to small struggling groups as well as organize the chaos of different students working on different lessons by monitoring progress through a classroom computer. Khan asserts that his approach takes passivity out of the classroom by requiring students to interact with the computer. Eric Schmidt, Google's CEO, extols the Academy as a game changer by building a platform that could completely alter

American classrooms. Along the lines of the open source philosophy, Khan argues he will never put a price on his service, which is
why his company is nonprofit. He has also been clear that he is not
about changing schooling but rather improving how people learn
around the globe (Thompson, 2011). This rhetoric however does
not include the selling of depersonalized data to third party entities
(Herold, 2014).

The Academy's website notes: "We may share anonymous or
aggregate data to improve our services and learn more about our
users...In certain occasions, Khan Academy may work with business partners to improve our services or offerings. We may dis-
close automatically collected and other aggregate non-personal
information to authorized business partners to conduct research
on online education" (Khan Academy Privacy Notice, 2014). After
Khan Academy's privacy policy was analyzed by two experts—Joel
Reidenberg, a law professor at Fordham University, and Khaliah
Barnes, a lawyer for the Electronic Privacy Information Center, a
Washington based advocacy group—it was concluded that when
compared to other virtual support products, they scored the lowest.
Khan Academy is basically able to gather unlimited information
about users and disclaim any responsibility for it. Mr. Reidenberg
further confirmed that the Academy's privacy policy clearly indicates that advertisers may use tracking and surveillance technologies that "automatically route user information to the third party"
(Herold, 2014).

As a former hedge fund manager, Khan comes from a very
data-centric sphere, so it is only logical that his Academy's paradigm includes what Khan refers to as arming "the teachers with
as much data as possible" so they can make their interactions with
students as productive as possible (Khan, 2011). The obvious is
that the same data used to track students' progress can also track
teacher performance. Teacher effectiveness, for instance, could be
mapped through the analysis of students' scores as they move from
one learning module and one class to the next. Its practice and use
of data collection and analysis is consistent with my discussion of
KDD (see chapter 4), as Khan academy gathers data from every
Khan academy user around the world, given the fact that millions
of students are using the site every month watching 100,000 to
200,000 videos a day (Khan, 2011). Khan Academy is armed with

a massive dataset to scour in all types of imaginable and unimaginable ways. Furthermore, Khan intends to mine data about how people learn and where they get stuck to discover previously invisible learning patterns with the goal of creating customized lessons that are perfectly keyed to each student's learning style. It is no surprise that Khan is now considering starting his own private school (Thompson, 2011).

Virtual schools, including MOOCs and Khan Academy, are helping students gain access to privileged knowledge that was once limited to Ivy Leagues and the affluent, but they do not help them to progress beyond "user" status where their data is freely collected, used, and sold. More problematic is the fact that they are moving toward what Hans Magnus Enzensberger called "a fully industrialized educational system…In that process, education will become a mass media, the most powerful of all, and a billion-dollar business" (1974, p. 6). These education experiments seem to point to a new schooling model based on the industrialized economy where education will become analogous with an assembly line. Instruction would become a standardized commodity produced for a mass, global market. The fact that virtual schools can enroll hundreds in a class and MOOCs have the capacity to enroll hundreds of thousands of students in a single course confirms the fact that education is becoming a mass media product.

The looming of a fully industrialized educational ecosystem requires a critical perspective to balance our democratic options. As Julian Assange indicates, in this network revolution only the skilled will be able to freely project their truly independent voice (Assange et al., 2012). As I have just outlined, inequalities are taking new forms and it is the state's responsibility to help level the playing field. This simply cannot happen without serious efforts to break free from neoliberalism, whose policies and practices prevent creative and critical thinking for social justice in the digital age. A critical theory of technology for schooling would provide a conduit for these skills to identify and respond to new forms of struggle, a topic I address in chapter 6.

6

Toward a Critical Theory of Technology for Schooling

The impact of the information revolution on schooling reform strategies is that it has opened the door to private corporations. Those dominating charitable education funding, dubbed "venture philanthropists," are made up of investors rather than donors who seek returns in the form of sweeping changes to public schooling. These investors are also at the helm of mega corporations including Walmart, Microsoft, Facebook, and other Wall Street and Silicon Valley billionaires. The overarching goal behind much of the movement is to use the rhetoric that technological disruption has necessitated radical change in how we educate children to justify and legalize the funneling of public funds into the private sector. It is of little surprise that the reform rhetoric is toward privatization of public money in the form of expanding all types of charter schools, including virtual schools. Such schools are able to better realize the neoliberal agenda for education including recruiting nonunion teachers and corporate principals, building sophisticated data accountability systems, weakening tenure and seniority protection, and even reimaging the teaching profession all together. A case in point lies with the much-publicized recent reform efforts in New Jersey.

The combined effort of New Jersey governor, Chris Christie, the New Jersey major, Cory Booker, and educational tech philanthropist, Mark Zuckerberg, from Facebook were to not just reform but bring "transformational change" to the failing school system of inner city Newark, New Jersey. Zuckerberg was looking for a city that was ready to revolutionize education and Booker as well as Christie were looking to turn Newark into a symbol of educational excellence for the whole nation. After 200 million dollars of donated funds and a billion dollars in public funding, the New Jersey school system along with the surrounding community is no better, and some would argue worse off than before the reform efforts (Russakoff, 2014). As reported by Dale Russakoff in the *New Yorker* (2014), at the heart of the plan was to make Newark the charter school capital of the nation. This would be achieved by using an unfettered neoliberal, market driven approach such as imposing reform from the top down so as to keep teachers' unions and machine politicians (i.e., politicians interested in controlling politics for private rather than public ends) out of the decision making process. In the case of Newark, Zuckerberg pledged 100 million dollars contingent on matching funds. As the matching funds rolled in, they were transferred to the new Foundation for Newark's Future. Interestingly in order to sit on the board you had to contribute a minimum of five million dollars, which left out local foundations and voices. The first 20 million went to various education specialists, all part of the tight-knit neoliberal reform movement. From there the strategy was to close public schools and open charters along with specialty schools. Some community members likened colocation (i.e., the placement of charters in unused space in district schools) to colonization so that powerful interests could get their hands on the district's billion dollars. When students move to charters, public money leaves with them destabilizing the traditional public schools they leave. The example of Newark is echoed by the investigative report of Lee Fang (2011), who revealed that just like the push for charter schools in Newark, the virtual schooling movement is pressed by a tech venture capitalist agenda that siphons money from the public sector into the hands of educational entrepreneurs via virtual schools.

Schooling in the contemporary era has the potential to radically help society adjust to technology's evolution, but the agenda of education venture philanthropists and capitalists is not the solution. Likewise, scholars and other education stakeholders have not been successful in harnessing technology in ways that address its multifaceted reach. A point missing from both sides of the education reform debate is that following the argument presented by Best and

Kellner (2001), we are moving to an era of posthumanism where technology is becoming more human and the human species is becoming more technological. Turkle (1997) takes a similar position when she identifies cyberspace as an emancipatory agent where machines and humans are becoming more alike than different and where people are provoked to consider postmodern ideas about the instability of meaning and the lack of universal and knowable truths.

These prognostics serve as the rationale for introducing a critical theory of technology for schooling, to argue that schooling must become a more active mediator in the information revolution and it's impact. In addition to considering venture capitalism, we must also take into account real life–virtual life (RL–VL) and human–machine mergers for social justice and democratic ends.

I begin with an explanation of the intersection among schooling, technology, and identity. This is followed by a sketch of an initial critical theory of technology for schooling that includes its constitutive elements and some concrete applications, and closes with some thoughts about the future for a virtualized and hybridized society. This chapter does not present a full theoretical elaboration of a critical theory of technology for schooling but rather introduces the idea to foster further scholarly developments. In using the term critical theory, I employ the practices of the Frankfurt School and British Cultural Studies to analyze how artifacts of digital online culture impact society. Up to this point, I have used critical theory to interrogate the categories of hegemonic and counterhegemonic forces by demonstrating some of the ways identities have changed, how ideologies are transposed into digital online culture, exposed the pilfering of education dollars by private corporations, and in doing so, outlined several new iterations of social inequalities. In response to these realities, I now apply critical theory to technology in the service of schooling for social justice ends. It is with this in mind that I move beyond the neoliberal agenda for schooling and draw on the writings of Dewey, Rousseau, Freire, Marcuse, and Illich to discuss how technology can be used to overcome the changing societal conditions currently impacting students' abilities to live a good life by moving from object to subject positions.

As the struggle between hegemonic forces and counterhegemonic movements become more embedded into technology and society, we are seeing the remaking of ontological states. The way we live our life is defined for us, and is taken for granted as "normal" and invisible. In an introduction to Andrew Feenberg's broader philosophical critical theory of technology, Veak noted that "power is concretized through technologically mediated organizations that prevent their citizens from meaningful political participation" (2006, p. xiv). In essence, we are heading into a struggle by proxy: in the mist of cyberculture, the domination and manipulation over our digital lives is gradually mutating into deeper layers of representation. Feenberg illustrates this point when he notes:

> I call those aspects of technological regimes which can best be interpreted as direct reflections of significant social values the "technical code" of the technology. Technical codes define the object in strictly technical terms in accordance with the social meaning it has acquired. These codes are usually invisible because, like culture itself, they appear self evident. For example, if tools and workplaces are designed today for adult hands and heights, that is only because children were expelled from industry long ago with design consequences we now take for granted. Social regimes reflect this social decision unthinkingly, as is normal, and only scientific investigation can uncover the source of the standards in which it is embodied. (Feenberg, 1991, p. 88)

It is within this new arena that our core values have to be safeguarded and entrusted into the hands of the official knowledge acquisition and dissemination body that schooling represents. Schooling has not fully recognized that it is entangled in this neoliberal, technological and identity dynamic. As discussed in chapter 3, the multiplying of our identities resulting from the expansion of technology in our lives is altering who we are as humans. Given the fact that the schooling environment is the site where, for most, identity formation is broadened and crystallized, it is worth analyzing the intersection of schooling with identity and technology.

Figure 6.1 is designed to aid in mapping the intersection of schooling, technology, and identity. The model's open three-dimensional rectangular shape (aka orthogonal parallelepiped), encased within an open cylinder, represents schooling practitioners. These practitioners are composed of four types, each of which represents a different actor within the schooling environment.

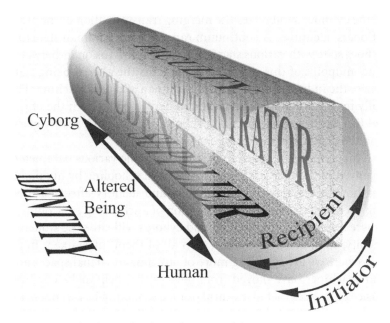

Figure 6.1   Schooling-technology-identity model.

The student facet includes learners inside or outside the academic environment. This comprises individuals[1] as well as groups of individuals learning in a classroom, on their own, or through a physical or virtual platform. The faculty facet encompasses participants involved in schooling directly or indirectly as creators and diffusers of knowledge in the learning process. The administrator facet includes facilitators of the formal or informal schooling mechanism. The term supplier identifies individuals, groups, and corporations that provide goods or services for the schooling process and are external to its structural framework. This involves physical suppliers such as textbook publishers as well as virtual ones such as designers of virtual schooling content or amateur YouTube training videos. They are providers of schooling tools but are not involved in the schooling process itself.

The cylinder enveloping schooling practitioners represents technology that they interact with either as initiators (i.e., participation in blogs, social media, as well as programmers), recipients (i.e., those who passively engage with technology including social media lurkers and casual users), or, alternatively, both. The length of the cylinder symbolizes the merging transformation of the practitioners' identities: A continuum ranging from a human state to a cyborg state with various stages of technological fusion in-between. The midpoint of this graduation pinpoints the altered-being state where the individual is equally part human and part machine. The fully machine cyborg state indicated here includes both the physical (i.e., hardware, biomechanical body parts, virtual reality glass) and the virtual (software, cyberspace).

This model is intended to help visualize the various parameters involved in the merger of technology with schooling by highlighting how technology impacts identity and identity affects schooling. In essence, it shows the projection of a schooling environment where humans, altered-beings, and cyborgs will either be students, faculty, staff, or suppliers and even all of them intermixed. In an age where we are spending more of our time in virtual spaces and our machines have moved from devices that help make our lives easier to devices that often think for us, schooling has an opportunity to guide the fusion of humans, virtualization, and technology by balancing the rationalistic, structured logic of our machine[2] side with the authentic, emotional, creative intuition of our human side. As machines are taking a stronger position in our lives, our left-brain logic and right-brain creativity have been transposed to our present condition. They are no longer just convenient devices or support tools, rather they are becoming indispensable, almost an appendage to our practical daily routines.

Beyond the individual, society is relying on virtualization and other technological advancements to serve many of its primary functions. New cultural policies and practices have accompanied our normative machine logic in the form of relinquishing individual autonomy and responsibility to make room for safety and protection. This process dictates that in order to be safe we must accept the conditions that ensure surveillance and transparency over freedom and privacy. The polarity between these forms is further played out in virtualized practices of obediently accepting "terms and conditions" required by much of virtualized culture versus challenging these gatekeepers and holding tech corporations accountable.

Despite the fact that the line between humans and machines continues to be debated, I argue that as the human–machine merger proceeds down its logical path, humans will need to hold on to their intuitive, authentic selves. This portion of our identities is defined by the values of freedom, liberation, and openness, which enable our creativity to translate into problem solving, invention, and aesthetics. These organic, chaotic, and emotional characteristics enable great thoughts, great inventions, and bold humanitarian actions.

A critical theory of technology for schooling argues for education to take an active role in the human–machine reality. This can be accomplished by providing suggestions for how "schooling users" can both embrace the logical, obedient machine part of their identity while preserving and fostering their free, unfiltered, open one. I will begin by first outlining the theory's constitutive elements followed by highlighting some areas where schooling can improve its stance when it comes to technological integration.

Constitutive Elements

Since schooling rests at the nexus of these mergers, one of the first steps toward identifying its position is to recognize what constitutes its population's technological identity. We are now in a situation where the learning process already includes hardware, software, and digital tools of various kinds. Technology supplements us by reinforcing logical capacities as a legitimate part of our identity. Our technological characteristics, however, are not limited to the tangible. They also include the Internet, as it is the medium in which this side of us thrives. The Web is a pure digital construct and naturally fosters logical processing better than intuitive thinking as evidenced by the fact that virtual representations are built on codes, structures, and rules. This portion of our identity fits well with traditional schooling, as seen in practices such as the patterns of standardized curriculum, time management both in time allotted to discrete subjects and the breakdown of those subjects throughout the school day, as well as the grading structure and the classical pedagogical format. More recently some of these practices have been co-opted by the neoliberal schooling agenda that turns them into spectacles. Both faculty and administrators are transformed into accountants frenzied about keeping track of their students, establishments, and own performance ratings. The result is a complete quantification of schooling that distracts from what its purpose should be. Schooling has not yet capitalized on individual agency within virtualization as a powerful cultural tool to break free from these damaging practices. Once we psychologically move past neoliberal spectacles, schooling can begin to embrace new potentials. The work of Paulo Freire and Herbert Marcuse sheds some light on how to manage this transition.

Although Paulo Freire did not theorize about the Internet, his teachings seem to apply to today's struggles. He observed that people are uncompleted human beings and through consciousness can become more whole. At the time of Freire's writing, he implicated the Brazilian education system as an oppressor. Today, schooling is still the oppressor only the forms of oppression have changed. In light of such realities, he argues for the development of one's power to critically perceive the way they exist in the world by coming to see the world not as a static reality but as a reality in the process of transformation ([1970]2000, p. 83). The transformative process is applicable to today's schooling population, as they too must free themselves of their current psychological condition by seeing "the back of the show." The ideology, hegemony, and control exerted over schools through technology policies and practices as well as their present neoliberal indoctrination must be made visible and challenged. They must also be made aware that new schooling models such as virtual schooling are just another iteration of the same problem.

Education philosopher Herbert Marcuse shows a path toward this end. He argued for new modes of realization corresponding to the new capabilities of society ([1964]1991, p. 4). This includes the restoration of individual thinking that is now absorbed by mass communication and indoctrination, and schooling itself follows such a path, as it has become an established neoliberal tool. Drawing on Marcuse's work, a society trained to engage in critical and original thought might first learn how to harness its machine and virtualized attributes giving them ultimate control over their own minds. Schooling must lay the groundwork for the intellectual and emotional aptitudes to guide us through this task. It is against the tech interests of those monetizing schooling to teach the very skills that could turn on them. The best hope for such training is within schooling entities outside of corporate interests (i.e., public schools).

In order to deconstruct cultural codes, schooling must impart new competencies and forms of literacy (J. S. Brown, 2002; Buckingham, 2008; Kellner & Share, 2007). Media literacy, information literacy, and computational thinking skills top the list. Thus, a critical theory of technology for schooling includes these skill sets. In an increasingly visual society where users are barraged with a multitude of media images, an understanding of how such images affect our values, attitudes, ideas, thinking, and general ways of being is imperative. Critical media literacy is not just about making distinctions between reliable and unreliable sources: It is about understanding who produces media, how and why they do so, how these media represent the world, and how they create meanings. It is also about empowering citizens to effectively read media messages and produce media themselves so that they can become active initiators and recipients (Giroux, 2010; Jenkins, 2009; Kellner, 1998; Kellner & Share, 2005; 2007; Poster, 1995). I would like to broaden this point to include an understanding of how our virtual environments, digital companions, and tech capitalists affect our values, attitudes, ideas, thinking, and general ways of being. The teaching of these expanded critical media literacy skills would foster new aptitudes toward dealing with our layered and often ambiguous mergers as well as corporate practices that prey on various forms of digital illiteracy and lack of consciousness.

Another emerging skill is the ability to efficiently find quality information among a sea of options. Information studies training in the areas of finding, organizing, evaluating, storing, and retrieving information is essential. The ability to use the language of machines in the form of "tags" is critical to online life. A great majority of Web activity is keyword or "tag" based necessitating training on how to use precise, specific, and narrow language that helps us to better employ our machines toward democratic ends. The more specific the language, the more accurate the results for users, whereas when the language is vague the results are often general. People need to become digital bricoleurs. For example, using a keyword in a search engine brings a number of links to the information related to this keyword. At this point, the keyword itself becomes a tool as it expands to build more and more information. Judgment is inherently critical to becoming an effective digital bricoleur. Bricolage in this case involves abilities to find something that can be turned into a tool to build something else (J. S. Brown, 2002). If access to information is key to democratic participation, tags and the language of search is one of the gatekeepers.

Finally, in response to Turkle's push for the general population to attain formal programming skills (see chapter 2), I propose that training in computational thinking would be more appropriate. By computational thinking, I am referring to the "if, then" axiomatic thinking tradition that is characteristic of today's computer programmers. It would be better to equip students with the ability to solve problems when it comes to a machine's full affordances. Such thinking skills, however, can be taught outside of programming. Technologist are already offering an introduction to this type of thinking with the project "code.org," which uses drag and drop programming within a broader storytelling framework as a learning tool (What Most Schools Don't Teach, 2014). Although this initiative is commendable, its goal is to create the next generation of programmers. I would rather see this mode of thinking taught within a broader critical thinking curriculum. Furthermore, the fostering of such cognitive skills is needed to more fully anticipate options within a machine-saturated world. It should be noted that computational thinking skills must also coexist with bricolage skills to maximize students' intellectual maturity as they face the digital age. Now that I have outlined initial thoughts on what constitutes a critical theory of technology for schooling, I turn to several contemporary areas of improvement where schooling can strengthen its position.

Some Concrete Applications

This theoretical construction challenges normative practices in schools by presenting alternative actions it can take to position itself at the forefront of the debates outlined in this book. Furthermore, this theory fits nicely with four areas of improvement that can be achieved in the immediate future to bolster the institution's readiness. Running through each area is the notion of ethical accountability in light of the realities outlined throughout this book. Critical thinking literacy for digital online culture is one of the first improvements that begins schools' shift in perspective by resetting its core values toward technological consciousness. Social justice battles still relevant today, also afflict our virtual society, constituting another area where schooling can improve awareness. The poaching of schooling data and its expansion demands drastic improvement by schools' regulatory bodies. The last area of improvement addressed here is for schooling to take a decisive role in the current virtualization and globalization of economic and social life by setting up precedents of openness and transparency. It must also resist privatization under the guise of modernization.

Discussions around training for virtualized democratic participation begins with challenging education's core mission, which, per the US Department of Education, is to "promote student achievement and preparation for global competitiveness by fostering educational excellence and ensuring equal access" (U.S. Department of Education | Mission, 2011). I have established that schooling is currently creating a labor force and in the case of big data using students to strengthen capitalist institutions. I would like to recognize that there is some value to equipping students to participate economically within society; however this agenda is not balanced with the ethical mandate to educate for personal freedom, consciousness, and democracy. In the case of big education data, it is done without the learner's knowledge or permission.

Contemporary schooling is caught between two opposite roles. On one end is the all-encompassing economic focus to create acquiescent workers and technology consumers, and on the other end, the development of active participants for humanity and freedom. This tension could be better negotiated if education were to reset its core values to foster the sparks of Freire and Marcuse's notions of consciousness. A newly established core value system would allow every student to be trained for virtualized democratic participation by receiving instruction in how to consciously and critically participate. This includes systematic training in issues around domination and manipulation by using critical media literacy, information studies, and computational thinking skills to facilitate the interrogation of social justice realities as they relate today around friction, KDD, the repersonalization of identity, and surveillance. Schoolings' current level of technology integration and use does not move students beyond the status of users, and in the case of flipped classrooms and MOOCs, it uses them as free labor elevating large corporations like Amazon above the universities; at least they compensate their "mechanical turks" (Amazon Mechanical Turk | Welcome, 2013).

Virtualization has layered another environment in which the citizenry must be aware of continued social justice inequities in relation to gender, race, and class. Underrepresented groups' voices are especially silent in the areas of computer programming, interface designing, as well as contributing to virtual discourses. The theoretical construct outlined here can be applied to the politics of virtual representation to better address the cultural and psychological barriers blocking their full participation in digital online culture. Wikipedia serves as one example of this problem's pervasiveness and persistence.

Wikipedia, one of the best examples of a massive, global collaborative effort toward knowledge construction and dissemination, represents the meritocratic ideals embedded in so much of digital online culture. Regardless of one's age, ethnicity, culture, socioeconomic background, political ideology, or sexual orientation all contributions are welcome. Over 1.5 million people in practically every country have contributed to Wikipedia's 23 million entries; yet still, nine of ten Wikipedians are male (Gardner, 2013). This exemplifies the problem that despite widespread opportunities to be part of these important cultural creations, certain groups still do not engage. It is expected that such inequalities will enlarge along with our multiplying identities to include altered beings, cyborgs, and others who fall on the human-machine-identity continuum.

Another area in need of attention is the current practices in place to monetize schooling related data. Every student and educator should be protected from infringement as it pertains to their learning and teaching performance. The general population has yet to realize the pervasiveness of their personal data being collected as well as the monetary worth of these online actions. As discussed in chapter 4, everything from likes, searches, to posts are collected, mined, and traced. With the potential value of one's learning not yet fully tapped, we can expect myriad entrepreneurs racing to mine this digital gold (SumAll | Analytics for Marketers, n.d.). National protection of our learning and teaching identities upholds the democratic promise that the state will be a defender of public interest. This should inspire the creation of national standards to protect electronic education records and transactions. Just as the United States HIPPA Privacy Rule (U.S. Department of Health & Human Services | The Privacy Rule, n.d.) outlines national standards to protect individuals' medical records and students' learning habits, equal protection should be given to struggles and victories.

The last, but certainly not final, area to address is the cry for educational technology to allow for ubiquitous, free access to education. The ability to manage high volumes of simultaneous interactions across the planet is enabling more open-access, free, high quality knowledge acquisition opportunities. However, not enough public institutions are seizing this opportunity in the interest of students. Initial reform endeavors such as MOOCs and Khan Academy, although far from ideal, demonstrate what is possible through the use of the globalized network. Contemporary mobile technology in this case offers the ability to overcome low quality communication infrastructures as it pertains to Third World countries. Schooling has the potential to better reach underserved groups including those from low-tech societies, those with limited Web access, and those oppressed due to their race, gender, or social class. These current reform endeavors represent the globalized potential of education today. Mirroring Appadurai's –scapes (1996), schooling has illustrated its ability and interest to extend beyond local boundaries, thus enabling users to remedy problems of distance, time, culture, and language like never before. Societies seem to be ready for realizing Ivan Illich's dream for deschooling. Illich ([1971]2000) argued for a new approach to incidental or informal education where an education system would "have three purposes; it should provide all who want to learn with access to available resources at any time in their lives; empower all who want to share what they know to find those who want to learn it from them; and, finally furnish all who want to present an issue to the public with the opportunity to make their challenge known" (p. 56). For Illich this would of course take place outside the control of technocrats and use "modern technology to make free speech, free assembly, and a free press truly universal, and therefore, fully educational" (p. 56). The effective and ethical harnessing of technology in schools would present an opportunity to steer societies toward an Illichean endeavor.

The Future

The last 20 years has been marked by radical changes in techno-logical inventions, yet the state of technology is still in its inception and we can expect more changes to come. The hardware, software, social networks, and other virtual environments of today may be entirely different in the near future. This means technology is a moving target. Once institutions are wired and equipped they must be upgraded and transformed to address the next iteration followed by a period of training and adjustment. Schooling has faced this very challenge, and as I discussed earlier in this chapter, US schools have done quite well in keeping up with infrastructure and equip-ment. However, I also demonstrated that it is time for schools to elevate their own consciousness, reassess its ethical stance, and shift its philosophy from an informational capitalist mindset to one of personal empowerment and freedom. Schooling must also staunchly defend its position in society by strongly resisting priva-tization and upholding the state as the responsible party for educat-ing its citizenry.

The most challenging aspect of any type of education reform is that change is often politicized around the political economy of schooling, is slow paced, is often highly contested, and is far more complex that it often seems. Reformation in the name of technol-ogy, however, may provide a unique opportunity, as it is one of the few sectors where neoliberals and other stakeholders are open to experiment. Since their motives are often on the assumption of future profits, the change emanating from them must be moni-tored. This requires an increase in the general public's political and personal engagement. Furthermore, policy makers are interested in keeping the country relevant and competitive within a digitized, global society and technology is uniquely positioned as an agent of change. With this in mind, I would like to turn to suggestions for future research related to further developing this theory.

Schooling Bill of Rights for a Virtualized and Hybridized Society

As I close this book, the film *Blade Runner* (De Lauzirika & Deeley, 1982) comes to mind. Its megalopolis with the cohabita-tion of humans and a new population of Replicants (i.e., cyborgs), indistinguishable from humans, seems to be around the corner for us. In the near future, maybe classrooms will no longer look like they do today, they may even be nonexistent or radically different. Perhaps the student body will be composed of humans, hybrids (i.e., human–machines), or even thinking and learning robots. Maybe the professor will not be fully human anymore. There is a never-ending array of possibilities for what the future holds, and even if we do not know exactly what shape it will take, we ought to prepare for what it could be. The future is seeping in, one invention at a time, either physical or virtual, they both quickly take new forms and soon smartphones will become a thing of the past and something more immersive will latch on to our human identities.

Major tech inventions seem to set the tone of our era; the graduation of their impact is never quite visible at first. The first airplanes were designed for a single person and were precarious, being made of Balsa wood and paper, they then evolved into today's powerful jetliners to transport hundreds, and matured into a cultural staple. Today, the digital revolution has been maturing into a sprawling network influencing everything in its path. I have taken you on this explorative journey ranging from understanding RL and VL as well as human–machine identity, as they present themselves today, to an analysis of current schooling challenges and future possibilities.

I have argued that schooling ought to be a role model for how to respond to the societal changes from technocratic developments and mediate its cultural implications. This will even have greater importance as we redefine what it means to be human. A mediator position implies that schooling, whatever future form it takes, ethically represents both sides of this reality. Schooling will invariably be faced with questions on how to respond to these iterations of humanity as they manifest among the student population and faculty. Social justice issues will arise related to fairness as it applies to varying learning and performance capabilities depending on whether one has the money for and access to such technological enhancements.

A set of guiding principles for schooling is in order to address both technology initiators (designers, programmers, manipulators, distributors, creators) and technology recipients (users). Such guidelines would address issues around technology, identity, ethical responsibilities (political, social, and individual), as well as the morality of privacy and democracy. They would encompass values of freedom and rights when it comes to knowledge acquisition and dissemination. Finally, they would uphold the ethics of fairness and respect as it relates to these populations. Thus, the future direction for a critical theory of technology for schools is to include a bill of rights designed to protect the natural rights of liberty of students and educators. More specifically, such a bill would outline schooling's responsibilities and help to better guarantee a number of personal freedoms including circumscribing tech corporations' influence, providing guidance for democratic, moral online living, and providing insight on how to respond fairly to the RL–VL and human–machine mergers.

Furthermore, in light of the new iterations and forms of social injustice, a schooling bill of rights for a virtualized and hybridized society would help education remain focused on upholding civil liberties, social justice, and democratic ideals. These mergers have moved at such a fast pace that schooling has yet to take a definitive position on issues that impact identity construction as it pertains to these mergers. A bill of rights would give schooling greater clarity on its position and responsibilities.

Final Thoughts

In this book, I have sought to begin theorizing how schooling should understand, respond to, and live the information revolution. The extent to which our identities are being altered, manipulated, and commodified by technological experiences is of particular concern. Common cultural practices around one's willingness to give up civil liberties in exchange for "free of charge" policies and to open one's life to the Web in general and tech capitalists in particular are becoming the norm. Most alarming is the fact that schooling is contributing to the problem rather than working toward protecting the citizenry from it. In response, I have argued for a critical theory of technology for schooling to remind education of what its quintessential mission should be: educating for freedom, democracy, consciousness, and a good life while upholding the highest ethical standards in both policy and practice.

This chapter sketched initial theoretical ideas to foster further scholarly developments. For that purpose, I have outlined future

directions as a path for improvement on the subject. As we become
more altered by our machines, virtual environments, and all-per-
vasive technologies in our lives, it is critical to consider Manuel
Castells' observation that whoever wins the battle over people's
minds will win (2010); it is the state's responsibility to protect and
equip the minds of its citizenry.

The Internet, the world's largest structured web of people along
with its open unregulated digital citizenry, is the terrain where
these battles of the mind are now being fought. The conundrum
lies in the fact that corporations are using cyberspace to control
virtual territories including the information they hold according to
their own terms, all in the name of an open, connected world. At
first glance, little appears wrong with local control. However, when
this practice is scaled to meet the size of Facebook's population, it
becomes increasingly problematic. Despite the fact that tech corporations are moving to be at the helm of schools, the population's
apathy in this area[3] results in relinquished control over an ever-
growing slice of their lives. Technocracy is seeping into the virtual,
pushing away democratic representation for its "virtual residents,"
who have not yet developed a sense of digital citizenship. Schooling
can help the public recognize the importance of digital citizenship
as it pertains to rights, responsibilities, and fair representation to
maintain a sense of virtual democracy.

Ultimately, technocrats would like society to turn to technology
as a method for solving social problems. This solutionism ideology,
as Morozov (2013) puts it. is "an intellectual pathology that recognizes problems as problems based on just one criterion: whether
they are 'solvable' with a nice and clean technological solution at
our disposal" (p. 3), thereby transferring the hard work of thinking
and acting for ourselves to a computer program or application. A
critical theory of technology for schooling is ultimately a tool for
preserving a harmonious balance between such perfectionist ideology and the imperfection of human nature that defines who we are.
We are at a point where the lack of a digital footprint in the cloud is
becoming an impediment to our identity and subsequently to our
citizenship. It is with this in mind that schooling needs theoretical
tools to help prepare for the fundamental changes that are taking
shape as we live the information revolution.

Notes

2 A Case Study: Sherry Turkle and the Psychological Role of Computers

1. The term technology is used here to convey the fact that Turkle's point is larger than human–computer interaction or the Internet.
2. A framework for a critical theory of technology for schooling is outlined in chapter 6.

3 Down the Rabbit Hole: Identity and Societal Mutation

1. Although tweeting and texting are mediums of language alteration today, I recognize these are ephemeral and will changes as new media tools come along.
2. Especially in the cases where users do not specify in their profile that they want to limit diffusion to their friends.
3. See chapter 6 on schooling.

4 Manufactured Consciousness and Social Domination

1. Surveillance culture is not limited to the United Sates. Over the last decade, it has taken root in various Western countries such as England with its pervasive use of cameras throughout the city.
2. As of the writing of this chapter.
3. In February 2012, US congress passed a law that by 2015 it will open the national airspace to drones.
4. This attitude is consistent with my discussion of identity in chapter 3.
5. Lulz is a pluralization of Laugh Out Loud (lol) referring to amusing jokes, images, and pranks often at someone else's expense, typically through embarrassment (Coleman, 2011; Olson, 2012).
6. Anonymous also uses hacking to achieve its goals.

5   Virtualization and Neoliberal Restructuring of Education

1. As discussed in chapter 1, with the fifth discontinuity, humans no longer maintain a superior position in the world. Technology is becoming more human and the human species is becoming more technological.
2. As of this writing, Pearson's Common Core contract was facing legal challenges.
3. Coursera is a company that partners with top universities in the world to offer free online courses.
4. Skilled crowd refers to people who have a basic skill set and have met prerequisites for the online course in which they are enrolled.

6   Toward a Critical Theory of Technology for Schooling

1. The term individual indicates a singular human entity, altered or otherwise.
2. The term machine is used to refer to all technological representations, either physical or virtual.
3. A recent *Atlantic Monthly* article reported that when Facebook users were asked to vote on a new privacy policy, voter turnout was 0.038 percent (Madrigal, 2012).

References

50 for the future: The most influential people to watch in cyberspace (1995, February 27). *Newsweek*, 125(9), 42. Retrieved April 20, 2013, from http://web.ebscohost.com/ehost/detail?sid=379b200a-4800–4fca-8e76-88631babf2e3%40sessionmgr111&vid=5&hid=119&bdata=JnNpdGU9ZWhvc3QtbGl2Z Q%3d%3d#db=mth&AN=9502237605.

Aday, S., Farrell, H., Lynch, M., Sides, J., & Freelon, D. (2012). Blogs and bullet II—New media and conflict after the Arab Spring (No. 80). Peaceworks. United States Institute of Peace. Retrieved May 31, 2013, from http://www.usip.org/files/resources/PW80.pdf.

Amazon Mechanical Turk | Welcome (2013). Amazon Mechnical Turk—Artificial Artificial Intelligence. Retrieved May 3, 2013, from https://www.mturk.com/mturk/welcome.

Anderson, C. (2012, June 22). Danger room | How I accidentally kickstarted the domestic drone boom. Wired.com. Retrieved May 1, 2013, from http://www.wired.com/dangerroom/2012/06/ff_drones/all/.

Andrews, L. (2012, February 5). Facebook is using you. *The New York Times*, SR7. Retrieved April 10, 2013, from http://www.nytimes.com/2012/02/05/opinion/sunday/facebook-is-using-you.

Andrews, S., Burrough, B., & Ellison, S. (2014, May 1). The Snowden saga: A shadowland of secrets and light. *Vanity Fair* (May). Retrieved June 23, 2014, from http://www.vanityfair.com/politics/2014/05/edward-snowden-politics-interview.

Appadurai, A. (1996). *Modernity at large: Cultural dimensions of globalization*. Public Worlds series. Minneapolis, MN: University of Minnesota Press.

Arad, A., Feige, K., & Alonzo, V. (Prod.) (2008). *Iron man*. Dir. J. Favreau. Paramount Pictures. Retrieved April 29, 2013, from http://www.imdb.com/title/tt0371746/companycredits.

Arafeh, S., Levin, D., Rainie, L., & Lenhart, A. (2002). The digital disconnect: The widening gap between Internet-savvy students and their schools (qualitative study). American Institutes for Research (AIR) for Pew Internet & American Life Project. Retrieved April 11, 2013, from http://www.pewinternet.org/Reports/2002/The-Digital-Disconnect-The-widening-gap-between-Internetsavvy-students-and-their-schools.aspx.

Assange, J., Appelbaum, J., Müller-Maguhn, A., & Zimmermann, J. (2012). *Cypherpunks freedom and the future of the Internet*. New York, NY: OR Books. Retrieved April 10, 2013, from http://www.contentreserve.com/TitleInfo.asp.

Augmented reality in tourism: 10 best practices (2014). Digital Tourism Think Tank. Retrieved June 17, 2014, from http://thinkdigital.travel/best-practice /augmented-reality-in-tourism/.

Austin, S. & Rack, B. J. (Prod.) (1991). *Terminator 2: Judgment day*. Dir. J. Cameron. Tri-Star Pictures. Retrieved April 18, 2013, from http://www.imdb .com/title/tt0103064/?ref_=sr_1.

Baard, M. (2004, April 19). The news, one entry at a time. WIRED (Culture: Lifestyle). Retrieved June 25, 2014, from http://archive.wired.com/culture /lifestyle/news/2004/04/63120.

Baraniuk, R. (2006). Richard Baraniuk on open-source learning. Retrieved April 26, 2013, from http://www.ted.com/talks/lang/eng/richard_baraniuk_on _open_source_learning.html.

Barbara, J. (2013, March 3). Google glasses the beginning of the end of gadgets? *Forbes*. Retrieved April 9, 2013, from http://www.forbes.com/sites /julietbarbara/2012/03/03/are-google-glasses-the-beginning-of-the-end-of -gadgets/.

Baron, N. & Ling, R. (2007). Emerging patterns of American mobile phone use: Electronically-mediated communication in transition. Presented at the Mobile Media 2007, Sydney, Australia.

Bartiromo, M. (2009, December). Inside the mind of Google. *CNBC* Original. Retrieved April 10, 2013, from http://www.cnbc.com/id/33831099.

Baudrillard, J. (1991). Simulacra and science fiction. Trans. A. B. Evans. *Science Fiction Studies, Science Fiction and Postmodernism*, 18(3), 309–313. Retrieved April8,2013,fromhttp://www.depauw.edu/sfs/backissues/55/baudrillard55art .htm.

———(1994). Simulacra and simulation. Trans. S. F. Glaser. *The body, in theory*. Ann Arbor, MI: University of Michigan Press.

Benkler, Y. (2011). A free irresponsible press: Wikileaks and the battle over the soul of the networked fourth estate. *Harvard Civil Rights—Civil Liberties Law Review*, 46(2), 311–397. Retrieved April 9, 2013, from http://harvardcrcl.org /wp-content/uploads/2009/06/Benkler.pdf

Best, S. & Kellner, D. (1991). Postmodern theory: Critical interrogations. New York, NY: Guilford Press.

———(2001). Critical perspectives. *The postmodern adventure: Science, technology, and cultural studies at the third millennium*. New York, NY: Guilford Press.

Bethke, B. (2004, December 7). Cyberpunk! Information database—The cyberpunk project. Retrieved May 1, 2013, from http://project.cyberpunk.ru/idb /cyber_punk.html.

Bilton, N. (2012, February 21). Google to sell heads-up display glasses by year's end. *The New York Times*. Retrieved April 8, 2013, from http://bits.blogs .nytimes.com/2012/02/21/google-to-sell-terminator-style-glasses-by-years -end/.

———(2013, April 28). Brain computer interfaces inch closer to mainstream. *The New York Times*. Retrieved May 22, 2013, from http://bits.blogs.nytimes

.com/2013/04/28/disruptions-no-words-no-gestures-just-your-brain-as-a
-control-pad/.

Bissell, T. (2008, November 3). Annals of technology—The grammar of fun: CliffyB
and the world of the video game. *The New Yorker*, 80. Retrieved May 6, 2013, from
http://www.newyorker.com/reporting/2008/11/03/081103fa_fact_bissell.

Blumer, H. (1986). *Symbolic interactionism: Perspective and method*. Berkeley,
CA: University of California Press.

De Bont, J., Parkes, W., Curtis, B., & Molen, G. (Prod.) (2002). *Minority Report*.
Dir. S. Spielberg. Twentieth Century Fox Film Corp. Retrieved April 23, 2013,
from http://www.imdb.com/title/tt0181689/?ref_=sr_1.

Bottari, M. (2013, October 2). From junk bonds to junk schools: Cyber schools
fleece taxpayers for phantom students and failing grades. PR Watch. Retrieved
June 5, 2014, from http://www.prwatch.org/news/2013/10/12257/junk-bonds
-junk-schools-cyber-schools-fleece-taxpayers-phantom-students-and-faili.

Bowles, S. & Gintis, H. (1976). *Schooling in capitalist America: Educational reform
and the contradictions of economic life*. New York, NY: Basic Books.

Bradshaw, P. (2010, August 26). Scott Pilgrim vs the world. *The Guardian*.
Retrieved April 9, 2013, from http://www.guardian.co.uk/film/2010/aug/26
/scott-pilgrim-vs-the-world-review.

Bridges, W. (1991). *Managing transitions: Making the most of change*. Reading,
MA: Perseus Books.

Britten, F. (2011, September 20). Brands embrace an "Augmented Reality."
The New York Times. Retrieved April 9, 2013, from http://www.nytimes
.com/2011/09/21/fashion/fashion-embraces-augmented-reality-technology
.html?pagewanted=all&_r=0.

Brown, E. (2012, September 28). Transient electronics melt away in the body.
Los Angeles Times. Retrieved April 10, 2013, from http://articles.latimes
.com/2012/sep/28/science/la-sci-biodegradable-electronics-20120929.

Brown, J. S. (2002). Growing up digital: How the web changes work, education,
and the ways people learn. *UDSLA Journal*, 16(2). Retrieved April 11, 2013,
from http://www.usdla.org/html/journal/FEB02_Issue/article01.html.

Buchheit, P. (2014, February 19). 4 ways privatization is ruining our education system. Salon.com. Retrieved June 5, 2014, from http://www.salon
.com/2014/02/19/4_ways_privatization_is_ruining_our_education_system
_partner/.

Buckingham, D. (Ed.) (2008). *Introducing identity. Youth, identity, and digital
media*, The John D. and Catherine T. Macarthur Foundation series on Digital
Media and Learning. Cambridge, MA: MIT Press.

Business Analytics and Business Intelligence Software (2012). SAS—The Power
to Know. Retrieved April 29, 2013, from http://www.sas.com/

Cannon, L. (2000). *President Reagan: The role of a lifetime*. New York, NY: Public
Affairs.

Carlson, S. (2005). The net generation goes to college. *The Chronicle of Higher
Education*, 52(7), A34. Retrieved April 11, 2013, from http://chronicle.com
/article/The-Net-Generation-Goes-to/12307.

Carr, D. (2012, January 12). A glimpse of Murdoch unbound. *The New York Times*, p. B1. Retrieved from http://www.nytimes.com/2012/01/30/business /media/twitter-gives-glimpse-into-rupert-murdochs-mind.html?_r=0.

Carr, N. G. (2011). *The shallows: What the Internet is doing to our brains*. New York, NY: W.W. Norton.

Carroll, L. ([1865]2009). *Alice's adventures in wonderland*. New York, NY: Sterling.

Castells, M. (2010). *The power of identity. The information age: Economy, society, and culture*. Malden, MA: Wiley-Blackwell.

Cavanagh, S. (2014, May 2). Pearson wins major contract from common-core testing consortium. *Education Week—Marketplace K-12*. Retrieved June 14, 2014, from http://blogs.edweek.org/edweek/marketplacek12/2014/05/pearson _wins_major_contract_from_common-core_testing_consortium .html?cmp=SOC-SHR-FB.

Christie, M. (2004). Computer databases and aboriginal knowledge. *Learning Communities: International Journal of Learning in Social Contexts*, 1, 4–12.

Clinton, B. (2005). *My life: The early years*. New York, NY: Vintage Books.

Cody, A. (2014, January 6). 15 months in virtual charter hell: A teacher's tale. Education Week Teacher—Living in Dialogue. Retrieved June 6, 2014, from http://blogs.edweek.org/teachers/living-in-dialogue/2014/01/15_months _in_virtual_charter_h.

Cohen, J. D., Dunbar, K., & McClelland, J. L. (1990). On the control of automatic processes: A parallel distributed processing account of the Stroop Effect. *Psychological Review*, 97(3), 332–361.

Coleman, G. (2011, April 6). Anonymous: From the Lulz to collective action. The New Everyday: A Media Commons Project. Retrieved May 1, 2013, from http://mediacommons.futureofthebook.org/tne/pieces/anonymous-lulz -collective-action.

Compensation Information for Ronald J. Packard, Chief Executive Officer of K12 INC (2014). Salary.com. Retrieved June 7, 2014, from http://www1.salary.com /Ronald-J-Packard-Salary-Bonus-Stock-Options-for-K12-INC.html.

Computer History Museum (2006a). Internet History—1962–1992. Exhibits. Retrieved April 22, 2013, from http://www.computerhistory.org/internet _history/.

Computer History Museum (2006b). Internet History—1980's. Exhibits. Retrieved April 22, 2013, from http://www.computerhistory.org/internet _history/internet_history_80s.html.

Cook, J. (2005, January 11). CBS News fires 4 in erroneous Bush story, investigators cite "myopic zeal." *Chicago Tribune*. Retrieved April 10, 2013, from http://arti-cles.chicagotribune.com/2005-01-11/news/0501110453_1_mary-mapes-cbs -news-executives-chief-executive-louis-boccardi/2.

Cooley, C. H. ([1902]2012). *Human nature and the social order*. Stockbridge, MA: HardPress Publishing.

Cottom, T. McMillan (2014). 4-Profits R Us. *On Campus*, 33(4), 7–9. Retrieved June 5, 2014, from https://www.aft.org/emags/oc/oc_summer2014/index. html#/8/.

Coursera | About Us (n.d.). Coursera—Explore Courses. Retrieved May 3, 2013, from https://www.coursera.org/about.

Coutu, D. (2003). Technology and human vulnerability: A conversation with MIT's Sherry Turkle. *Harvard Business Review*, 81(9), 1–9.

Crichton, M. (Prod.) (1994). Dir & Prod. B. Levinson. *Disclosure*. Warner Bros. Retrieved June 20, 2014, from http://www.imdb.com/title/tt0109635/?ref_=ttco_co_tt.

Cuban, L. (2001). *Oversold and underused computers in the classroom*. Cambridge, MA: Harvard University Press. Retrieved April 10, 2013, from http://site.ebrary.com/id/10315841.

Cuban, L., Kirkpatrick, H., & Peck, C. (2001). High access and low use of technologies in high school classrooms: Explaining an apparent paradox. American Educational Research Journal, 38(4), 813–834. Retrieved April 10, 2013, from http://aer.sagepub.com/cgi/doi/10.3102/00028312038004813.

Culatta, R. (2011). Behaviorist learning theory. Retrieved June 17, 2014, from http://www.innovativelearning.com/teaching/behaviorism.html.

Curnutt, H. (2009). A fan crashing the party: Exploring reality-celebrity in MTV's Real World franchise. *Television & New Media*, 10(3), 251–266. Retrieved May 28, 2013, from http://tvn.sagepub.com/cgi/doi/10.1177/1527476409334017.

Danna, A. & Gandy, O. H. (2002). All that glitters is not gold: Digging beneath the surface of data mining. *Journal of Business Ethics*, 40(4), 373–386. Retrieved April 10, 2013, from http://link.springer.com/article/10.1023%2FA%3A10208 45814009.

Daw, D. (2011, October 24). What makes Siri special? *PC World*. Retrieved April 9, 2013, from http://www.pcworld.com/article/242479/what_makes_siri_special _.html.

Debord, G. ([1967]2004). *The society of the spectacle*. Trans. K. Knabb. London, UK: Rebel Press.

Dewey, J. ([1916]2009). *Democracy and education*. Radford, VA: Wilder Publications.

Diana, C. (2013, January 27). Talking, walking objects. *The New York Times*, SR1. Retrieved April 11, 2013, from http://www.nytimes.com/2013/01/27/opinion /sunday/our-talking-walking-objects.html?pagewanted=all.

Dick, P. K. (1996). *Do androids dream of electric sheep?* New York, NY: Ballantine Books.

Duhigg, C. (2012, February 19). How companies learn your secrets. *The New York Times*, MM30. Retrieved April 10, 2013, from http://www.nytimes .com/2012/02/19/magazine/shopping-habits.html?pagewanted=all&_r=0.

Emerson, R. M. (1976). Social exchange theory. *Annual Review of Sociology*, 2, 335–362.

Enzensberger, H. M. (1974). *The consciousness industry: On literature, politics and the media*. A Continuum Book. New York, NY: Seabury Press.

———(1975). The industrialization of the mind. *The Urban Review*, 8(1), 68–75. Retrieved April 9, 2013, from http://link.springer.com/article/10.1007%2FBF 02172457?LI=true#page-1.

———(1982). The industrialization of the mind. In B. Armstrong (Ed.), *Critical essays* (p. 9). New York, NY: The Continuum Publishing Company.

Erikson, E. H. (1980). *Identity and the life cycle.* New York, NY: Norton.

Ertmer, P. A. (2005). Teacher pedagogical beliefs: The final frontier in our quest for technology integration? *Educational Technology Research and Development,* 53(4), 25–39. Retrieved April 11, 2013, from http://link.springer.com/10.1007/BF02504683.

Fact sheet: Digital promise initiative (2011, September 15). The White House. Retrieved April 23, 2013, from http://www.whitehouse.gov/the-press -office/2011/09/15/fact-sheet-digital-promise-initiative.

Fang, L. (2011, November 16). How online learning companies bought America's schools. *The Nation.* Retrieved June 13, 2014, from http://www.thenation.com /article/164651/how-online-learning-companies-bought-americas-schools

Fayyad, U., Piatetsky-Shapiro, G., & Smyth, P. (1996). Advances in knowledge discovery and data mining. *American Association for Artificial Intelligence,* 17(3), 37–54.

Feenberg, A. (1991). *Critical theory of technology.* New York, NY: Oxford University Press.

Feldman, L. (2007). The news about comedy: Young audiences, the Daily Show, and evolving notions of journalism. *Journalism,* 8(4), 406–427. Retrieved April 10, 2013, from http://jou.sagepub.com/content/8/4/406.short.

Foege, A. (2013). *The tinkerers: The amateurs, DIYers, and inventors who make America great.* New York, NY: Basic Books.

Fogg, B. J. (2003). *Persuasive technology: Using computers to change what we think and do.* The Morgan Kaufmann series in Interactive Technologies. Burlington, MA: Morgan Kaufmann Publishers.

Foucault, M. (1986). Of other spaces. Trans. J. Miskowiec. Diacritics, 16(1), 22–27.

Fredrickson, B. (2013, March 23). Your phone vs. your heart. *The New York Times,* SR14. Retrieved April 24, 2013, from http://www.nytimes.com/2013/03/24 /opinion/sunday/your-phone-vs-your-heart.html?_r=0.

Freire, P. ([1968]2000). *Pedagogy of the oppressed* (30th anniversary ed.). New York, NY: Bloomsbury Academic.

Freud, S. ([1923]1989). The ego and the id (J. Strachey, Ed.). The standard edition of the complete psychological works of Sigmund Freud. New York, NY: Norton.

Friedman, T. L. (2013, January 26). Revolution hits the universities. *The New York Times,* SR1. Retrieved April 11, 2013, from http://www.nytimes .com/2013/01/27/opinion/sunday/friedman-revolution-hits-the-universities .html.

Gabler, N. (2011, August 14). The elusive big idea. *The New York Times,* SR1. Retrieved April 26, 2013, from http://www.nytimes.com/2011/08/14/opinion /sunday/the-elusive-big-idea.html?pagewanted=all&_r=0.

Gardner, S. (2013, January 13). Wikipedia, the people's encyclopedia. *Los Angeles Times.* Retrieved April 11, 2013, from http://articles.latimes.com/2013/jan/13 /opinion/la-oe-gardner-wikipedia-20130113.

Gee, J. P. (2005). Learning by design: Good video games as learning machines. E-Learning and Digital Media, 2(1), 5–16. Retrieved May 6, 2013, from http://www.wwwords.co.uk/pdf/freetoview.asp?j=elea&vol=2&issue=1&year=2005&article=2_Gee_ELEA_2_1_web.

Gee, J. P. & Hayes, E. R. (2011). Language and learning in the digital age. Abingdon: Routledge.

Gergen, K. J. (1991). The saturated self: Dilemmas of identity in contemporary life. New York, NY: Basic Books.

Gibson, J. J. ([1979] 1986). The ecological approach to visual perception. Hillsdale, NJ: Lawrence Erilbaum Associates.

——— The theory of affordances. In R. Shaw & J. Bransford (Eds.), Perceiving, acting, and knowing: Toward an ecological psychology (pp. 67–82). Hillsdale, NJ: Lawrence Erlbaum.

Gibson, W. ([1984]2004). Neuromancer. New York, NY: Ace Books.

Giddens, A. (1991). Modernity and self-identity: Self and society in the late modern age. Palo Alto, CA: Stanford University Press.

Giroux, H. A. (1981). Schooling and the Myth of Objectivity: Stalking the politics of the hidden curriculum. McGill Journal of Education / Revue des sciences de l'éducation de McGill, 16(003). Retrieved June 13, 2014, from http://mje.mcgill.ca/article/view/7420.

———(2004). Cultural studies, public pedagogy, and the responsibility of intellectuals. Communication and Critical/Cultural Studies, 1(1), 59–79. Retrieved April 4, 2013, from http://www.tandfonline.com/doi/abs/10.1080/147914204 2000180926.

———(2010). The mouse that roared: Disney and the end of innocence (updated and expanded ed.). Lanham, Md: Rowman & Littlefield Publishers.

Gitlin, T. (2003). The whole world is watching: Mass media in the making & unmaking of the new left. Berkeley, CA: University of California Press.

Glass, G. (2009). The realities of K-12 virtual education (Policy Brief). National Education Policy Center. Retrieved June 14, 2014, from http://nepc.colorado.edu/publication/realities-K-12-virtual-education.

Glenn, D. J. (1989). MIT research heavily dependent on defense department funding. The Tech Online Edition, 109(7). Retrieved April 9, 2013, from http://tech.mit.edu/V109/N7/glenn.07o.html.

Goffman, E. (1959). The presentation of self in everyday life. New York, NY: Anchor Book.

Goodenow, R. (1996). The cyberspace challenge: Modernity, post-modernity and reflections on international networking policy. Comparative Education, 32(2), 197–216. Retrieved April 11, 2013, from http://www.tandfonline.com/doi/abs/10.1080/03050069628849.

Gray, L., Thomas, N., & Lewis, L. (2010). Teachers' use of educational technology in U.S. public schools: 2009 (NCES 2010–040). U.S. Department of Education, National Center for Education Statistics. Retrieved April 11, 2013, from http://nces.ed.gov/pubsearch/pubsinfo.asp?pubid=2010040.

Greenhow, C. & Robelia, B. (2009). Informal learning and identity formation in online social networks. Learning, Media and Technology, 34(2),

119–140. Retrieved April 11, 2013, from http://www.tandfonline.com/doi /abs/10.1080/17439880902923580.

Guynn, J. (2012, March). Facebook pledges to help advertisers by making ads more prominent. *Los Angeles Times*. Retrieved April 10, 2013, from http:// articles.latimes.com/2012/mar/01/business/la-fi-facebook-advertisers -20120301.

Hancock, L. (2012). When big data is bad data. *Columbia Journalism Review*. Retrieved May 6, 2013, from http://www.cjr.org/behind_the_news/the _press_and_standardized_tes.php?page=all.

Hanson, E. M. (1997). Educational decentralization: Issues and challenges. Occasional Paper No. 9 Chile: Partnership for Education Revitalization in the Americas. Santiago, Chile: Inter-American Dialogue & PREAL.

Harcup, T. (2011). Alternative journalism as active citizenship. *Journalism*, 12(1), 15–31. Retrieved April 10, 2013, from http://jou.sagepub.com/content/12/1/15. short.

Hardy, Q. (2012, December 3). Big data's role is still evolving. *The New York Times*, B8. Retrieved April 10, 2013, from http://bits.blogs.nytimes.com/2012/11/28 /jeff-hawkins-develops-a-brainy-big-data-company/.

Harel, I. & Papert, S. (1991). Constructionism: Research reports and essays, 1985–1990. Norwood, NJ: Ablex Pub. Corp. Retrieved from http://books .google.com/books?id=2jMNAQAAMAAJ&dq=kafai%20minds%20in%20 play&source=gbs_similarbooks.

Harvey, D. (2007). A brief history of neoliberalism (1st ed.). Oxford; New York: Oxford University Press.

Helft, M. (2010, October 22). Marketers can glean private data on Facebook. *The New York Times*. Retrieved April 8, 2013, from http://www.nytimes .com/2010/10/23/technology/23facebook.html.

Heller, N. (2013, May 20). Laptop U: Is college moving online? *The New Yorker*, 80. Retrieved June 5, 2014, from http://www.newyorker.com /reporting/2013/05/20/130520fa_fact_heller.

Henn, S. (2010, September 30). No political "promoted" tweets and trends this election season. Marketplace's Steve Henn reports. NPR. Retrieved April 8, 2013, from http://www.marketplace.org/topics/business/no-political -promoted-tweets-and-trends-election-season.

Hernandez, G. A., Eddy, K. J., & Muchmore, J. (2001). Insurance weblining and unfair discrimination in cyberspace. *SMU Law Review*, 54(4), 1953–1972. Retrieved April 10, 2013, from http://heinonline.org/HOL/LandingPage?col lection=journals&handle=hein.journals/smulr54&div=91&id=&page.

Herold, B. (2014, April 16). Prominent ed-tech players' data-privacy policies attract scrutiny. *Education Week*. Retrieved June 17, 2014, from http://www .edweek.org/ew/articles/2014/04/16/28privacy_ep.h33.html.

Holland, D. C. (1998). *Identity and agency in cultural worlds*. Cambridge, MA: Harvard University Press.

Holland, D., Jr., Lachicotte., W., Skinner, D., & Cain, C. ([1998]2001). *Identity and agency in cultural worlds*. Cambridge, MA: President and Fellows of Harvard College.

Hopmann, D. N. & Stromback, J. (2010). The rise of the media punditocracy? Journalists and media pundits in Danish election news 1994–2007. *Media, Culture & Society*, 32(6), 943–960. Retrieved April 10, 2013, from http://mcs .sagepub.com/cgi/doi/10.1177/0163443710379666.

How a K¹² online education works | K12 (2014). k12.com. Retrieved June 13, 2014, from   http://www.k12.com/what-is-k12/how-k12-education-works#.U5tOuy _LGA4.

Hsu, D. D. (1995). Negroponte reflects on media lab's first ten years. *The Tech*, 115(47), 14–15.

Hudson, M. (1999, November). Education for change: Henry Giroux and transformative critical pedagogy. Solidarity—Against the current, 83. Retrieved June 13, 2014, from http://www.solidarity-us.org/site/print/1734.

Huerta, L., Rice, J. K., Shafer, S. R., Barbour, M. K., Miron, G., Gulosino, C., & Horvitz, B. (2014). *Virtual Schools in the U.S. 2014: Politics, Performance, Policy, and Research Evidence.* Boulder, CO: National Education Policy Center. Retrieved June 6, 2014, from http://nepc.colorado.edu/publication /virtual-schools-annual-2014.

Hwang, S.-W., Tao, H., Kim, D.-H., Cheng, H., Song, J.-K., Rill, E., Brenckle, M. A., et al. (2012). A physically transient form of silicon electronics. *Science*, 337(6102), 1640–1644. Retrieved April 11, 2013, from http://www.sciencemag .org/cgi/doi/10.1126/science.1226325.

Ichinose, C. (2014, January 28). A teacher's experience: What I learned working in online schools. *Education Week Teacher.* Retrieved June 7, 2014, from http://www.edweek.org/tm/articles/2014/01/28/fp_ichinose.html

Illich, I. ([1971]2000). *Deschooling society.* London, UK: Marion Boyars Publishers Ltd.

Internet Advertising: The online ad attack (2005, April 27). *The Economist.* Retrieved April 22, 2013, from http://www.economist.com/node/3908700.

Internet Advertising: The ultimate marketing machine (2006, June 6). *The Economist.* Retrieved April 22, 2013, from http://www.economist.com /node/7138905.

Ive, J. (2007). Product designer (1967-) Winner of the Design Museum's Inaugural Designer of the Year Award in 2003. British Council Design Museum. Retrieved May 1, 2013, from http://designmuseum.org/design/jonathan-ive.

Jackson, R. (2011). Culture, identity, and hegemony: Continuity and (the lack of) change in US counterterrorism policy from Bush to Obama. *International Politics*, 48(2/3), 390–411.

Jacobson, N. & Kilik, J. (Prod.) (2012). *The Hunger Games.* Dir. G. Ross. Lionsgate. Retrieved April 30, 2013, from http://www.imdb.com/title /tt1392170/?ref_=sr_2.

Jameson, F. (1991). *Postmodernism, or, the cultural logic of late capitalism.* Durham, NC: Duke University Press.

Jenkins, H. (2008). Convergence culture: Where old and new media collide. New York, NY: New York University Press.

——(2009). Confronting the challenges of participatory culture: Media education for the 21st century. Cambridge, MA: MIT Press.

Johnson, B. (2010, January 10). Privacy no longer a social norm, says Facebook founder. *The Guardian*. Retrieved April 10, 2013, from http://www.guardian.co.uk/technology/2010/jan/11/facebook-privacy.

Johnson, S. (2006). *Everything bad is good for you: How today's popular culture is actually making us smarter*. New York, NY: Riverhead Books.

Jonas-Dwyer, D. & Pospisil, R. (2004). The millennial effect: Implications for academic development. HERDSA 2004 conference proceedings (pp. 194–207). Presented at the 27th HERDSA Annual Conference. Retrieved April 5, 2013, from http://www.herdsa.org.au/wp-content/uploads/conference/2004/papers/jonas-dwyer.pdf.

Jones, S. (1995). Hyper-punk: Cyberpunk and information technology. *The Journal of Popular Culture*, 28(2), 81–92.

——(1997). *Virtual culture: Identity and communication in cybersociety*. London, UK: Sage Publications.

K12 virtual teacher salary (2014). Glassdoor.com. Retrieved June 7, 2014, from http://www.glassdoor.com/Salary/K12-Virtual-Teacher-Salaries-E42734_D_KO4,19.htm.

Katz, J. M. (1981). *Why don't you listen to what I'm not saying?* (1st ed.). Garden City, NY: Anchor Press.

Kay, P. & Kempton, W. (1984). What is the Sapir-Whorf hypothesis? *American Anthropologist*, 86(1), 65–79.

Kellner, D. (1998, December). Boundaries and borderlines: Reflections on Jean Baudrillard and critical theory. Illuminations: The Critical Theory Website. Research Resource. Retrieved April 11, 2013, from http://www.uta.edu/huma/illuminations/kell2.htm.

——(2003a). *Media culture: Cultural studies, identity, and politics between the modern and the postmodern*. New York, NY: Routledge.

——(2003b). *Media spectacle*. New York, NY: Routledge.

——(2005). Critical theory and education: Historical and metatheoretical perspectives. In I. Gur-Ze'ev (Ed.), *Critical theory and critical pedagogy: Toward a new critical language in education* (pp. 49–69). Haifa, Israel: University of Haifa. Retrieved April 10, 2013, from http://construct.haifa.ac.il/~ilangz/critical-pedagogy-critical-theory-today.pdf.

——(2008). *Guys and guns amok: Domestic terrorism and school shootings from the Oklahoma City bombing to the Virginia Tech massacre*. The Radical Imagination Series. Boulder, CO: Paradigm Publishers.

——(2011). Cultural studies, multiculturalism, and media culture. In G. Dines & J. M. Humez (Eds.), *Gender, race, and class in media: A critical reader* (3rd ed.). Thousand Oaks: SAGE Publications.

———(2012a). *Media spectacle and insurrection, 2011: From the Arab uprisings to Occupy everywhere*. Critical Adventures in New Media. New York, NY: Bloomsbury.

——(2012b). The Murdoch media empire and the spectacle of scandal. *International Journal of Communications*, 6, 1169–1200. Retrieved April 10, 2013, from http://ijoc.org/ojs/index.php/ijoc/article/view/1613/754.

Kellner, D., & Share, J. (2005). Toward critical media literacy: Core concepts, debates, organizations, and policy. *Discourse: Studies in the Cultural Politics of Education*, 26(3), 369–386. Retrieved April 11, 2013, from http://www.tandfonline.com/doi/abs/10.1080/01596300500200169.

———(2007). Critical media literacy, democracy, and the reconstruction of education. In D. P. Macedo & S. R. Steinberg (Eds.), *Media literacy: A reader* (pp. 3–23). New York, NY: Peter Lang.

Kelley, K. (2007). On the next 5,000 days. Retrieved April 26, 2013, from http://www.ted.com/talks/kevin_kelly_on_the_next_5_000_days_of_the_web.html.

Kennedy, G. E., Judd, T. S., Churchward, A., Gray, K., & Krause, K.-L. (2008). First year students' experiences with technology: Are they really digital natives? *Australasian Journal of Educational Technology*, 24(1), 108–122. Retrieved April 11, 2013, from http://www.eric.ed.gov/ERICWebPortal/search/detailmini.jsp?_nfpb=true&_&ERICExtSearch_SearchValue_0=EJ832712&ERICExtSearch_SearchType_0=no&accno=EJ832712.

Kennedy, K. & Molen, G. (Prod.) (1993). *Jurassic Park*. Dir. S. Spielberg. Universal Pictures. Retrieved April 18, 2013, from http://www.imdb.com/title/tt0107290/?ref_=sr_1.

Kennedy, K., Parkes, W., & Curtis, B. (Prod.) (2001). *A.I. Artifical Intelligence*. Dir. S. Spielberg Warner Bros. Retrieved April 23, 2013, from http://www.imdb.com/title/tt0212720/?ref_=sr_2.

Khan Academy | Learn almost anything for free. (2013). Khan Academy. Retrieved May 3, 2013, from https://www.khanacademy.org/.

Khan Academy | Khan Academy privacy notice (2014, May 8). Khan Academy. Retrieved June 17, 2014, from http://www.khanacademy.org.

Khan, S. (2011). Let's use video to reinvent education. Retrieved April 26, 2013, from http://www.ted.com/talks/salman_khan_let_s_use_video_to_reinvent_education.html.

Khatchadourian, R. (2010, June 7). A reporter at large—No secrets—Julian Assange's mission for total transparency. *The New Yorker*. Retrieved May 31, 2013, from http://www.newyorker.com/reporting/2010/06/07/100607fa_fact_khatchadourian.

Kirkham, C. (2012, July 30). For-profit colleges get scathing indictment n senate report. *Huffington Post*. Retrieved June 16, 2014, from http://www.huffingtonpost.com/2012/07/30/for-profit-colleges-senate-report.

Kittlaus, D., Cheyer, A., & Gruber, T. (2011). Siri. Apple Inc. [Original author SRI International].

Klein, J. (2003). *The natural: The misunderstood presidency of Bill Clinton*. New York, NY: Broadway Books.

Koller, D. (2012). What we are learning from online education.. Retrieved April 26, 2013, from http://www.ted.com/talks/daphne_koller_what_we_re_learning_from_online_education.html.

Kübler-Ross, E. (1997). *On death and dying*. New York, NY: Touchstone.

Kushner, David. (2012, May 7). Annals of technology—Machine politics—The man who started the hacker wars. *The New Yorker.* Retrieved April 10, 2013, from http://www.newyorker.com/reporting/2012/05/07/120507fa_fact _kushner.

Kushner, Donald (Prod.) (1982). *Tron.* Dir. S. Lisberger. Buena Vista. Retrieved April 18, 2013, from http://www.imdb.com/title/tt0084827/?ref_=sr_2.

Lakoff, G. (2004). *Don't think of an elephant!: Know your values and frame the debate: The essential guide for progressives.* White River Junction, VT: Chelsea Green Pub. Co.

Lakoff, G. & Wehling, E. (2012). *The little blue book: The essential guide to thinking and talking democratic* (1st Free Press Trade Paperback ed.). New York: Free Press.

Landau, J., Breton, B., and McLagen, J. (Prod.) (2009). *Avatar.* Dir. & Prod. J. Cameron. Twentieth Century Fox Film Corp. Retrieved April 23, 2013, from http://www.imdb.com/title/tt0499549/?ref_=sr_1.

Larson, E. (1994). *The naked consumer: How our private lives become public commodities.* New York, NY: Penguin Books.

Di Laurentis, D. (Prod.) (1968). *Barbarella.* Dir. R. Vadim. Paramount Pictures. Retrieved April 18, 2013, from http://www.imdb.com/title/tt0062711/? ref_=sr_2.

De Lauzirika, C. & Deeley, M. (Prod.) (1982). *Blade Runner.* Dir. R. Scott. Warner Bros. Retrieved April 18, 2013, from http://www.imdb.com/title /tt0083658/?ref_=sr_1.

Layton, L. & Brown, E. (2011, November 26). Virtual schools are multiplying, but some question their educational value. *Washington Post.* Retrieved June 16, 2014, from http://www.washingtonpost.com/local/education/virtual-schools -are-multiplying-but-some-question-their-educational-value/2011/11/22 /gIQANUzkzN_story.html.

Leary, M. R. & Tangney, J. P. (Eds.) (2003). *Handbook of self and identity.* New York, NY: Guilford Press.

Lederman, J. (2012, October 2). *Education chief wants textbooks to go digital.* Washington, DC: The Associated Press. Retrieved May 3, 2013, from http:// www.lexisnexis.com/lnacui2api/api/version1/getDocCui?oc=00240&hl=t&h ns=t&hnsd=f&perma=true&lni=56R0-VTX1-JBGK-G0KS&hv=t&csi=30447 8&hgn=t&secondRedirectIndicator=true.

Lee, S., & McBride, S. (2007). *Neo-liberalism, state power and global governance.* Dordrecht: Springer. Retrieved June 17, 2014, from http://public.eblib.com /EBLPublic/PublicView.do?ptiID=372364.

Leland, J. (2012, March 11). Adventures of a teenager polyglot. *The New York Times*, MB1. Retrieved April 23, 2013, from http://www.nytimes. com/2012/03/11/nyregion/a-teenage-master-of-languages-finds-online -fellowship.html?pagewanted=all.

Lévi-Strauss, C. (1966). *The savage mind.* Chicago, IL: University of Chicago Press.

Lewin, T. (2012, November 20). College of the future could be come one, come all. *The New York Times*, A1. Retrieved April 11, 2013, from http://www.nytimes

.com/2012/11/20/education/colleges-turn-to-crowd-sourcing-courses
.html?pagewanted=all&_r=0.

Lewis, E. (Prod.) (1960). *Spartacus.* Dir. S. Kubrick. Universal Pictures. Retrieved
April 30, 2013, from http://www.imdb.com/title/tt0054331/?ref_=sr_3.

Lievrouw, L. A. (2011). *Alternative and activist new media.* Digital Media and
Society Series. Malden, MA: Polity Press.

Lockley, L. C. (1950). Notes on the history of marketing research. *Journal of
Marketing,* 14(5), 733–736. Retrieved April 10, 2013, from http://www.jstor.org
/stable/1246952.

Loeb, P. S. (2005). Editorial foreword. *Journal of Nietzsche Studies,* 30(1), v–vii.
Retrieved April 9, 2013, from http://muse.jhu.edu/journals/journal_of
_nietzsche_studies/v030/30.1loeb01.html.

Lohr, S. (2012, February 29). For impatient web users, an eye blink is just too
long to wait. *The New York Times,* A1. Retrieved April 8, 2013, from http://
www.nytimes.com/2012/03/01/technology/impatient-web-users-flee-slow
-loading-sites.html?pagewanted=all&_r=0.

Lopate, L. (2011, November 9). Privatizing education. The Leonard Lopate
show. WNYC 93.9FM. Retrieved June 10, 2014, from http://www.wnyc.
org/story/172745-privatizing-education/?utm_source=sharedUrl&utm
_media=metatag&utm_campaign=sharedUrl.

Madrigal, A. C. (2012, June 19). The perfect technocracy: Facebook's attempt
to create good government for 900 million people. The Atlantic. Retrieved
April 11, 2013, from http://www.theatlantic.com/technology/archive/2012/06
/the-perfect-technocracy-facebooks-attempt-to-create-good-government
-for-900-million-people/258484/.

Marcuse, H. ([1964]1991). One-dimensional man: Studies in the ideology of
advanced industrial society (5th ed.). Boston, MA: Beacon Press.

Markoff, J. (2012, November 24). Learning curve: No longer just a human trait.
The New York Times, A1. Retrieved April 11, 2013, from http://www.nytimes
.com/2012/11/24/science/scientists-see-advances-in-deep-learning-a-part-of
-artificial-intelligence.html.

Mathews, J. (2013, October 18). Vociferous debate over profits highlights split
in school reform movement. *Washington Post.* Retrieved June 4, 2014, from
http://www.washingtonpost.com/local/education/surprising-split-in-school
-reformer-monolith/2013/10/27/0da9ea9a-3c16-11e3-b7ba-503fb5822c3e
_story.html.

McChesney, R. (2014). Rupert Murdoch: Not silent, but deadly. *Monthly Review,*
66(2). Retrieved June 24, 2014, from http://monthlyreview.org/2014/06/01
/rupert-murdoch-not-silent-but-deadly.

McLuhan, M. ([1964]1994). *Understanding media: The extensions of man.*
Cambridge, MA: MIT Press.

McLuhan, M. & Fiore Q.([1967]2005). *The medium is the massage.* Berkley, CA:
Ginko Press.

McNamara, M. (2007). Assessing the globalization decentralization nexus:
Patterns of education and reform in Mexico, Chile, Argentina and Nicaragua.

In S. Lee & S. McBride (Eds.), *Neo-liberalism, state power and global governance in the twenty-first century* (pp. 61–76). Dordrecht, Netherlands: Springer.

McQueen, R. (2011). Joichi Ito set to lead Media Lab. *The Tech Online Edition*, 131(26). Retrieved April 9, 2013, from http://tech.mit.edu/V131/N26/joichi-interview.html.

Mead, G. H. (1967). *Mind, self & society from the standpoint of a social behaviorist.* (C. W. Morris, ed.). Chicago, IL: University of Chicago Press.

Menand, L. (2012, July 9). *A critic at large—Seeing it now—Walter Cronkite and the legend of CBS News. The New Yorker*, 88. Retrieved May 5, 2013, from http://www.newyorker.com/arts/critics/atlarge/2012/07/09/120709crat_atlarge_menand.

Mencimer, S. (2011, November). Jeb Bush's cyber attack on public schools. *Mother Jones*. Retrieved June 16, 2014, from http://www.motherjones.com/politics/2011/10/jeb-bush-digitial-learning-public-schools.

Mezrich, B. (2010). *The accidental billionaires: The founding of Facebook, a tale of sex, money, genius, and betrayal.* New York, NY: Anchor Books.

Miron, G., Huerta, L., Rice, J. K., Cuban, L., Horvitz, B., Gulosino, C., & Shafer, S. R. (2013). *Virtual schools in the U.S. 2013: Politics, performance, policy, and research evidence.* Boulder, CO: National Education Policy Center. Retrieved June 17, 2014, from http://nepc.colorado.edu/publication/virtual-schools-annual-2013.

Miron, G. & Urschel, J. (2012). *Understanding and improving full-time virtual schools: A study of student characteristics, school finance, and school performance in schools operated by K12 Inc.* Boulder, CO: National Education Policy Center. Retrieved June 17, 2014, from http://nepc.colorado.edu/publication/understanding-improving-virtual

Mizukochi, S. (2009, September 3). *Mobile culture & Japanese identity.* Personal Interview.

Morozov, E. (2013, March 3). The perils of perfection, SR1. *The New York Times.* Retrieved April 11, 2013, from http://www.nytimes.com/2013/03/03/opinion/sunday/the-perils-of-perfection.html.

Morris-Suzuki, T. (1988). *Beyond computopia: Information, automation, and democracy in Japan.* Japanese Studies. New York, NY: Kegan Paul International; Routledge, Chapman, and Hall.

Moy, E. (1993). Media lab to get $2.65M from HP. *The Tech*, 113(46), 1–10.

Murphy, D., Bryce, I., Di Bonaventura, L., DeSanto, T., & Bates, K. (Prod.) (2007). *Transformers.* Dir. M. Bay. Paramount Pictures. Retrieved April 23, 2013, from http://www.imdb.com/title/tt0418279/?ref_=sr_4.

National Archives and Records Administration (2000, November 16). *The Clinton presidency: Historic economic growth.* The White House. Retrieved April 23, 2013, from http://clinton5.nara.gov/WH/Accomplishments/eightyears-03.html.

Nelson, T. H. (1987). *Computer lib/dream machines.* Richmond, WA: Tempus Books/Microsoft Press.

Newman, K. S., Fox, C., Roth, W., Mehta, J., & Harding, D. (2005). *Rampage: The social roots of school shootings.* New York, NY: Basic Books.

Nietzsche, F. W. ([1883–1885]2012). *Thus spoke Zarathustra* (W. Kaufmann, trans.). Hollywood, FL: Simon & Brown.

Norman, D. A. (1988). *The psychology of everyday things*. New York, NY: Basic Books.

O'Connor, J. (2012, September 11). Florida investigates K12, nation's largest online educator | StateImpact Florida. http://stateimpact.npr.org. Retrieved June 7, 2014, from http://stateimpact.npr.org/florida/2012/09/11/florida -investigates-k12-nations-largest-online-educator/.

Oberly, N. (2003, Winter). reality, hyperreality (1). University of Chicago. Retrieved April 9, 2013, from http://csmt.uchicago.edu/glossary2004/reality-hyperreality.htm.

Olmos, L., Torres, C. A., & Van Heertum, R. (Eds.). (2011). Preface: Globalization and education. *Educating the global citizen in the shadow of neoliberalism thirty years of educational reform in North America* (pp. ii–xi). Oak Park, IL: Bentham eBooks. Retrieved April 11, 2013, from http://site.ebrary.com /id/10504680.

Olson, P. (2012). *We are Anonymous: Inside the hacker world of Lulzsec, Anonymous, and the global cyber insurgency*. New York, NY: Little, Brown and Co.

An open letter from San Jose State U.'s Philosophy Department (2013, May 2). *The Chronicle of Higher Education*. Retrieved June 5, 2014, from http://chronicle .com/article/The-Document-Open-Letter-From/138937/.

Papandrea, M.-R. (2007). Citizen journalism and the reporter's privilege. *Minnesota Law Review*, 91 (Boston College Law School Research Paper No. 110). Retrieved May 5, 2013, from http://papers.ssrn.com/sol3/papers. cfm?abstract_id=932681.

Pariser, E. (2011). Beware online "filter bubbles." Ted Talks—TED2011. Retrieved June 24, 2014, from http://www.ted.com/talks/eli_pariser_beware _online_filter_bubbles.

Paumgarten, N. (2012, May 14). The world of surveillance—Here's looking at you—Should we worry about the rise of the drone? *The New Yorker*. Retrieved April 10, 2013, from http://www.newyorker.com /reporting/2012/05/14/120514fa_fact_paumgarten.

Peppers, D. & Rogers, M. (1997). *The one to one future: Building relationships one customer at a time*. New York, NY: Currency Doubleday.

Perlroth, N. & Bilton, N. (2012, February 16). BITS: An easy sweep of user data from devices. *The New York Times*, B4. Retrieved April 10, 2013, from http:// query.nytimes.com/gst/fullpage.html?res=9B07E4D7163FF935A25751C0A9 649D8B63.

Person, L. (1998). Notes toward a postcyberpunk manifesto. Slahdot. technology-related news website. Retrieved April 9, 2013, from http://news.slashdot.org /story/99/10/08/2123255/notes-toward-a-postcyberpunk-manifesto.

Phippen, A., Sheppard, L., & Furnell, S. (2004). A practical evaluation of Web analytics. *Internet Research*, 14(4), 284–293. Retrieved April 10, 2013, from http://www.emeraldinsight.com/10.1108/10662240410555306.

Piaget, J. ([1954]1986). *The child's construction of reality*. New York, NY: Ballantine Books.

Platt, M. (Prod.) (2010). *Scott Pilgrim vs. the World*. Dir. E. Wright. Universal Pictures. Retrieved April 24, 2013, from http://www.imdb.com/title /tt0446029/.

Poster, M. (1995). *The second media age*. Cambridge, UK; Cambridge, MA: Polity Press; B. Blackwell.

———(2006). Postmodern virtualities. In M. G. Durham & D. Kellner (Eds.), *Media and cultural studies keyworks* (pp. 611–625). Malden, MA: Blackwell.

Prensky, M. (2006). *"Don't bother me Mom, I'm learning!": How computer and video games are preparing your kids for twenty-first century success and how you can help!* (1st ed.). St. Paul, MN: Paragon House.

Priest, D. & Arkin, W. M. (2011, September 6). Top secret america: Are we safer? Frontline—News Documentary Series. PBS. Retrieved April 9, 2013, from http://www.pbs.org/wgbh/pages/frontline/are-we-safer/.

Q3 2014—K12 Inc. Earnings Conference Call (2014, April 29). Thompson Reuters Streetevents. Retrieved June 13, 2014, from http://webcache.googleusercontent.com/search?q=cache:pBSFln6n4GgJ:phx.corporate-ir.net/External.File %3Fitem%3DUGFyZW50SUQ9MjMxODY1fENoaWxkSUQ9LTF8VHlwZT 0z%26t%3D1+&cd=1&hl=en&ct=clnk&gl=us.

Quillen, I. (2011, August 10). Media companies move into digital-education space. *Education Week*, 30(37), 18. Retrieved June 10, 2014, from http://www .edweek.org/ew/articles/2011/08/10/37newscorp-s1.h30.html.

Quinn, J. (2009, April 15). Bankers to receive huge bonuses despite financial crisis. *The Telegraph*. Retrieved June 15, 2014, from http://www.telegraph .co.uk/finance/recession/5154915/Bankers-to-receive-huge-bonuses-despite -financial-crisis.html.

Reagan, R. (1983, March 23). Strategic defense initiative speech. Address to the Nation on Defense and National Security. Retrieved April 22, 2013, from http://www.reagan.utexas.edu/archives/speeches/1983/32383d.htm.

Reeves, B. & Nass, C. (1996). *The media equation: How people treat computers, television, and new media like real people and place*. Cambridge, UK: Cambridge University Press.

Research aims to restore amputee limb function (2004). *MIT News*. Retrieved April 9, 2013, from http://web.mit.edu/newsoffice/2004/limbloss.html.

Rheingold, H. (1991). *Virtual reality*. New York, NY: Summit Books.

Rich, M. (2014, June 10). Delay urged on actions tied to tests by schools. *The New York Times*. Retrieved June 14, 2014, from http://www.nytimes .com/2014/06/11/education/gates-foundation-urges-moratorium-on -decisions-tied-to-common-core.html.

Richtel, M. (2011, January 29). Egypt cuts off most Internet and cell service. *The New York Times*, A13. Retrieved April 10, 2013, from http://www.nytimes .com/2011/01/29/technology/internet/29cutoff.html.

Robelen, E. (2000). Election notebook. *Education Week*, 19(42). Retrieved April 9, 2013, from http://www.edweek.org/ew/articles/2000/07/12/42camnote.h19.html.

Robins, K. & Webster, F. (1999). *Times of the technoculture: From the information society to the virtual life.* New York, NY: Routledge.

Roddenberry, G. (1966–1969). *Star Trek.* NBC.

Rodgers, S. & Thorson, E. (2000). The interactive advertising model: How users perceive and process online ads. *Journal of Interactive Advertising,* 1(1), 42–61.

Roeper, R. (2011, March 24). Sucker punch: A confusing house-of-horrors story with busty women. *Chicago Sun-Times.* Retrieved April 9, 2013, from http://www.suntimes.com/news/roeper/4489929-452/sucker-punch-a-confusing-house-of-horrors-story-with-busty-women.html.

Rojek, C. (2001). *Celebrity.* London, UK: Reaktion Books.

Rosenfeld, K. N. (2010). "Terminator" to "Avatar": A postmodern shift. *Jump Cut: A Review of Contemporary Media,* 52, 14. Retrieved June 17, 2014, from http://www.ejumpcut.org/archive/jc52.2010/RosenfeldAvatar/.

Rousseau, J.-J. ([1762]1979). Emile: Or, on education (A. Bloom, Trans.). New York: Basic Books.

Rubin, P. (2014, May 20). The inside story of Oculus Rift and how virtual reality became reality | Gadget lab. WIRED. Retrieved June 17, 2014, from http://www.wired.com/2014/05/oculus-rift-4/.

Rudin, S., De Luca, M., Brunetti, D., & Chaffin, C. (Prod.) (2010). *The Social Network.* Dir. C. Chaffin. Columbia Pictures. Retrieved April 23, 2013, from http://www.imdb.com/title/tt1285016/?ref_=sr_1.

Russakoff, D. (2014, May 19). Schooled. *The New Yorker.* Retrieved June 8, 2014, from http://www.newyorker.com/reporting/2014/05/19/140519fa_fact_russakoff.

Russell, M., Bebell, D., O'Dwyer, L., & O'Connor, K. (2003). Examining teacher technology use: Implications for preservice and inservice teacher preparation. *Journal of Teacher Education,* 54(4), 297–310. Retrieved April 13, 2013, from http://jte.sagepub.com/cgi/doi/10.1177/0022487103255985.

Saltman, K. J. (2010). *The gift of education: Public education and venture philanthropy* (1st ed.). New York: Palgrave Macmillan.

Saul, S. (2011, December 12). Online schools score better on wall street than in classrooms. *The New York Times.* Retrieved June 14, 2014, from http://www.nytimes.com/2011/12/13/education/online-schools-score-better-on-wall-street-than-in-classrooms.html.

Savage, C. (2012, March 12). U.S. relaxes limits on use of data in terror analysis. *The New York Times,* A1. Retrieved April 10, 2013, from http://www.nytimes.com/2012/03/23/us/politics/us-moves-to-relax-some-restrictions-for-counterterrorism-analysis.html.

School-Principal-Salary (2014). Salary.com. Retrieved June 7, 2014, from http://swz.salary.com/SalaryWizard/School-Principal-Salary-Details.aspx.

Scott, A. O. (2010, August 13). This girl has a lot of baggage, and he must shoulder the load. *The New York Times*, C11. Retrieved April 9, 2013, from http://www .nytimes.com/2010/08/13/movies/13scott.html?pagewanted=all&_r=0.

Scott, A. O. (2011, March 24). Well, here they are, wherever this may be. *The New York Times*, C8. Retrieved April 9, 2013, from http://movies.nytimes .com/2011/03/25/movies/sucker-punch-from-zack-snyder-review.html.

Seltzer, W. & Thacher, R. (Prod.) (1973). *Soylent Green*. Dir. R. Fleisher. Metro-Goldwyn-Mayer (MGM). Retrieved April 29, 2013, from http://www.imdb .com/title/tt0070723/?ref_=fn_al_tt_1.

Sengupta, S. (2012, March 31). On Facebook, "Likes" become ads. *The New York Times*. Retrieved April 10, 2013, from http://www.nytimes.com/2012/06/01 /technology/so-much-for-sharing-his-like.html?pagewanted=all&_r=0.

Sharkey, B. (2010, August 13). Movie review: Scott Pilgrim vs. the world. *Los Angeles Times*. Retrieved April 9, 2013, from http://articles.latimes.com/2010 /aug/13/entertainment/la-et-scott-pilgrim-20100813.

——(2011, March 25). Movie review: Sucker punch. *Los Angeles Times*. Retrieved April 9, 2013, from http://articles.latimes.com/2011/mar/25/entertainment /la-et-sucker-punch-20110325.

Shields, R. (2003). *The virtual*. New York, NY: Routledge.

Shuler-Donner, L. & Winter, R. (Prod.) (2000). *X-Men*. Dir. B. Singer. Twentieth Century Fox Film Corp. Retrieved April 29, 2013, from http://www.imdb .com/title/tt0120903/?ref_=fn_al_tt_5.

Silver, J. & Cracchiolo, D. (Prod.) (1999). *The Matrix*. Dir. A. Wachowski & L. Wachowski. Warner Bros. Retrieved April 23, 2013, from http://www.imdb .com/title/tt0133093/?ref_=sr_1.

Silver, J., Hill, G., Malerba, R., Molfenter, H., & Woebcken, C. (Prod.) (2006). *V for Vendetta*. Dir. A. Wachowski & L. Wachowski. Warner Bros. Retrieved April 30, 2013, from http://www.imdb.com/title/tt0434409/?ref_=sr_1.

Singel, R. (2009, September 23). Newly declassified files detail massive FBI data mining project. *Wired Magazine*. Retrieved April 10, 2013, from http://www .wired.com/threatlevel/2009/09/fbi-nsac/.

Singer, A. (2012, September 4). Pearson "Education"—Who Are These People? *Huffington Post*. Retrieved June 4, 2014, from http://www.huffingtonpost .com/alan-singer/pearson-education-new-york-testing-_b_1850169.html.

——(2014, May 7). The pseudo-science of common core and high-stakes testing. *Huffington Post*. Retrieved June 14, 2014, from http://www.huffington-post.com/alan-singer/common-core-pseudoscience_b_5280441.html.

Singer, N. (2011, November 13). Face recognition makes the leap from sci-fi, BU3. Retrieved April 9, 2013, from http://www.nytimes.com/2011/11/13/business /face-recognition-moves-from-sci-fi-to-social-media.html.

Slack, J. D. (1984). The information revolution as ideology. *Media Culture Society*, 6, 247–256.

Snyder, D. (Prod.) (2011). *Sucker Punch*. Dir.& Prod. Z. Snyder. Warner Bros. Retrieved April 24, 2013, from http://www.imdb.com/title/tt0978764 /?ref_=sr_1.

Solove, D. (2002). Access and aggregation: Privacy, public records, and the constitution. *Minnesota Law Review*, 86(6). Retrieved April 10, 2013, from http://papers.ssrn.com/sol3/papers.cfm?abstract_id=283924.

Stallman, R. (2002). The GNU project and the GNU manifesto. In J. Gay (Ed.), *Free software, free society: Selected essays of Richard M. Stallman* (pp. 15–39). Boston, MA: Free Software Foundation.

———(2010). *Free software, free society: Selected essays of Richard M. Stallman* (J. Gay, Ed.). Boston, MA: Free Software Foundation.

Stanley, J. & Crump, C. (2011, December). Report: Protecting privacy from aerial surveillance: Recommendations for government use of drone aircraft. American Civil Liberties Union. Retrieved April 10, 2013, from http://www.aclu.org/technology-and-liberty/report-protecting-privacy-aerial-surveillance-recommendations-government-use.

Stelter, B. (2012, May 28). You can change the channel, but local news is the same. *The New York Times*. Retrieved April 10, 2013, from http://www.nytimes.com/2012/05/29/business/media/local-tv-stations-cut-costs-by-sharing-news-operations.html?pagewanted=all.

Stepanek, M. (2000, April 3). Weblining: Companies are using your personal data to limit your choicesand force you to pay more for products. *Bloomberg Businessweek*. Retrieved April 10, 2013, from http://www.businessweek.com/2000/00_14/b3675027.htm.

Streitfeld, D. (2012, February 12). Erasing the boundaries. *The New York Times*, B1. Retrieved April 9, 2013, from http://www.nytimes.com/2012/02/13/technology/keeping-consumers-on-the-digital-plantation.html.

Stroop, J. R. (1935). Studies of interference in serial verbal reactions. *Journal of Experimental Psychology*, 18(6), 643–662. Retrieved April 29, 2013, from http://content.apa.org/journals/xge/18/6/643.

Stryker, S. (1980). *Symbolic interactionism: A social structural version.* The Benjamin/Cummings Series in Contemporary Sociology. Menlo Park, CA: Benjamin/Cummings Pub. Co.

Stryker, S. & Burke, P. J. (2000). The past, present and future of identity theory. *Social Psychology Quarterly*, 63(4), 284–297.

SumAll | Analytics for marketers (n.d.). SumAll. Retrieved May 4, 2013, from https://sumall.com/.

Tajfel, H. (1974). Social identity and intergroup behavior. *Social Science Information*, 13(2), 65–93.

Tapscott, D. (1999). *Growing up digital: The rise of the Net generation.* New York, NY: McGraw-Hill.

Taylor, C. (1989). *Sources of the self: The making of the modern identity.* Cambridge, MA: Harvard University Press.

Teacher salary (2014). Glassdoor.com. Retrieved June 7, 2014, from http://www.glassdoor.com/Salaries/teacher-salary-SRCH_KO0,7.htm.

Teacher salary—Average K-12 Teacher Salaries (2014). PayScale.com. Retrieved June 7, 2014, from http://www.payscale.com/research/US/All_K-12_Teachers/Salary.

Technology | Guiding principles. (2011, September 16). The White House. Retrieved April 28, 2013, from http://www.whitehouse.gov/issues/technology.

Thomas, E. & Golberg, J. (Prod.) (2010). *Inception*. Dir. & Prod. C. Nolan. Warner Bros. Retrieved April 23, 2013, from http://www.imdb.com/title/tt1375666/?ref_=sr_1.

Thompson, C. (2011, July 15). How Khan Academy is changing the rules of education. *Wired Magazine*. Retrieved April 13, 2013, from http://www.wired.com/magazine/2011/07/ff_khan/.

Thompson, K. (2009, December 30). Drone porn: The newest YouTube hit. *Huff Post World—The Blog*. Retrieved April 10, 2013, from http://www.huffingtonpost.com/keith-thomson/drone-porn-the-newest-you_b_407083.html.

Thuraisingham, B. (2002). Data mining, national security, privacy and civil liberties. *ACM SIGKDD Explorations Newsletter*, 4(2), 1–5. Retrieved April 10, 2013, from http://portal.acm.org/citation.cfm?doid=772862.772863.

Tomlinson, R. (n.d.). The first email. OpenMap. Retrieved April 22, 2013, from http://openmap.bbn.com/~tomlinso/ray/firstemailframe.html.

Toppo, G. (2012, November 28). Online schools spend millions to attract students. *USA Today*. Retrieved June 16, 2014, from http://www.usatoday.com/story/news/nation/2012/11/28/online-schools-ads-public-/1732193/.

Torres, C. A. (1989). The capitalist state and public policy formation: Framework for a political sociology of educational policy making. *British Journal of Sociology of Education*, 10(1), 81–102. Retrieved April 13, 2013, from http://www.tandfonline.com/doi/abs/10.1080/0142569890100106.

———(2005). No child left behind: A brainchild of neoliberalism and american politics. *New Politics*, 10(2), 94–100. Retrieved April 13, 2013, from http://newpol.org/content/no-child-left-behind-brainchild-neoliberalism-and-american-politics.

———(2009). *Education and neoliberal globalization*. Routledge research in education. New York, NY: Routledge.

Trebay, G. (2012, February 14). Model struts path to stardom not on runway, but on YouTube. *The New York Times*, A1. Retrieved April 23, 2013, from http://www.nytimes.com/2012/02/14/us/kate-upton-uses-the-web-to-become-a-star-model.html?pagewanted=all&_r=0.

Turkle, S. (1997). *Life on the screen: Identity in the age of the Internet*. New York, NY: Touchstone.

———(2003). ITS | Welcome page. MIT initiative on technology and self. Retrieved April 22, 2013, from http://web.mit.edu/sturkle/techself/.

———(2005). *The second self: Computers and the human spirit*. Cambridge, MA: MIT Press.

———(2009). *Simulation and its discontents*. Cambridge, MA: The MIT Press.

———(2012a). *Alone together*. New York, NY: Basic Books.

———(2012b). Connected, but alone? Retrieved April 26, 2013, from http://www.ted.com/talks/sherry_turkle_alone_together.html.

Turner, G. (2004). *Understanding celebrity*. London, UK: SAGE.

————(2006). The mass production of celebrity: "Celetoids," reality TV and the "demotic turn." *International Journal of Cultural Studies*, 9(2), 153–165. Retrieved May 28, 2013, from http://ics.sagepub.com/cgi/doi/10.1177/1367877906064028.

————(2010). Approaching celebrity studies. *Celebrity Studies*, 1(1), 11–20. Retrieved May 28, 2013, from http://www.tandfonline.com/doi/abs/10.1080/19392390903519024.

U.S. Department of Education | Mission (2011, October 10). ED.gov. Retrieved May 4, 2013, from http://www2.ed.gov/about/overview/mission/mission.html?src=ln.

U.S. Department of Health & Human Services | The privacy rule. (n.d.). hhs.gov. Retrieved May 4, 2013, from http://www.hhs.gov/ocr/privacy/hipaa/administrative/privacyrule/index.html.

VanHampton, T. (2012, May 18). Virtual reality goes to school. *The New York Times*, AU4. Retrieved April 16, 2013, from http://www.nytimes.com/2012/05/20/automobiles/virtual-reality-goes-to-school.html?_r=0.

VanHeertum, R. & Torres, C. A. (2011). Educational reform in the U.S. in the past 30 years: Great expectations and the fading American dream. In L. Olmos, C. A. Torres, & R. Van Heertum (Eds.), *Educating the global citizen in the shadow of neoliberalism thirty years of educational reform in North America* (pp. 3–27). Oak Park, IL: Bentham eBooks. Retrieved April 12, 2013, from http://site.ebrary.com/id/10504680.

Veak, T. J. (2006). Introduction. In T. J. Veak (Ed.), *Democratizing technology: Andrew Feenberg's critical theory of technology* (pp. ix–xxii). Albany, NY: State University of New York Press.

Vedder, A. (1999). KDD: The challenge to individualism. *Ethics and Information Technology*, 1(4), 275–281. Retrieved April 10, 2013, from http://link.springer.com/article/10.1023%2FA%3A1010016102284.

Vega, T. (2013, April 7). Sponsors now pay for online articles, not just ads. *The New York Times*. Retrieved April 13, 2013, from http://www.nytimes.com/2013/04/08/business/media/sponsors-now-pay-for-online-articles-not-just-ads.html?pagewanted=all.

Vygotskiĭ, L. S. (1978). *Mind in society: The development of higher psychological processes* (M. Cole, V. John-Steiner, S. Scribner, & E. Souberman, Eds.). Cambridge, MA: Harvard University Press.

Wall, A. (2013). History of search engines: From 1945 to Google today. Search Engine History. Retrieved April 22, 2013, from http://www.searchenginehistory.com/.

Wark, M. (2004). *A hacker manifesto.* Cambridge, MA: Harvard University Press.

Weischedel, B., & Huizingh, E. K. R. E. (2006). Website optimization with web metrics. CEC '06 Proceedings of the 8th international conference on Electronic commerce (pp. 463–470). Presented at the ICEC 2006, ACM Press. Retrieved April 10, 2013, from http://dl.acm.org/citation.cfm?id=1151525.

Weisman, R. (2006). Frank Moss named new director of MIT media lab. *The Tech*, 126(4), 19.

Welch, A. (1998). The end of certainty? The academic profession and the challenge of change. *Comparative Education Review*, 42(1), 1–14. Retrieved April 13, 2013, from http://www.jstor.org/stable/1188783.

Weld, D., Adar, E., Chilton, L., Hoffmann, R., Horvitz, E., Koch, M., Landay, J., et al. (2012). Personalized online education—A crowdsourcing challenge. The Association for the Advancement of Artificial Intelligence. Retrieved April 10, 2013, from http://www.cs.washington.edu/people/faculty/weld/publications/.

Wells, J., & Lewis, L. (2006). Internet access in U.S. public schools and classrooms: 1994–2005 (NCES 2007–020). U.S. Department of Education, National Center for Education Statistics. Retrieved April 10, 2013, from http://nces.ed.gov/pubsearch/pubsinfo.asp?pubid=2007020.

Wenger, E. (1999). *Communities of practice: Learning, meaning, and identity. Learning in doing.* Cambridge, UK: Cambridge University Press.

What most schools don't teach (2014). Code.org. Retrieved June 25, 2014, from http://code.org/.

Williams, R. (1977). *Marxism and literature.* Oxford, UK: Oxford University Press.

Wilson, G. (2004). Internet pop-up ads: Your days are numbered—The supreme court of California announces a workable standard for trespass to chattels in electronic communications. *Loyola of Los Angeles Entertainment Law Review*, 567. Retrieved April 10, 2013, from http://digitalcommons.lmu.edu/elr/vol24/iss3/4/.

Wingfield, N. (2013, February 17). Oculus rift headset aims for affordable virtual reality. *The New York Times*, B1. Retrieved April 16, 2013, from http://www.nytimes.com/2013/02/18/technology/oculus-rift-headset-aims-for-affordable-virtual-reality.html?pagewanted=all&gwh=1FCEB8D8C86A55D977BE6E9028A9FE03.

Wiske, M. (1985). Book Review. *Harvard Educational Review*, 55(2), 236–240.

Wollstonecraft, M. ([1792]2012). A vindication of the rights of woman. Philadelphia, PA: Empire Books. Wong, J. (2006). Control and professional development: Are teachers being deskilled or reskilled within the context of decentralization? *Educational Studies*, 32(1), 17–37. Retrieved June 6, 2014, from   http://www.tandfonline.com/doi/full/10.1080/03055690500415910#.U5EHOy_LGA4.

Wyer, K. (2012, March 27). 10 Questions: Leah Lievrouw on the loss of online privacy. *UCLA Today*. Retrieved April 10, 2013, from http://today.ucla.edu/portal/ut/10-questions-231158.aspx.

Yager, E. M. (2006). *Ronald Reagan's journey: Democrat to Republican.* Lanham, MD: Rowman & Littlefield.

Yin, S. (2011, October 13). Verizon Wireless now collecting your web, location, app data. *PC Magazine*. Retrieved April 10, 2013, from http://www.pcmag.com/article2/0,2817,2394625,00.asp.

Young, J. (2012). Providers of free MOOC's now charge employers for access to student data. *The Chronicle of Higher Education.* Retrieved April 10, 2013, from http://chronicle.com/article/article-content/136117.

Yurkanon, E. (2001, April 11). Technical history of ARPANET. *Technical Histories of Network Protocols.* Retrieved April 22, 2013, from http://www.cs.utexas.edu/users/chris/nph/ARPANET/ScottR/arpanet/timeline.htm.

Zakon, R. (2011, December 30). Hobbes' Internet timeline 10.2. The definitive ARPAnet & Internet history. Retrieved April 22, 2013, from http://www.zakon.org/robert/internet/timeline/.

Zhang, J. (2009). Comments on Greenhow, Robelia, and Hughes: Toward a creative social web for learners and teachers. *Educational Researcher,* 38(4), 274–279. Retrieved April 10, 2013, from http://edr.sagepub.com/content/38/4/274.full.

Zimmerman, J. (2006, November 3). Designing for the self. Lecture presented at the Human Computer Interaction Seminar (CS547), Stanford University. Retrieved April 9, 2013, from http://www.youtube.com/watch?v=H1S0OykQHXA.

Ziskin, L., Bryce, I., & Curtis, G. (Prod.) (2002). *Spider-Man.* Dir. S. Raimi. Columbia Pictures. Retrieved April 29, 2013, from http://www.imdb.com/title/tt0145487/?ref_=sr_3.

Zucchino, D. (2012, March 18). Stress of combat reaches drone crews. *Los Angeles Times.* Retrieved April 9, 2013, from http://articles.latimes.com/2012/mar/18/nation/la-na-drone-stress-20120318.

Index

Page numbers in italics denote information in figures.

A.I. Artificial Intelligence (film), 44–5
abstraction of realities
   augmented reality, 1, 3, 6–8, 78,
      80–1
   hyperreality, 6, 8, 11–12, 48,
      78–83, 88
   real life reality, 7
   virtual reality, 1, 3, 5–6, 8–11, 19
   See also simulacrum/simulacra
Acquisti, Alessandro, 75
Advanced Research Agency Network
   (ARPANET), 4, 36, 40
advertising, 95–100, 131, 143
affordance theory, 18–19, 70, 73,
   109, 160
altered beings, 124–5, 156, 162
Anderson, Chris, 107
Anonymous (cyber group),
   111–12, 143
APEX Learning, 136
Apollo Group, 137
Appadurai, Arjun, 16, 163
Apple, 47, 70–1
   Macintosh, 4, 22–3, 59
   Siri, 71, 128
apps, 1–2, 7–8, 47, 69, 71
Arab Spring, 43, 117
Are We Safer? (documentary), 107
Arkin, William, 107
artifacts
   and affordance theory, 70
   cyberpunk, 38
   emotional, 72

and identity, 18–19
new media, 16, 26–8, 38, 99,
   106, 153
viral, 67–8
Assange, Julian, 113, 118, 149
augmented reality, 1, 3, 6–8, 78, 80–1
authenticity
   and depersonalization of data, 101
   and digital conformity, 53–4
   in film, 37
   in friction model, 94
   and portability/fragmentation,
      74, 85
   and schooling, 156–7
   Turkle on, 46, 51, 53–4, 58
Avatar (film), 11, 48
avatars, 5, 8, 46, 57, 81–2, 139

Baard, Mark, 116–17
Baraniuk, Richard, 15–16
Barbara, Juliette, 74
Barbarella (film), 37
Barnes, Khaliah, 148
Baudrillard, Jean, 8, 51, 80–1, 83, 88,
   92, 97
Bedortha, Darcy, 138–9
Best, Steven, 25–6, 64, 76, 128–9,
   152–3
Bethke, Bruce, 37
Biden, Joe, 118
Blade Runner (film), 37–8, 164–5
Bluetooth technology, 75
Blumer, Herbert, 64, 69

Booker, Cory, 151
Bowles, Samuel, 132, 134
Bradshaw, Peter, 81
bricolage, 60, 123, 126, 160
Bridges, Jeff, 38
Brin, Sergey, 96
Brinkley, Douglas, 116
Browning, Emily, 81
Burke, Peter J., 64
Burners-Lee, Tim, 40
Bush, George W., 42, 51, 114, 116, 133
Bush, Jeb, 136

Cain, Carole, 18
capitalism
  and celebrity culture, 68
  and cloud computing, 89, 93
  Frankfurt School's critique of, 95
  and friction, 89, 93, 119
  high-tech, 96–101, 111, 119–20, 143,
    159, 166
  information, 92, 95, 164
  and neoliberalism, 24
  and schooling, 15, 130–6, 143–6,
    152, 159, 161
  and technology, 23–5
  and virtualization, 89
Carnoy, Martin, 136
Carr, Nicholas, 67, 83, 85–7
Carroll, Lewis, 63
Castells, Manuel, 143, 167
celebrity culture, 22, 28, 65–8, 91, 97,
  109–10
Cera, Michael, 80
ChoicePoint, Inc., 97
Christie, Chris, 151–2
Christie, Michael, 70
class, social, 47, 57–8, 199, 42–3, 162–3
Clinton, Bill, 40–2, 51, 129
cloud computing
  defined, 88–9
  and fiction, 93–110
  and locus of data control, 46–7
  and schooling, 134, 167
  and technological progress, 3, 46–7,
    71, 88–9

and the technomensch, 88–9
and virtual reality, 10
cognitive framing, 27, 69, 97, 109, 136
Cohen, Jonathan D., 78
Cold War, 34–6
Coleman, Gabriella, 111
computer technology, use of
  the term, 1
computers
  and abstraction of realities, 6–11
  in film, 37–8, 44–5
  hackers, 14, 33, 55–6, 76, 96, 111–12
  and identity, 17–19
  information revolution, 4
  Macintosh, 4, 22–3, 59
  McLuhan on, 15
  as a second self, 33
  supercomputers, 34, 36, 79
  terminology, 13
  Turkle on, 22–3, 31–3, 49–50, 55–6,
    58–60
  types of technology, 1–2
  See also cyberspace; human-
    machine merger
Connections Education, 131, 136
conservatism, 34–5, 43, 113–14
constructivist psychology, 17, 20,
  64–5, 72, 92
convergence culture, 27
Cooley, Charles, 65–7
Coursera, 131, 144
creative commons, 14–15. See also
  open source movement
creativity, 89, 149, 156–7
Cronkite, Walter, 116
crowdsourcing, 144–5
cultural intersections, 11–12, 13,
  13–16
culture
  celebrity, 22, 28, 65–8, 91, 97,
    109–10
  convergence, 27
  cyberpunk, 37–8
  virtual, 3, 11–14, 20, 49
  See also artifacts; digital online
    culture

cyber activism, 111–13
cyberpunk, 33, 35–8, 78–9
cyberspace
    and abstraction, 6
    Advanced Research Agency
        Network (ARPANET), 4, 36, 40
    analytics, 100–3
    browsers, 40, 94
    complexity of, 4–5
    "consensual hallucination" of, 4–5
    early years of, 11–12, 36, 40
    and fragmentation, 73–9, 83–5, 88,
        94, 95, 101
    as "free," 100
    and hybridization, 75, 88–9, 153,
        164–6
    as infinite, 4–6
    multiuser domains, 5, 10, 32, 39, 57
    open source movement, 14–15, 34,
        54, 143, 147–8
    and portability, 73–5, 88, 126
    Web 2.0, 15, 22, 44, 67–8, 88, 111, 117
    See also cloud computing; digital
        online culture; knowledge
        discovery in databases (KDD);
        social networking
cyborgs, 26, 44, 49, 124, 128, 156, 162
    in film, 37, 41–2, 164

Daily Show with Jon Stewart, The
    (television program), 116, 118
data
    big data, 133, 144–6
    data mining, 15, 95, 100–10, 145–6
    data movement, 97–101
    data-centric teaching, 146–9
    depersonalization and
        repersonalization of, 101–5
    and friction model, 94
    poached, 89, 94, 94, 97, 161
    recycled, 94, 95
    sold, 94, 95, 102, 149
    willingly provided, 93–4, 94, 95–6
    See also knowledge discovery in
        databases (KDD)
Debord, Guy, 46, 107–8, 120

democracy
    and capitalism, 119–20, 140, 153
    and friction, 93
    and journalism, 113–14
    and privacy, 99, 105, 109
    and schooling, 2–3, 133–4, 140, 149,
        159–3, 166
    virtualized, 14, 25, 134, 161, 167
Dewey, John, 134, 139, 153
Dick, Philip K., 37. See also Blade
    Runner (film)
digital conformity, 53–4, 84
digital online culture, 26–8
    and affordance theory, 18
    artifacts of, 99, 153
    and commodification, 99
    critical thinking literacy for, 161
    cultural codes of, 143
    and cyber activists, 112
    defined, 12
    in film, 81
    and fragmentation, 74
    and the Frankfurt school, 91, 97, 99
    and freedom, 119
    and identity, 21, 31, 63, 65–8, 74–7,
        81, 88
    and journalism, 118
    and multiplicity/parallelity, 76–7
    and portability, 74
    and privacy, 106
    and race, 57
    and schooling, 51, 60, 153, 160–2
    and the self, 65–8
    and social justice, 162
    terminology of, 13
    Turkle on, 61
    and virtual culture, 11–16
    See also cyberspace; virtualization
Digital Promise (education initiative),
    43, 51, 123
Disclosure (film), 9
drones and drone technology, 44,
    76–7, 107–10, 112
    non-military use of, 108–9
    Remotely Piloted Aircraft (RPA), 76
    unmanned aerial vehicles (UAVs), 108

Duhigg, Charles, 103
Duncan, Arne, 147

education. *See* schooling
Eisgruber, Christopher L., 144–5
Elder Scrolls (video game), 8
Enzensberger, Hans Magnus, 91–2, 95, 99, 149
Evans, Arthur B., 80

Facebook
    and celebrity culture, 97
    and data mining, 15, 94, 98
    in film, 49
    and filter bubbles, 117
    and gender, 56–7
    and individualism, 15
    and privacy, 54, 96–7, 110, 170n3
    and schooling, 137, 151
Fairness Doctrine, 113–14
Falwell, Jerry, 35
Fang, Lee, 139, 152
Feenberg, Andrew, 154
firing the customer, 105
flipped classrooms, 146–7, 162
Ford, Harrison, 37
Foucault, Michel, 76, 88
fragmentation
    and abstraction of reality, 27, 88
    in friction model, *94*, 95
    and identity, 83–5, 101
    and portability, 73–9
    Turkle on, 48–50
framing, cognitive, 27, 69, 97, 109, 136
Frankenstein Syndrome, 25
Frankfurt School, 91–2, 95, 99, 149, 153
Free Software Foundation (FSF), 34
Freire, Paulo, 15, 68, 139, 153, 158, 161
Freud, Sigmund, 17
friction
    in the cloud, 93–105
    and data acquisition, 103, 110, 119
    defined, 93
    model of, *94*
Friedman, Thomas, 144

Gabler, Neil, 83–6
Galloway, Scott, 14
Gee, James Paul, 127
"geek," use of the term, 49
gender, 55–6
Gergen, Kenneth, 74, 76, 83–5
Gibson, William
    on cyberspace, 4
    Neuromancer, 4, 14, 37–8
Giddens, Anthony, 21, 64–5
Gintis, Herbert, 132, 134
Giroux, Henry, 122–4
Goffman, Erving, 20, 46
Goodenow, Ronald, 128
Google, 54, 98–9, 110
    ads, 99–100, 119, 137
    Google Earth, 9
    Google Glass, 5, 27, 78
    search engine, 69, 98, 117
    Street View, 128
    See also Schmidt, Eric
Gresham's law, 84
Gross, Bill, 99

hackers, 14, 33, 79, 96
    and cyber activist groups, 111–12
    in film, 38, 45
    first-generation, 111–12
    and gender, 56
    and neoliberal education, 55
Hanson, E. Mark, 137
Hayes, Elisabeth, 127
Henn, Steve, 14
hero-worship, 66–7
heterotopias, 76
Hewlett Packard, 41
Holland, Dorothy, 18, 100
Hotz, George, 96
human-machine merger, 1, 153
    cyborgs, 26, 44, 49, 124, 128, 156, 162
    in film, 37, 41–2, 164–5
    and identity, 26, 72, 75, 83, 88, 156–7, 165
    and inequalities, 162
    and schooling, 156–7, 162, 165

Turkle on, 31–3, 49, 59–60
Hunger Games, The (film), 109
hybridization, 75, 88–9, 153, 164–6
hyperreality, 6, 8, 12, 48, 78–83, 88

IBM, 34, 100
Idealab, 99
identity
    and celebrity culture, 65–8
    critiquing, 83–7
    defined, 63–5
    and digital online culture, 63, 65–8,
        74, 76–7, 81, 88
    and fragmentation, 73–5
    and hero-worship, 66–7
    and human-machine merger, 26,
        72, 75, 83, 88, 156–7, 165
    and hybridization, 73–5
    and hyperreality, 78–83
    and inequality, 162
    looking glass self theory of, 65–6
    and multiplicity, 76–8
    and new technology, 69–73
    and parallelity, 76–8
    and portability, 73–5
    psychology of, 17–18, 20, 65–73, 77
    and self-reflexivity, 64
    teacher/student, 134–44
    and the technomensch, 87–9
    theories of, 16–17, 65–6
    Turkle on, 21–4, 26, 49–53, 76
    virtualization and, 19, 17–21, 27–8,
        79–82, 88
    and worldviews, 64–5, 69
Illich, Ivan, 153, 163
immaterial exploitation, 95
Inception (film), 49
information capitalism, 92, 95
Internet. *See* cyberspace
Ito, Joichi, 48
Ive, Jonathan, 70–1

Jameson, Frederic, 22, 74
Jenkins, Henry, 27, 122–3
Jones, Steve, 36–7
journalism

activist, 111, 117–18, 143
alternative, 111, 114–18
blogs as, 116–17
and the Fairness Doctrine, 113–14
and media conglomerates, 114
participatory, 111, 113, 117
Jurassic Park (film), 42

K12 Inc., 130–1, 136, 138–41
Kaplan, 131, 140
Katz, Judith Milstein, 20
Kellner, Douglas
    on cyberpunk culture, 36–7
    on identity, 64
    on media spectacle, 22, 68,
        107–8, 114
    on a multiperspectival approach, 52
    on posthumanism era, 152–3
    on schooling, 122, 124, 128, 152–3
    on technology, 25–6, 76
    on violence, 21–2
Kelly, Kevin, 67, 87
keywords, 159–60
Khan, Sal, 146–9
Khan Academy, 144, 146–9, 163
Kleinrock, Leonard, 36
Kline, Charley, 36
knowledge discovery in databases
    (KDD)
    data mining, 15, 95, 100–10, 145
    defined, 94
    and depersonalization of data,
        101–2
    and friction, *94*, 94–5
    and national security, 107
    and schooling, 142, 145, 148
    and social justice, 161
Koller, Daphne, 144–6
Kübler-Ross, Elisabeth, 85

Lachicotte, William, Jr., 18
Lakoff, George, 27, 69, 97
Lévi-Strauss, Claude, 60
Lievrouw, Leah, 102, 110–12
Lisberger, Steven, 38
Luddism, 23

Marcuse, Herbert, 99, 153, 158, 161
mass communications, 91–2
Massachusetts Institute of
    Technology (MIT)
    and defense department funding, 35
    impact on Turkle, 28, 31, 33–4, 36,
        38, 57
    Initiative on Technology and Self
        (ITS), 28, 31
    Media Lab, 41, 44, 48
    and open source movement, 34
    prosthetic limbs project, 44, 49
    "Things that Think" initiative, 41
massive open online courses
    (MOOCs), 131, 135, 138–9,
    144–6, 149, 162–3
Matrix, The (film), 44–5, 91, 102–3
McChesney, Robert, 114
McLuhan, Marshall, 15–16, 18–20,
    52, 69
McNamara, Michael, 136
Mead, George Herbert, 65
media literacy, 27, 120, 159, 161
media spectacle, 66, 68
Microsoft, 4, 100, 136, 151
"Millennials," use of the term, 69
Minority Report (film), 44–5, 103
Mizukochi, Shin, 72
mobile applications (apps), 1–2, 7–8,
    47, 69, 71
Morozov, Evgeny, 167
Morris-Suzuki, Tessa, 92
Moss, Frank, 48
multiple realities, 1–3, 9, 23, 82
multiplicity, 76–8
multitasking, 46, 77–8
multiuser domains, 32
    MOOS, 5, 10, 39, 57
    MUDS, 5, 10, 32, 39, 57
    Second Life, 5
    World of Warcraft, 5
Murdoch, Rupert, 114, 135

Nass, Cliff, 19, 70
National Education Policy Center
    (NEPC), 140–2

National Science Foundation
    (NSF), 36
National Security Association (NSA),
    107, 110
Negroponte, Nicholas, 41, 48
Nelson, Ted, 19, 70
neoliberalism
    and big data, 133, 144–6
    and decentralization, 136–8
    defined, 2–3
    and deskilling of teachers, 138–42
    and inequalities, 149
    and innovation, 24
    and privatization, 29, 121, 134–8,
        151–2
    schooling agenda of, 3, 51, 55, 121,
        133, 151–4, 157–8
    and students as products/
        consumers, 142–4
    and teacher/student identity,
        134–44
    and technology, 38, 92, 111–12, 130,
        134–5, 143–4
    and Turkle, 28, 32–3, 39
Newman, Katherine S., 21–2
Nietzsche, Friedrich, 37, 87
Nixon, Richard, 69
No Child Left Behind (education
    legislation), 51, 133
Norman, Don, 70

Obama, Barack, 42–3, 47, 51, 133
Oberly, Nicholas, 79–80
Oculus Rift (virtual reality headset),
    5, 9
O'Malley, Bryan Lee, 80
open source movement, 54, 143
    creative commons, 14–15
    Free Software Foundation (FSF), 34
    and Khan Academy, 147–8

Packard, Ron, 139
Page, Larry, 96
Papert, Seymour, 17
parallelity, 76–9, 88
Pariser, Eli, 117

Pearson, 131, 135, 137
Piaget, Jean, 17
Pines, Steven, 135
Pirate Bay (BitTorrent site), 112
Pole, Andrew, 103
Pope, Bill, 81
portability, 73–5, 88, 126
Poster, Mark, 9
posthumanism, 25–6, 87, 153
post-idea world, 83–4
postmodernism
    in film, 48
    Jameson on, 22
    multiplicity, 76–8
    and schooling, 123
    Turkle on, 22–3, 39, 46, 49–52, 55, 123, 153
Priest, Dana, 107
privacy
    and data depersonalization, 100–1
    Facebook, 96–7
    laws, 101, 109, 163
    and schooling, 146, 148
    and surveillance, 54–5, 105–13
    and "terms and conditions," 156
    Turkle on, 13, 54–5, 84, 96
    and virtualization, 14, 52, 91, 93, 119, 156
prosthetic limbs, 44, 48–9
psychological immersion, 5–6
psychological virtual reality, 10
psychology
    constructivist, 17, 20, 64–5, 72, 92
    consumerism, 99
    and hyperreality, 11
    identity research, 17–18, 20, 65–73, 77
    and schooling, 121, 129, 139, 158, 162
    and technological change, 31–3, 37, 55–9, 65–73, 81, 85–6

race, 17, 26, 28, 56–8, 60, 162–3
Race to the Top (education initiative), 51, 133
Rather, Dan, 116
Reagan, Ronald, 34–5, 40
real life reality, 7

"Real World, The" (television program), 66–7
reality television, 66–7, 109
Reeves, Byron, 19, 70
Reidenberg, Joel, 148
Remotely Piloted Aircraft (RPA), 76–7. See also drones and drone technology
Rheingold, Howard, 8, 19
Rich Site Summary (RSS), 12–13
Robins, Kevin, 23–6, 105–6
Rousseau, Jean-Jacques, 139, 147, 153
Russakoff, Dale, 152

Saltman, Ken, 2
Sandel, Michael, 138
Sapir–Whorf hypothesis, 69
Schmidt, Eric, 96, 147–8
schooling
    and big data, 144–6
    bill of rights, 164–6
    and capitalism, 15, 130–6, 143–6, 152, 159, 161
    and class warfare, 142–3
    and compensation, 139–40
    and data mining, 162–3
    and data-centric teaching, 146–9
    decentralization of, 136–8
    Kellner on, 122, 124, 128, 152–3
    massive open online courses (MOOCs), 131, 135, 138–9, 144–6, 149, 162–3
    and neoliberalism, 3, 51, 55, 121, 133–44, 151–4, 157–8
    and pedagogy, 121, 123–4, 127, 135, 157
    and postmodernism, 123
    privatization of, 121, 134–8, 151–2
    reform, 151–67
    teacher/student identity, 134–44
    Turkle on, 58–61, 121, 123, 129
    use of the term, 124
    virtual schools, 130–42, 149, 151–2, 155, 158
    virtualization of, 121, 126–7, 129–32, 142

"schooling users," use of the term, 124
schooling-technology-identity model,
    154, *155*, 155–6
Schwarzenegger, Arnold, 41
science fiction
    A.I. Artificial Intelligence (film),
        44–5
    Avatar (film), 11, 48
    Barbarella (film), 37
    Blade Runner (film), 37–8, 164–5
    Inception (film), 49
    Jurassic Park (film), 42
    Matrix, The (film), 44–5, 91, 102–3
    Minority Report (film), 44–5, 103
    Neuromancer (Gibson), 4, 14, 37–8
    Scott Pilgrim vs. the world (film),
        80–1
    and simulacrum/simulacra, 80–3
    Soylent Green (film), 102–3
    Star Trek (television series), 37
    Sucker Punch (film), 80–3
    Terminator 2: Judgment Day
        (film), 41–2
    Transformers (film), 48
    Tron (film), 37–8
    V for Vendetta (film), 112
    See also cyberpunk
Scott, A. O., 81–2
Scott, Ridley, 37
Scott Pilgrim vs. the world (film), 80–1
self-censorship, 54–5
September 11, 2001 terrorist attacks,
    105–7, 109–10
Sharkey, Betsy, 81–2
Shibuya, Steve, 82
Shields, Rob, 9, 11
Siegel, Eric, 103
simulacrum/simulacra, 7, 51, 80, 92
simulation
    as abstraction of reality, 6–7, 11–12
    and augmented reality, 7
    defined, 6, 7
    and drone technology, 108
    in film, 45
    and hyperreality, 79–80

and simulacrum/simulacra, 80
Turkle on, 42–3, 51–3, 56–61, 76
and virtual culture, 12
and virtual reality, 8, 10–11
Skinner, Debra, 18
Slack, Jennifer, 14
smartphones, 7–8
    and data, 94, 104
    and human-machine merger, 49,
        75, 78
    and identity, 1–2, 72, 88
    and surveillance, 106
    and technological progress, 47, 125
Snowden, Edward, 107
Snyder, Zack, 81–2
social justice, 3, 118–20, 149, 153,
    161–2, 165–6
social media. *See* social networking
Social Network (film), 49
social networking, 2, 15, 22, 43–4
    and celebrity culture, 22
    and commodification, 95–6
    communication through, 73, 106
    and data-mining, 15, 84
    and information acquisition, 94
    and media spectacle, 68
    as news sources, 115
    and objectification of women, 57
    and schooling, 155
    and self-representation, 53–4, 66
    and social change, 43
    Twitter, 14, 56, 73, 94, 98, 110, 117
    See also Facebook
Soylent Green (film), 102–3
Spartacus (film), 112
Spielberg, Steven, 42, 45
Stallman, Richard, 34
Star Trek (television series), 37
Strategic Defense Initiative
    (SDI), 34–5
Stroop, John Ridley, 77–8
Stryker, Sheldon, 39, 64
Sucker Punch (film), 80–3
superhero movies, 80–1
surveillance

adware as first step toward, 98
countersurveillance, 110–13
and friction, 93
normalizing, 24, 29
and politics/political economy,
    105–10
and safety, 106, 156
and schooling, 148, 161
Turkle on, 54–5
symbolic interactionism, 28, 64,
    69–70

Target, 103
Taylor, Charles, 16–17
Tea Party, 43
technology, use of the term, 1–2
technomensch, 87–8
Terminator 2: Judgment Day
    (film), 41–2
textbooks, 15–16, 60, 147, 155
Thurn, Sebastian, 144
Torres, Carlos Alberto, 132–4
Transformers (film), 48
transient electronics, 128–9
transparency
    and economics, 109–10
    normalization of, 93, 96, 106,
        119, 143
    and safety, 156
    and schooling, 156, 161
    Turkle on, 59
Tron (film), 37–8
Turkle, Sherry
    Alone together, 32, 45–52, 54, 57–8,
        84, 86
    on authenticity and digital
        conformity, 53–4
    background and publications,
        28, 31–2
    on gender, race, and class, 56–8
    on identity, 21–4, 26, 49–53, 76
    *Life on the screen: Identity in the age
        of the Internet*, 10–11, 22–3, 32,
        38–42, 44–6, 49–52
    on multilifing, 46, 77

on postmodernity, 22–3, 39, 46,
    49–52, 55, 123, 153
on privacy, 13, 54–5, 84, 96
on relationships, 33, 48–54,
    83–4, 484
on schooling, 58–61, 121, 123, 129
*The second self: Computers and the
    human spirit*, 32–9, 45, 56, 58
Simulation and its discontents, 32,
    42–5
on surveillance and self-censorship,
    54–5
on technology's influence, 72, 74,
    83–7, 121
on virtualization, 10–11, 19, 32, 39,
    42–3, 52

übermensch, 37, 45, 87–8
Udacity, 131

V for Vendetta (film), 112
video games and gamers, 6–10, 21, 44,
    56, 81–2, 126
violence, 21–2
viral, going, 65–8, 146
"virtual," use of the term, 9–10
virtual culture, 3, 11–14, 20, 49
    defined, 12
    See also digital online culture
virtual reality, 1, 3, 5–6, 19
    categories of, 10
    defined, 8–11
virtual schools, 130–42, 149, 151–2,
    155, 158
virtualization
    defined, 10
    and democracy, 134, 161–2
    in film, 81–3
    and identity, 19, 17–21, 27–8,
        79–82, 88
    and individual agency, 158
    of schooling, 121, 126–7, 129–32, 142
    and schooling bill of rights, 164–6
    Turkle on, 10–11, 19, 32, 39,
        42–3, 52

war and wars
  Afghanistan, 44, 107–8
  drones used in, 44, 76–7,
    107–10, 112
  Iraq, 44, 107–8, 114–15
  journalism coverage of, 114–15
  Vietnam, 114
Waze (application), 7
Web 2.0, 15, 22, 44, 67–8, 88, 111, 117
weblining, 104–5
Webster, Frank, 23–6, 105–6
Wikileaks, 117–18, 143

Wikipedia, 162
Williams, Raymond, 115
Winstead, Mary Elizabeth, 80
Winthrop, John, 35
Wiske, Martha Stone, 58
Wollstonecraft, Mary, 139
World Wide Web. *See* cyberspace
worldviews, 16, 64–5, 69
Wright, Edgar, 81

Zimmerman, John, 19
Zuckerberg, Mark, 96, 151–2